T0278485

Dirty Real

Dirty Real

EXILE ON
HOLLYWOOD AND VINE
WITH THE
GIN MILL COWBOYS

Peter Stanfield

REAKTION BOOKS

Dedicated to the memory of Steve Neale
With gratitude to David Lusted and Lawrence Jackson –
nonpareils among readers
This one is for Julie – play on, Sidney x

Published by
REAKTION BOOKS LTD
Unit 32, Waterside
44–48 Wharf Road
London N1 7UX, UK
www.reaktionbooks.co.uk

First published 2024
Copyright © Peter Stanfield 2024

Printed and bound in Great Britain
by TJ Books Ltd, Padstow, Cornwall

A catalogue record for this book is available from the British Library

ISBN 978 1 78914 862 6

Contents

Introduction:
Dirt for Dirt's Own Sake

I know nothing of his life after he left the university. He cut
himself off from all decent society. He was perversely bound
to sink in the social scale, to declass himself. I'm afraid my
son had a *nostalgie de la boue* – a nostalgia for the gutter. He
tried to cover it over with fancy talk about re-establishing
contact with the earth, becoming a poet of the people,
and such nonsense. His real interest was dirt for dirt's own
sake. I brought him up to be pure in thought and desire, but
somehow – somehow he became fascinated with the pitch
that defileth. And the pitch defiled him.

Ross Macdonald, *The Galton Case* (1959)

The setting is Hibbing, Minnesota, 1957, just a few pages
into Anthony Scaduto's *Bob Dylan: An Intimate Biography*
(1971), and the author is introducing his reader to the girl who will
become Dylan's high school love, Echo Helstrom. She's fifteen
years old, and Bob, a year older, has yet to make any impression
on her. He was then a 'clean-cut goody-goody kid', she said, who
lived over the tracks from her on the well-to-do side of town.[1] Their
paths eventually crossed at the drugstore. Echo told it this way:

'He walked in with another boy, John Buckland, and they came over and started talking to us. Picking us up, I guess. I think I had on my motorcycle jacket and a pair of jeans. Very uncouth, for Hibbing.'[2] Pre-dating The Crystals' 'He's a Rebel', The Shangri-Las' bad-boy melodramas, Janis Ian's 'Society's Child' and a thousand other teen operas, the events recalled by Echo flip the bad-boy trope with the girl in denim and leather and from the wrong side of town. Echo and Bob then bond over their shared enthusiasm for the blues and together tear-up Hibbing on his motorcycle.

Before Bobby Zimmerman graduated, a transformation occurred and the girls in school now viewed him with the same nervous desire he held for Echo Helstrom. The nice boy had turned into a hoodlum in his 'big boots and tight pants' – he's good-bad, but he's not evil.[3] In his memoir, Dylan recalls of Echo that 'Everybody said she looked like Brigitte Bardot, and she did.'[4]

Whatever the truth in the scenario, Scaduto is organizing Dylan's biography along familiar lines. Zimmerman's change – from nice kid to the rough protagonist in girl group teen fantasies – follows the same path as that taken by the young man in Ross Macdonald's detective story *The Galton Case* (1959). From small town to metropolis, from suburbia to city, the journey – a transformation from bourgeois student to Beat poet – is a rite of passage. Here, the sooty mask of dirty face and scuffed boots hides the real, the better to perform the authentic. The middle-class dropout resurfacing as a bohemian artist, poet, painter, troubadour or film-maker is the shadow figure who flits through the following pages of *Dirty Real*, both as a protagonist in the films and as a persona adopted by the film-makers themselves. The films' characters, as with the actors, writers and directors, were costumed in the pitch that defileth and showed too an acute nostalgia for the gutter none had known at first hand. For a cool moment they almost turned Hollywood into an image of themselves. This book is about that moment, the people who made it and their films.

'Don't Bogart that joint'

In its June 1966 edition, *Playboy* pulled itself onto the already heavily laden Humphrey Bogart bandwagon with the feature '"Here's Looking at You, Kid" – The Bogart Boom', providing a quiz, film and book list on its subject alongside two lengthy appreciations of the man, the career, the myth and the cult by the *New York Times* film critic Bosley Crowther and the London *Observer*'s Kenneth Tynan. The latter dealt with the myth; he had met the man once, but they hadn't got along. Tynan wrote that he 'preferred the lines' Bogart's scriptwriter gave him 'to the ones ad-libbed that night'.[5] Tynan had done his homework, having read 83 accounts of Bogart in magazines and books, but he was still unimpressed by the man and was even less enthralled by the hagiographies. Having first seen Bogart in *The Petrified Forest* (1936), aged ten, Tynan had long been a fan:

> We rooted for Bogart because, although he got second billing, he never said 'Yes, Boss' as if he meant it. He was nobody's man but his own. And this extended to his relationship with the audience. You had to take him on his own terms. He never stooped to ingratiation, and though his bullying was silken, it was also icy. In latter-day terminology, he was 'inner-directed', steering by a private compass that paid no attention to storm signals from outside. Moreover,

if the needle led him (as it usually did) into a hail of bullets, he would die with a shrug: no complaints, no apologies, no hard feelings of any kind. And this, in an age when stars were supposed to emote and be vibrant, was something else we admired. It reflected, in part, the emotional tact of a man who seemed genuinely repelled by sentimentality; and in part the professional assurance of an actor who knew damned well that he could get along without it. Either way it was revolutionary and we relished it.[6]

Because his characters did not seek favours, were not obsequious or deferential, apologetic or resentful, Bogart's performances were at odds with the conventions of the day, especially his peers' delivery of cheap sentiment, which was made to seem tritely out of date in the face of his stoicism. Against them, Bogart appeared contemporary. His currency with audiences in the 1960s was intensified, according to Tynan, by what the profilers and biographers wrote were his defining characteristics of a hatred of phonies and a prizing of loyalty.[7]

Discussing Bogart's sparring with James Cagney in *Angels with Dirty Faces* (1938) and *The Roaring Twenties* (1939), Tynan wrote, 'The contrast of styles was beautiful to watch. It was Bogart the wily debunker versus Cagney the exultant cavalier.'[8] With his 'built-in shit detector', the 'verdict, on points, went to Bogart's sewage snarl'.[9] With *The Maltese Falcon* (1941), Bogart went from second fiddle to lead, from villain to anti-hero:

The Hammett private eye was the first antihero. No Batman he: Operating in a corrupt society, he was not above using corrupt means. He was a cynic to whom nothing human, however squalid, was alien; a man soured but still amused by the intricate depravity of his fellow creatures; and he could, on occasion, be extremely brutal. In short, he was virtually indistinguishable from the Bogart gangster in every respect but one: He was on the side of the law. From now on Bogart could be ruthless – he could even kill – with no loss of glamor and every appearance of moral rectitude. He could engage in mayhem and emerge untarnished. Still as fascinating as ever, he was no longer reprehensible. The farewell to overt criminality was what enabled Bogart to become a world star and a household god.[10]

Bogart's appeal to his cult followers, wrote Tynan, was that he was 'a loner who belonged to nobody, had personal honour . . . and would therefore survive. Compared to many of his Hollywood

Humphrey Bogart (*left*) in *The Petrified Forest* (dir. Archie Mayo, 1936).

colleagues, he seemed an island of integrity, not perhaps very lovable but at least unbought.'[11] Jean-Luc Godard paid 'tribute to the Bogart way of life' with *À bout de souffle* (1960), and Woody Allen did something similar with his 1969 theatrical production *Play It Again, Sam* (adapted as a film in 1972), about a character who lives vicariously through Bogart.[12] In between, Bogart became a regular in 'personality poster' catalogues alongside W. C. Fields, Mae West, Brigitte Bardot, and Peter Fonda and Dennis Hopper in *Easy Rider* – a readymade pin-up for every student's dormitory wall. University film clubs promoted the cult with 'Bogart Festivals', a revival to challenge Chaplin's, wrote Crowther.[13]

It had all begun, Crowther continued,

> as far back as the summer of 1956, when the small but selective Brattle Theater [in Cambridge, Massachusetts] booked a two-year-old Bogart film, *Beat the Devil*, and found it did something for the aggressively long-haired audience, made up largely of the summer population at Harvard, Radcliffe and MIT. It tickled sophisticated fancies with its wacky, slightly beat comedy.[14]

The next year, the theatre booked *Casablanca* (1942), which was a bigger hit with its patrons. In following years it programmed an ever greater number of his films, culminating in an annual two-week Bogart Festival. The Brattle 'has become the center of the Bogart cult in the U.S.', Crowther wrote in 1966.[15] He described the character Bogart's audience embraced as a 'bitter, bruising . . . disillusioned, disenchanted individual moving through what is generally an alien world'.[16] He appealed to 'today's younger generation', he wrote, because, like Bogey's characters, they are 'skeptical about idealism', wary of displaying virtues and 'suspicious of anyone who does . . . Today's young man, cynical and anxious about the way things are going in the world, sees in the character of Bogart a cheering model of firm contempt and cool aplomb. The young woman sees him as an image of masculine self-assurance and command.'[17]

For the film-makers of New Hollywood, Bogart was not only a figure they might identify with, he was also someone they would refract in their own anti-heroes – Clyde Barrow in *Bonnie and Clyde* (1967), George in *Easy Rider* (1969), Bobby Dupea in *Five Easy Pieces* (1970), Harry Collings in *The Hired Hand* (1971), Kansas in *The Last Movie* (1971), McCabe in *McCabe and Mrs Miller* (1971) and G.T.O. in *Two-Lane Blacktop* (1971).[18]

The link that Bogart provided between the Old and the New Hollywood is front and centre in a series of Jim Beam advertisements that ran through 1972 in the most popular magazines of the day. Dennis Hopper, dressed in his hippy cowboy raiment, is standing next to John Huston – director of two of the most celebrated Bogart performances, *The Maltese Falcon* and *The Treasure of the Sierra Madre* (1948) – who is attired as if on a safari. 'Generation gap? never heard of it', ran the tagline. The ad copy continued:

In 1941, a young maverick of a man directed his first motion picture. The man was John Huston.

The motion picture was *The Maltese Falcon*, a masterpiece that's had profound and lasting influence on the making of films.

In 1969, another young maverick of a man directed a motion picture, also his first.

This time it was Dennis Hopper and *Easy Rider*. Both the man and his film have made an extraordinary impact on the minds, imaginations and life styles of people everywhere.

Huston. And Hopper.

In *The Last Movie*, Hopper paid tribute to Huston's *The Treasure of the Sierra Madre* and Bogart's Fred C. Dobbs. Prospecting for gold in the Peruvian mountains, the film's flipped-out Americans had started their hunt with no more than a headful of Huston's movie to aid them in their adventure. Mavericks who bent Bogart's attitude and style were everywhere you cared to look as the 1960s turned into the 1970s.

The Treasure of the Sierra Madre and Fred C. Dobbs would leave their certain mark on Sam Peckinpah. He made direct references to the film in *Bring Me the Head of Alfredo Garcia* (1974) and indirectly in *The Wild Bunch* (1969), *The Ballad of Cable Hogue* (1970) and *Pat Garrett and Billy the Kid* (1973). These Peckinpah pictures featured characters at the end of their days who searched for fame or riches where there wasn't any and then found it, just as Dobbs unearthed gold, only then to lose it all. 'Bogey's Fred Dobbs in *Treasure*', wrote Crowther, is the 'epitome of the exhausted realist, grown suspicious and resentful of others and seeking madly for the security he has lost'.[19] Dobbs resonated, his name shared in three other films: in 1965, the screenplay for *The Great Sioux Massacre* was credited to 'Fred C. Dobbs', Marvin Gluck's alias of choice; in 1969, Jerry Lewis played 'Fred Dobbs' in *Hook, Line and Sinker*; and, the following year, Ian McShane played him in *Pussycat, Pussycat, I Love You*.

Elsewhere, Dobbs came out of his hole in the ground to appear in Eve Babitz's long acknowledgements in *Eve's Hollywood* (1974)

Dennis Hopper and John Huston advertisement for Jim Beam, 1972.

– or perhaps the author had posted a salute not to the character but to the place named after him, Fred C. Dobbs Café in West Hollywood, where surfer girls and those who throttled up and down the Strip hung out in 1966.[20] The café was memorialized in a tour poster of Hollywood's teen 'Hot Spots', sold for $1 via the Mothers of Invention album *Freak Out!* (1966): 'it used to be the best place to go to meet friends and dig the juke box until the heat blew it for us . . . or was it that bunch of outside idiots that started hanging around towards the end there, unable to maintain their coolness? The ruins are located at 8537 Sunset Blvd.'

A year later, on Fairfax, the 29-year-old owner of Gi Gi Studios, which provided space and models for amateur photographers with a yen to improve their artistry, asked to be identified as 'Fred C. Dobbs'. A *Los Angeles Times* piece wrote that he 'takes a hard line towards the customers, requiring models to stay 8 feet away from them at all times . . . Dobbs, who's been in the business for six years between acting assignments, admits having a callous view toward the models.'[21] Fred C. Dobbs was cited in numerous other *Los Angeles Times* articles, ranging from pieces on start-up airlines to the Mexican 1000 road race, contemporary gold prospecting, and a businessman's desire for money and sex that might best be personified if Raquel Welch played 'Fred C. Dobbs in a remake of *Treasure of the Sierra Madre*'.[22]

If Bogart and Dobbs provided Hollywood in the 1960s with one kind of anti-hero to celebrate and imitate, in the immediate aftermath of Beatlemania, rock 'n' roll provided further role models for those who lived where the action was, down on the Strip – The Standells, The Byrds, The Seeds, Love and The Doors.[23] Peter Fonda had read the runes; in 1965 he took acid with The Beatles and The Byrds.[24] The following year he appeared as a hoodlum motor-cyclist in Roger Corman's *The Wild Angels* (1966) and in early 1967 he released his own folk-rock single, one side a cover of Donovan's 'Catch the Wind' and the other an original composition, 'November Night', by a then unknown Gram Parsons. Not having much of a voice didn't help Fonda's hip aspirations, even with Hugh Masekela as his producer, and he dropped his attempt at a music career. He did, however, repay his debt to Parsons by securing a cameo for his group, International Submarine Band, in Corman's *The Trip* (1967).[25]

The outlaw motorcycle film gave Fonda and his peers – Dennis Hopper (*Glory Stompers*, 1967) and Jack Nicholson (*Hells Angels on Wheels*, 1967), alongside other children of Old Hollywood – a readymade anti-hero stance that would bury the beach movie up to its neck in sand.[26] *The Wild Angels* was the first in a sequence of films designed to evoke an air of the emerging counterculture: 'The next big area for teen-age films is protest,' one of American International Pictures's (AIP) directors said: 'Teen-agers identify with protest because they are in revolt against their parents.'[27] The hoodlum biker movie also provided a tenuous link with the ultimate rock 'n' roll outlaws, The Rolling Stones, whose recruitment of Hells Angels to run security at Altamont in 1969 proved calamitous.

In their early days, the band had been defined by George Melly, a keen student of the emerging British pop scene, as 'more one-dimensional' than The Beatles: 'They were about aggression expressed in sexual terms . . . Sex was still a weapon, a way to appal the suburbs,' he wrote.[28] Melly's younger contemporary Nik Cohn wrote that the Stones were 'the voice of hooliganism . . . like creatures from another planet, impossible to reach or understand but most exotic, most beautiful in their ugliness'.[29] But if the Stones were 'evil', as Cohn wrote, he then asked, 'what was so good about bad?'[30] In 1979, Nick Tosches looked back to when he was fifteen and first heard '(I Can't Get No) Satisfaction' blaring from a transistor radio as he sat on a New Jersey street corner with his friends:

It was unlike anything else to be heard that summer of 1965. Lurid, loud, and concupiscent, it was at once a yell of impotence and of indomitability. Its conspiratorial complaints sanctified our frustrations, and its vicious force promised deliverance . . . I was arrested for the first time that summer, for D&D.[31]

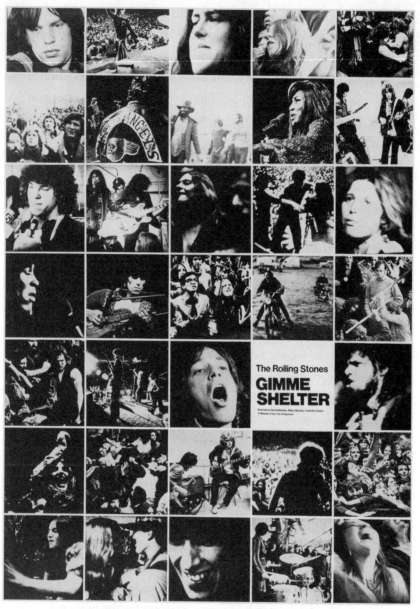

Poster for *Gimme Shelter* (dir. Albert Maysles, David Maysles
and Charlotte Zwerin, 1970).

Following 'Satisfaction', which dominated the airwaves in the summer of 1965, 'the Stones' project of radical self-definition was becoming a mass movement – against everything that kept the world within our reach and out of our grasp, everything that stopped us from making felt possibilities real,' as Robert Christgau wrote late in 1972 for *Creem* magazine.[32] By 1966, 'the "way of life" then-manager Andrew Loog Oldham had promised the Stones would carry forth fell into place,' wrote Greil Marcus. He continued:

> Bohemians roamed London, flashing contempt for all things bourgeois while toying with their ruling-class equivalents. They posited a duel between the sexes, choosing weapons of scorn and humor. Sensitive to the disasters of the world they passed through, they refused its claims anyway. They skirted decadence by the pace they kept, and avoided it because they were driven not by idle curiosity, or even narcissism, but by the most delicate and brutal shadings of lust.[33]

'Each pop generation must go further than the one before,' wrote Cohn, 'must feel as if it's doing everything for the first time. Always, it must be arrogant and vain and boorish. Otherwise, it's not being healthy and the whole essential teen revolt gets damned up.'[34] Most importantly, the Stones were independent and uncompromising, and because of this they 'threatened the structure' of the music business, 'in which pop was controlled by old men, by men over thirty'.[35] Youth helped to define the threat they held to the status quo, and so Cohn, as he wrote towards the end of the 1960s, thought that it was likely all over for The Rolling Stones: 'They weren't made to get old. They existed only to go bang one time, and then disappear again. And if they have any sense of neatness they'll get themselves killed in an air crash, three days before their thirtieth birthdays.'[36]

Brian Jones *did* die in 1969: that June, aged 27, a little before Cohn's book was published. Charlie Watts's wife, Shirley, had read the passage about the hypothetical air crash, and Stanley Booth, chronicler of the Stones' 1969 U.S. tour that would end with Altamont, overheard her say how terrible she found the idea: 'I was very upset and then I remembered Bill's already thirty, so that's alright.'[37] Booth thinks Jones's death changed The Rolling Stones: 'Yes,' says Lil (a barely anonymized Eve Babitz), 'now they know they will die.'[38] Figments of their own mortality might have informed the three albums released after Jones's death – *Let It Bleed* (1969), *Sticky Fingers* (1971) and *Exile on Main Street* (1972) – but the death they registered on these records was that of their younger selves. These were oblique attempts to account for an unwanted maturity even as they still rejected responsibility, and scorned the idea of dealing with the consequences of their actions – holding the gang together, against the odds, was what most mattered – and, as the most commercially successful working band of the day, took themselves, while loitering on Main Street, into self-imposed exile from the world that sustained their lifestyle.

An American who knew Bogart personally told Tynan: 'He never went around with hoods and bums. That's pure legend. He was an upper-class boy.'[39] Like Bogart, the Stones were not the thing itself. Being a band of outlaws was a role they played. The fantasy had them on the run, one step ahead of the police, when in reality they were grammar-school boys who had turned the tables and learned how to bully the prefects and torment their teachers. To some, they were, in Booth's memorable phrase, 'pacifist comrades of illegal sacraments' – sex, drugs and Jumpin' Jack Flash – served with a dark undertow of violent menace.[40]

In Donald Cammell and Nicolas Roeg's *Performance* (1970), rock 'n' roll and criminality were pulled together, the line drawn tight. The film was a culmination of the persona that Oldham had long fomented when, in their earliest days of fame, he drew parallels between the band and Anthony Burgess's 'droogs' in his novel *A Clockwork Orange* (1962). After attending a press conference held in New York in 1965, one commentator thought the Stones looked like 'five unfolding switchblades', and he left the event with 'the terrible feeling that if Kropotkin were alive in the 1960s he would almost certainly have had a press agent'.[41] For Oldham, the Stones were anarchic agents in the blurring of divisions – legal, social and cultural – expressed in the tagline he composed for the 'Get Off of My Cloud' marketing campaign: 'Rolling Stones – the dividing line between art and commerce'.[42] Where creativity met Mammon was the target New Hollywood's film-makers were aiming to land on, and, like the Stones, they too would don the accoutrements and attire of the outlaw and play out the role for all it was worth.

> Your advertising is just dandy. Folks'd never guess
> you don't have a thing to sell.

Bonnie Parker to Clyde Barrow in *Bonnie and Clyde* (1967)

8 December 1967: *Time* magazine has put *Bonnie and Clyde* on its cover using a commissioned Robert Rauschenberg montage of four black-and-white images from the film, overprinted in blocks and smudges of yellow, blue, pink and blood-red. The banner proclaims: 'THE NEW CINEMA: VIOLENCE . . . SEX . . . ART . . .'

If the contraction of sex and violence was nothing particularly noteworthy, the link with art was novel. Rauschenberg, it was reported, viewed the film on a Moviola, selected frames, and had them blown up and transferred to a silkscreen before treating the final image with coloured inks and paints, 'including splotches of bloodlike watercolor'.[43] He made nine montages before the editors at *Time* made their final choice: 'Though such characters as Bonnie and Clyde are not familiar images in Rauschenberg's art, his technique on *Time*'s cover is. It will be immediately identified as a "Rauschenberg" by those who know his work from museums and art galleries around the world.'[44] It was not Rauschenberg's design that was remarkable, given that it is no better than formulaic Pop art – more a pastiche of Warhol's *Disaster* silkscreens of an electric chair, a suicide jumper, car crashes and race riots, albeit colourized – by comparison to his own assemblages made of oils, found objects and kerbside detritus. It was, rather, his name and the work's easily identifiable play with commercial imagery, which pulled the film firmly into the discourse around the conflation of the fine and popular arts, that were noteworthy. The suggestion was that the movie itself should be viewed as Pop art as much as Rauschenberg's or Warhol's and that of their contemporaries Roy Lichtenstein, Ed Ruscha, Claes Oldenburg or James Rosenquist.

Time began its examination of contemporary film, 'The Shock of Freedom in Films', with three vignettes drawn from, respectively, Michelangelo Antonioni's *Blow-Up* (1966) – the lingering kiss between two girls; John Boorman's *Point Blank* (1967) – the play with time and space; and Arthur Penn's *Bonnie and Clyde* – the juxtaposition of comedy and bloody violence. Stefan Kanfer wrote: 'Differing widely in subject and style, the [three] films have

Warren Beatty and Faye Dunaway in *Bonnie and Clyde*
(dir. Arthur Penn, 1967).

several things in common. They are not what u.s. movies used to be like. They enjoy a heady new freedom from formula, convention and censorship. And they are all from Hollywood.'[45] Perhaps for the only time in the magazine's history, *Cahiers du cinéma*'s then editor, Jean-Louis Comolli, was quoted:

> Traditionally, a film was a form of amusement – a distrac-
> tion. It told a story. Today, fewer and fewer films aim to
> distract. They have become not a means of escape but a
> means of approaching a problem. The cinema is no longer
> enslaved to a plot. The story becomes simply a pretext.[46]

Whether or not that was the case for American movies, Kanfer argued that contemporary domestic films are 'now treating once-shocking themes with a maturity and candor unthinkable even five years ago'.[47] One reason given for this shift in represen-tation was the end of the universal audience that Hollywood once catered for and that self-censorship – the role of the Production

Code Administration – ensured was achievable (to upset no one being the goal and, by this means, to maximize attendance). With the waning of the regulator's control over content – *The Dirty Dozen* and *Bonnie and Clyde* in 1967 symptomatic of an escalation in violent imagery – Hollywood moved to manage audience diversity and the new representational strategies. Where narrative obfuscation and visual ambiguity had once enabled Code-enforced films to play to both a sophisticated and unsophisticated audience, adults and children, with more direct, unambivalent, scenarios, Hollywood adopted a classification system that was rolled out in 1968.

Kanfer summarized these shifts as taking place due to television having displaced movies with their 'former function of providing placebo entertainment'. If TV was now the universal medium, film countered the assault on its popularity by reconceiving its productions as being aimed at specific audiences within the mass. The baby boom demographic thus held an increasingly important place among Hollywood's new constituencies: 'movie attendance among the middle-aged is down,' wrote Kanfer, 'yet receipts are up – partly because cinema has become the favorite art form of the young.'[48]

Bonnie and Clyde's writers, Robert Benton and David Newman (both in their mid-thirties in 1966–7), were understood to be representatives of the younger generation Hollywood was wooing.[49] They were admirers of François Truffaut, especially of his films *Jules et Jim* (1962) and *Tirez sur le pianiste* (1960; *Shoot the Piano Player*), which they reimagined for their screenplay. Kanfer wrote that they were less interested in the historical characters than in imitating Truffaut's 'juxtaposition of dulcet tragedy and saline comedy'.[50] Though offered to them, neither Truffaut nor Godard were able or willing to make Benton and Newman's story into a

film, but Warren Beatty did back their screenplay, first as its producer and then as its star. By acquiring Benton and Newman's
script, Beatty also bought shares in the cultural stock market where
the Nouvelle Vague had first revealed the immense value in turning
the revenants of Hollywood's pulp productions – *Gun Crazy, They
Live by Night, Asphalt Jungle, Kiss Me Deadly, Detour* – or, for want
of an elevating term, *film noir*, into art cinema. French cinephiles
had also made a profit by transforming select star-laden studio
products into signature artworks, auteur masterpieces by Howard
Hawks, Alfred Hitchcock, Douglas Sirk, Nicholas Ray and Otto
Preminger. Similarly, and as self-consciously, Beatty's picture (the
film's heralded author) was 'an American movie', wrote Kanfer,
'that started out as a film for a French director whose best works
were echoes of American movies'.[51]

Kanfer considered *Bonnie and Clyde* to be a 'watershed picture,
the kind that signals a new style, a new trend'.[52] He was not wrong,
but it was a prophecy, not an observation. What would come next
could hardly be known to him, yet he was able to see how producers
of mid-budget films were gearing up for the change he predicted:

In the wake of *Bonnie and Clyde*, there is an almost euphoric
sense in Hollywood that more such movies can and will
be made . . . The old dinosaurs in the corner offices have
finally given way to younger dinosaurs. Robert Evans of
Paramount is 37. Richard Zanuck, Fox production chief,
is 34. David Picker, United Artists' vice president for production, is 36. Today the studios are frequently packagers,
providing money and facilities for small, independent
production teams.[53]

Hollywood's habit of casting thirty-year-olds to play teenagers was being extended into the studios' boardrooms. Nik Cohn would not have been fooled.

Midnight Cowboy (1969) begins with an image of a white screen – a screen on a screen. A Western gunfight is heard on the soundtrack, a chaotic mix of pistolshots, whoops and hollers, but there is no image to accompany the action. Instead, as the camera is pulled back the white space is revealed as a drive-in theatre's screen. Beneath it, and just behind its supporting pillars, four horses graze. In the foreground is a children's playground in which a young boy, wearing a cowboy hat, rides a mechanical horse. He is rocking vigorously back and forth. As the aural shoot-out fades it is replaced with a man, off-screen, singing 'Git Along, Little Dogies', the camera movement comes to a halt and the Big Tex Drive-In's vast, empty courtyard is exposed – no cars and no living person, other than the boy, to be seen.

When he finally appears, the singer of the old cowboy tune is taking a shower, scrubbing himself clean, preparing for a fresh start with a new Stetson and fancy cowboy boots. He's throwing in his job as a dishwasher and heading for New York City. Carrying his calfskin suitcase, he walks through town accompanied on the soundtrack by Harry Nilsson singing Fred Neil's 'Everybody's Talkin''. Before he arrives at the diner to collect his final paycheck and say his farewells, he passes an old cinema, now a used furniture emporium. On the awning is the last picture show to play there, 'J HN AYNE . . . THE A AMO'. The symbolism of the empty drive-in and blank screen, the ghost sounds of an old Western, the derelict theatre and Jon Voight's Joe Buck – 'the best-looking cowboy in the whole parade', as his grandmother said of him – riding a Greyhound bus across the country, going east to Babylon, is neither obscure nor abstract: Old Hollywood is dying, and the new is busy being born. Like so many of his fictional peers, Joe Buck made the gutter his home, bathed in dirt and danced with disease. Like Baudelaire, director John Schlesinger kneaded mud and from it made gold ('j'ai petri de la boue, et j'en ai fait de l'or'): *Midnight Cowboy* was the first X-rated film to be a box office smash, with three Academy Awards, for Best Picture, Best Director and Best Adapted Screenplay, and a hit soundtrack album to boot. Featuring male prostitution, gay sex – a little fellatio carried out below screen – and drug taking; a cast that included Warhol familiars Viva, Paul Morrissey, Joe Dallesandro, Taylor Mead and Ultra Violet; and with scenes and montage sequences composed as if borrowed from an underground film, Big Tex's blank screen, the tabula rasa, was set to be written over with shadows new and old.

Writing in 1965 about the need for an American art movie that would challenge both Europe's auteurs and the guardians of Old Hollywood, Dennis Hopper celebrated 'underground moviemakers' Bruce Conner and Andy Warhol. The former, he thought, was 'the most original talent':

> Bruce rarely shoots the film he edits. He takes quick cuts from many old movies and by juxtaposing them he makes much-more-than-interesting things happen. What a great idea for a major company to hire Conner. Turn him loose on the stockpile of films that lie decaying in the vaults of all the major studios, and make fresh films without the expense of shooting one foot of film. That's a multi-million-dollar idea. Have *you* had one lately?[54]

Along with Gregory Markopoulos and Taylor Mead, Warhol was part of the 'lust-rious underground movie set' and, according to Hopper, represented the 'drag-down-around-the-corner approach to cinema-come-lately American art film'.[55] Warhol, he wrote,

> behaves like a man who has never seen a camera or movie. He behaves like the inventor, Tom Edison. He sets people in front of a stationary camera and asks them to stare blankly into the lens, or the Empire State Building appears and disappears. Warhol doesn't edit. He merely connects white leader together, which explains the appearing and disappearing, exposed under or under-exposed, the total movie is eight hours. The underexposed part, one light-setting for the whole movie, is only three of those hours.[56]

Hopper had sat for Warhol's screen tests, but he didn't stare blankly into the camera's lens as instructed; instead, he emoted, performing like the professional actor he was. An early buyer of Warhol's art, Hopper in 1963 played host to the artist when he visited LA for his second show at the Ferus Gallery. Warhol described Hopper's house in Topanga Canyon as 'like an amusement park – the kind of whimsical carnival place you'd expect to find bubble-gum machines in. There were circus posters and movie props and red lacquered furniture and shellacked collages . . . it was the first whole house most of us had ever been to that had this kiddie-party atmosphere.'[57] The soirée Hopper held in his honour was, Warhol wrote, 'the most exciting thing that had ever happened to me'.[58]

Returning to LA in 1969, Warhol watched an early edit of *Easy Rider* at Peter Fonda's house. The rough cut was still without a synchronized music track, so Fonda played the records he planned to include on his hi-fi as the film unspooled. Warhol recalled that after the screening, Paul Morrissey had teased Fonda: 'What a great idea – making a movie about your record collection!' He continued:

> It was exciting to see young kids like Peter and Dennis [Hopper and Fonda were then respectively 33 and 29 years old; Warhol was 41] putting out the new youth image on their own terms. The idea of using rock that way made you think back to certain underground movies, but what made *Easy Rider* so new-looking was the Hollywood style of opening it up, getting it out, and moving it on the road . . . the exact image millions of kids were fantasizing – being free and on the road, dealing dope and getting persecuted.[59]

The underground films Warhol probably had in mind for their use of pop music were Jack Smith's *Flaming Creatures* (1963), Kenneth Anger's *Scorpio Rising* (1963) and *Kustom Kar Kommandos* (1965), Warren Sonbert's *Where Did Our Love Go?* (1966) and Bruce Conner's *Breakaway* (1966). They had all used recently recorded discs on their soundtracks.

To create a super-pop camp parade of homoeroticism, Anger used tracks by The Angels, The Crystals, Bobby Vinton and Ray Charles, among others, which he placed alongside images of motorcyclists in *Scorpio Rising* and a hot-rodder in *Kustom Kar Kommandos*. The Everly Brothers' cover of Gene Vincent's 'Be-Bop-a-Lula' was placed by Smith over the drag party sequence at film's end. Like Anger, Sonbert used an array of girl group records to accompany images of his friends, producing a lyrical document he described as 'Warhol Factory days . . . serendipity visits, Janis and Castelli and Bellevue glances . . . Malanga at work . . . glances at *Le Mépris* and *North by Northwest* . . . Girl rock groups and a disco opening . . . a romp through the Modern'.[60] Conner filmed Toni Basil dancing in various stages of undress to her then contemporary single 'Breakaway' (subsequently a Northern Soul classic). Shot in 16mm monochrome, Hopper and Dean Stockwell helped to light Basil; the images of her against a black background are fast-cut, producing a strobe-like effect or that of a nudie arcade loop rolling too quickly through the projector. The duration and rhythm of the pop song provided a timeframe, holding the kinetic, rapid-fire, fragmented shots together. Smith's and Conner's use of pre-recorded songs followed the teenpic exploitation film practice of using pop records to accompany a dance sequence, but there any similarity ended – in both cases the convention is unravelled and distorted.

Conversely, the licensed musical recordings in *Easy Rider* shared nothing with the teenpic's conventional use of pop as dance music, its source readily identifiable as coming from a phonograph, radio, television or live performance. *Easy Rider*'s musical soundtrack is all extradiegetic: it is not heard by the film's characters but exists for the sole pleasure of the film's viewers; no one is dancing to Steppenwolf. The volume of its muscular rock songs, Steppenwolf and Jimi Hendrix especially, which were played against the grandeur and spectacle of American landscapes, dwarfed the urban jukebox and transistor radio pop of the underground film-makers. But the link with the experiments of Smith, Anger, Sonbert and Conner, as Warhol intuited, was nevertheless there, and not just in the 16mm footage of Hopper, Fonda, Karen Black and Basil tripping out in

New Orleans, the lens flares, 360-degree pans, staccato flash-cut transitions and the fetishized montage of Captain America's bike overlaid with Steppenwolf's 'The Pusher'.

Writing in the *Village Voice*, rock critic Robert Christgau thought *Easy Rider* was the only film that used rock music well and 'does justice to its spirit'.[61] The music, he wrote, was

> not so much the culmination of a form as of a subculture. It would be difficult if not impossible to understand this subculture without intelligent reference to the music. In fact, *Easy Rider* is a double rarity – not only does it use rock successfully, it also treats the youth drop-out thing successfully. You can't have one without the other.[62]

The music's inherent authenticity confers on the film, Christgau suggested, a genuineness in its representation of contemporary youth culture: Hopper 'resisted pressure to commission a soundtrack because he understood the profound emotional value of known songs. He knew he could not make his movie honestly without real music.'[63] New Hollywood's film-makers would repeatedly play out this scenario of film and rock's mutually confirming authenticity.

This authenticity held a different truth to that found in Warhol, Smith, Anger, Sonbert and Conner. They drew from the overtly commercial and ephemeral, from a teenage girl culture that rock music defined itself against. That bias acted to suppress the complexity and vitality in pop that was aimed primarily at girls; for the entry on The Shangri-Las in her 1969 *Rock Encyclopedia*, Lillian Roxon wrote, 'It was the necrophilia of it all that shocked the adults, not the funkiness of three bitchy white girls who told it straight out that in motor-bike gangs you don't just hold hands. The Shangri-Las were akin to Clyde Barrow's Bonnie, in a reversal of the proverbial image, the velvet hands in the iron gloves.'[64] It was a stance that Echo Helstrom would have understood. The real truth, ignored by most rock critics, was that their favoured music existed on the same continuum as pop even if they appeared to be polar opposites. The authentic and the synthetic would invariably find meeting points along the scale on which they coexisted.

Tacit recognition of this fact meant that Christgau provided a way back along the line from *Easy Rider* to the underground film-makers. The movie and its music are 'romantic and unsophisticated', he wrote, with *Easy Rider* 'glorifying the outcasts and detesting and fearing the straights', a division shared with the dream pop of The Angels' 'My Boyfriend's Back', The Shangri-Las' 'I Can Never Go Home Anymore' and Carole King's 'He's a Bad Boy' – a confluence brought more starkly into focus by *Easy Rider*'s 'dark side', the killing of its heroes that was 'anticipated spiritually by all those teen death songs that don't seem quite so funny after all. Think about it. Isn't Tom Hayden the leader of the pack?'[65]

Refiguring countercultural leader Tom Hayden as a character in a Shadow Morton pop production pushed the authentic into an abstraction, but that play between the lyrical and the real is what Fonda and Hopper strove for in *Easy Rider*, a goal immeasurably aided by the film's use of rock music. The *Washington Post*'s Tom Rowe wrote that *Easy Rider* was a 'reflection of its generation . . . like a Bob Dylan song on celluloid', an image thought apt enough to be used as a quote-line in advertisements for the film.[66]

Reviewing *Easy Rider* for the counterculture paper *Los Angeles Free Press*, neophyte film-maker Paul Schrader was less impressed by its attempt to represent the day's key issues. Making a point of not joining in with the underground's 'instant and understandable' identification with the paranoia fuelled by *Easy Rider*, 'which is the staple item of the youth culture (often rightly so)', he took the film to task for being superficial in its politics and conventional in its narrative form:

> Instead of the musical redundancies of Max Steiner, we now have Jimi Hendrix and the Steppenwolf to reinforce every thematic passage. One could take such trite set-ups in a better spirit if Hopper hadn't revealed his sensitivity to be sophomoric at most every turn. He crudely intercuts the shoeing of a horse with the changing of a motorcycle tire, dwells on graffiti about Jesus in a jail and a statue of Christ in (of all places!) a whore-house.[67]

The film is essentially dishonest, he argued, because it feigns a profundity:

> If the mass media decides to exploit the Hopper-Fonda paranoia it will acquire something as worthless as last year's mod fashions and nude plays. Hopper and Fonda are too infatuated with the idea of themselves as pundits, Christs, martyrs, and Porky Pigs to examine their heroes, villains, or themselves – and this form of harmless paranoia is easily stolen and marketed throughout the media.[68]

Even with The Byrds' Roger McGuinn mimicking Dylan on the soundtrack, the ease with which the film's attitude and style might be appropriated, refashioned and resold made it more akin to a

Shangri-Las 45 than The Rolling Stones, its outlaw message readily repeatable and therefore saleable.

That parable of commercial exploitation had already been prefigured in the film *Head*, starring The Monkees, made a year earlier by *Easy Rider*'s financial backers Bert Schneider and Bob Rafelson and with a script by the latter and Jack Nicholson. The film was like an extended version of the album *The Who Sell Out* (1967), a self-reflexive examination of the pop star as commodity. *Head*, however, failed to find an audience; it didn't take The Monkees television following into the nation's movie theatres. Unlike The Who – self-determined *and* fabricated – The Monkees had no way out of the conundrum because they could not make a counter-play towards the authentic that was open to bands who were defined on their own terms before becoming pop stars.

When Schneider and Rafelson brought Steve Blauner on board as a partner, their company, Raybert, became BBS Productions. Blauner had worked alongside Schneider at Screen Gems and had been Bobby Darin's manager. The team knew pop culture from the inside, and with the success of *Easy Rider* as a model of sorts they shifted along the continuum away from the synthetic and ephemeral end of the market. The films that they produced under the BBS banner, *Five Easy Pieces* (1970), *The Last Picture Show, Drive, He Said, A Safe Place* (all 1971) and *The King of Marvin Gardens* (1972), all held an ambition to be something more than just another commercial product – perhaps even the American answer to the Nouvelle Vague.

Like Andrew Loog Oldham for The Rolling Stones, in 1966 The Byrds held an aspiration to make a film, though theirs would not be a story of youth in revolt à la *Clockwork Orange* or *Only Lovers Left Alive* (1964) that Oldham had planned for his charges. McGuinn instead had a personal ambition 'to make an experimental film using electronic colours', but for the band project, Carole Eastman, who had written the Monte Hellman Western *The Shooting* (1966) and would later provide the script for *Five Easy Pieces*, was hired to produce a scenario. An ex-dancer and model, Eastman was part of the band's social set and a good friend of the ex-wife of Jim Dickson, The Byrds' manager. In timely order, she produced a draft treatment based on the band's history, but beyond that the project remained undeveloped.[69]

The following year, 1967, The Byrds were in the studio working on the album that would become *The Notorious Byrd Brothers*. Among the tracks laid down that summer was the Gerry Goffin and Carole King composition 'I Wasn't Born to Follow', which would feature prominently in *Easy Rider*. The album was the last David Crosby would make with the band until their reunion album, recorded in 1972. Bad feelings had come to a head over the decision to exclude some of Crosby's songs, especially 'Triad', a sweet, floating tune about living with two lovers that was as much about breaking with the convention of the heterosexual couple as it was about Crosby's desire to be desired by more than one woman at a time.

Though a fully realized version of 'Triad' was recorded, it stayed in the vaults until the 1980s, and opinion differs over why it was not released until then.[70] One suggestion for its suppression was its (un)suitability for a band that still courted the pop charts and AM radio; certainly the song's description of the pleasures to be found in a three-way sexual liaison did not have the built-in ambiguity of 'Eight Miles High'. The latter's druggy allusions were easily countered with the banal idea that it was inspired by the experience of circling in an aeroplane over London. The planned denial of the obvious, so as not to incur controversy, was a policy shared with Production Code-era films, which worked on the premise that viewers took away different meanings from films. Sophisticated adult audiences might watch Bogart and Ingrid Bergman in *Casablanca* (1942) and read the elision between their embrace and their subsequent separation as the space in which the couple made love; other viewers might see the edit, if they saw it at all, as simply and innocently moving things along.[71] Similarly, in *Gilda* (1946), when Glenn Ford's character is told that Gilda (Rita Hayworth) had not done any of the things he believed she had, it is at once true and false – Gilda's infidelities never made it onto the screen, the most audiences saw was Hayworth removing her long black glove as she sang 'Put the Blame on Mame'. Gilda was innocent even if such fetishized displays signified the opposite, the film's planned ambiguity so well handled that it evaded the censor's scissors.

The meaning of 'Triad' was never so ambivalent, but what didn't work for The Byrds, still nominally a pop group, worked exceptionally well for the rock band Jefferson Airplane, who covered the song on their 1968 album *Crown of Creation* and released it as the B-side of a single. With Grace Slick filtering her inner Jeanne Moreau, the frisson in Crosby's plea for sexual liberation is immeasurably enhanced by a woman asking her lovers to embrace the idea of sharing a communal bed. Yet Slick's pleasure in being disreputable was a tease: her outlaw stance was already fully part of her and the band's personae, her sexual trespasses had already been factored into the scheme of things. This was less the case with other female singers.

Produced and arranged by Barry Manilow in 1973, Sally Kellerman's 'Triad' is a gorgeous, soulful version that is more radical than the Airplane's because their trade, their appeal, was, as they sang, in breaking the rules learned in school, outlawing themselves from Main Street, Amerika. There was nothing ambiguous about the line 'Up against the wall, motherfucker' in 'We Can Be Together' from their album *Volunteers* (1969). As 'Hot Lips' Houlihan in Robert Altman's *M*A*S*H* (1970), Kellerman's male fantasy object carried none of that radicalism; her plea for sexual licence was thus more unexpected and carried a greater charge in articulating untrammelled female desire.

The figure of the *ménage à trois* had entered American movies from Godard's *Bande à part* (1964) and Truffaut's *Jules et Jim*. The two women in these films, played by Anna Karina and Jeanne Moreau respectively, feel no guilt or shame (even if punished) for their transgression of monogamous relationships. *Bonnie and Clyde* filtered such a triad through the titular characters and C. W. Moss (Michael J. Pollard). The director, Arthur Penn, and producer, Warren Beatty, however, rowed back from Clyde and C. W. as lovers, an idea that had much salience in early drafts of the script. The romantic triangle of two men and one woman was amplified in *Butch Cassidy and the Sundance Kid* (1969) and provided a novel twist to what would otherwise have been generic fare. The triad would again be evoked (and repressed) in *Two-Lane Blacktop*, figure strongly in *The Hired Hand*, *Doc* (1971), *Dirty Little Billy* (1972) and in *Monte Walsh* (1970), with Moreau alongside Lee Marvin and Jack Palance. The trope was exhausted in *Little Fauss and Big Halsy* (1970), starring Robert Redford, whose character formed and reformed the apex of numerous love triangles as he rode his way across Arizona and California deserts on a dirt bike with Pollard alongside.

As it slipped away from the duality of boy-meets-girl, the figure of a trio of lovers also stepped around the tired Hollywood convention of the formation of the couple that was so readily and commonly used to resolve its narratives. The third party in the equation provided a dramatic tension that may or may not be contained at film's end. For the film-makers who used the trope, it also gave a hint of the sexual revolution that was readily accessible to rock stars – typified by Mick Jagger with Anita Pallenberg and Michèle Breton in *Performance* – which they felt predisposed to exploit.

That new permissiveness was programmed into the films that Schneider, Rafelson and Blauner would produce and those that would be delivered by Ned Tanen at Universal, which matched the budgets, talent and ethos of BBS. In an interview with *Show* magazine in March 1971, Tanen told their reporter:

> About 14 or 15 months ago I had been talking with Lou Wasserman, the president, about an idea where you could have a film program that would basically be only one segment of your overall motion picture operation. An autonomous operation that would not be responsible to – and I don't mean this negatively – the bureaucracy of the studio. After some months of discussion, the company asked me if I would go ahead with it, and I agreed to so long as I could do it the way I felt it should be done. If I was wrong, then I'd be wrong . . . It's probably the smallest operation in the history of motion pictures.[72]

At least as he pitched it to *Show*'s reporter, Tanen was in the business of supporting artists, selling films based on the director's vision and integrity, his sincerity and honesty:

The only films that really make it, with rare exceptions, are those that are the vision of a filmmaker and a commitment on the part of the filmmaker, to the exclusion of everything else. That's all he can care about. So when Dennis Hopper goes off to make this film, it's taking two years of his life, in which period he isn't making 10 cents. He's gambling that the film's really going to be worthwhile. When Peter Fonda does *The Hired Hand* – the first thing he's ever directed – he's putting a year and a half to two years of his life into that film. Now these men could command a lot of money going out picking up acting assignments. That's not what they want to do. And those are the kind of people I want to be in business with . . . When you deal with Monte Hellman, you have a guy who, given the choice of the film or his life, would lay down in the street and ask for a car to hit him. And Hopper is more that way than Hellman.[73]

The art of film was more important than life itself, so it was sold.

In his 1938 novel *I Should Have Stayed Home*, a sour tale of Hollywood extras, Horace McCoy's protagonist, a handsome young man who has left Georgia in search of adventure, fun and fame, looks back to the start of his journey from the point when he realized his dream has ended:

Ahead of me, on top of the Newberry store, a big neon sign flashed on and off. It was an outline map of the United States and these words kept appearing: 'ALL ROADS LEAD TO HOLLYWOOD – And the pause that refreshes. ALL ROADS LEAD TO HOLLYWOOD – And the pause that refreshes. ALL ROADS LEAD TO HOLLYWOOD –'[74]

The advertising was just dandy, who knew they had nothing to sell?

> I turned off Vine Street onto Hollywood Boulevard, going west, telling myself I was crazy to admit that even now it was too late. I hadn't stayed home, I was here, on the famous boulevard, in Hollywood, where miracles happen, and maybe today, maybe the next minute some director would pick me out passing by.[75]

For so many of the new generation of film-makers, Hollywood was already home. They hadn't strayed from the family hearth to pursue their dreams; they had no need to be picked out by a passing director. It was their world to inherit; the trick they pulled off was to suggest they had gained it by hard-scrabble labour, from experience earned on the road, with sweat and dirt honestly come by. In self-defined exile, with their privilege hiding in plain sight, they had this tale to tell, and they told it with glorious, splendid elan.

1

The Hired Hand: Circling Back to the End Again

The Hired Hand, a distinctly minor Western that evokes images
of a Haight-Ashbury hippie wearing boots and buckskins . . .
Director Fonda never knows when to leave the art-film shtick
alone. It's been a long time since one small movie about two
lonesome cowboys has embraced so many slow dissolves,
freeze-action stills, shots of dappled light through branches
and Marlboro silhouettes against a crimson sunset.[1]

Playboy, October 1971

On the bank of a river, beside a cigar-shaped sandbar, three
men start their day. As they rise they are momentarily
touched by the 'fragile blessing' of nature: the sound of running
water and birdsong, the morning mist dissipating with the sun's
heat. One man, Harris, builds a small fire while another, Collings,
fishes for breakfast. The youngest of the three, Dan, emerges last
and, still heavy with sleep, throws himself into the river's cold
waters. The men are at ease in one another's company and attend
to nothing but their immediate needs. No threat or fear is indi-
cated, just the recording of the rituals of routine that they practise
with a 'hard granular patience'.[2]

Time shifts for the men at a crepuscular pace; their morning is uneventful until the fishing line snags on an object floating downstream:

> He started pulling on the line and its bundle came heavily, weighty against the current and, lolling in its grip, a dark, sodden mass of clothing and hair and the white turn of a hand and then, suddenly clear, the whole botched boggle of a face.
>
> Dan stopped pulling and let his blanket slip. Harris winced, as though looking into bright light. Only Collings made no reaction.
>
> 'Aw gawd, it's a little girl', Dan said and started to pull on the line.
>
> 'Leave it be'. But Dan didn't hear him and the body came in almost to the shelf and could be seen clearly. Her hair had been chestnut and her dress once purple.
>
> Collings cut the line before Dan knew what he was doing.[3]

The morning's spell is broken, its promise of renewal rent, its waking 'dreams crumbled into death'.[4]

The opening of Alan Sharp's novel, based on his screenplay and published to coincide with the release of the film, is rendered in Peter Fonda's direction as a set of overlaid actions that are blurred and obscured by the play of sunlight jouncing on the river's surface. The scene falls further out of time with Bruce Langhorne's soundtrack of plucked and struck string instruments underscored by the droning buzz of a hurdy-gurdy. Lacking sustain, the musical notes hang briefly and then drop. In their place follows more of the same. Repetitious, dreamy. Sound and image combine into a gently pulsing kaleidoscopic atmosphere within which the men appear to float. The scene is languorous, extended and detached before the object caught in the line reveals itself to be a dead child. Time then pauses, folds back on itself, hangs suspended like the water drops clinging to the line that is raised above the river before it is cut by Collings. The action is a release, momentum is regained. The swirling body floats on, and the men break camp.

The body of the dead girl is an augury – Dan will be killed in the next scene and Collings's fate is sealed – but beyond the

Poster for *The Hired Hand* (dir. Peter Fonda, 1971).

figuration of dread it also signifies how conditional and tenuous the ties are that bind one person to another. Dan wants to retrieve the girl's body, to pull her from the river's clutches, to give her a proper burial. But Collings knows that she has been too long in the water and her body will fall apart in their hands. The river cannot give up her corporeal being without the image of lost innocence becoming as despoiled as the girl's putrefied flesh, but the idea itself cannot so readily float on. Once seen and identified, even as it spools away from view, her body will haunt the men (as it will also the reader and viewer).

Whether in the novel or on film, the opening scene is exquisite, so beautiful and delicate it might disintegrate with the slightest touch or from the gentlest of inquiries. It will find its own shape or no shape at all. It is indeed a blessed and fragile thing. The scene explores in miniature the themes that will be played out until the story itself is finished. But there is truly no end here, just a set of returns. The story places beginnings up against endings, motifs of leaving echoed as returns, moments of drift refigured at their most amorphous as points of decision or dedication to a task at hand. Burying Dan, Harris reads from the Gospel of Thomas over his grave:

> Disciples said to Jesus 'Tell us how our end will be?' Jesus said, 'Have you then delivered the beginning that you enquire about the end? For where the beginning is, there shall be the end. Blessed is he who shall stand at his beginning and he shall know the end and not taste death.'

Both Harris and Collings are mature and experienced enough to know the end, which they can taste as certainly as they can the 'rattlesnake spit and scorpion piss' that flavours the rotgut they drink, which is why they turn back and head for an uncertain sanctuary with Hannah and Martha, the wife and daughter Collings had fled from seven years earlier.

Hard and tight, like a knot in his gut, there is an ache in Harry Collings that will never be satisfied. The three men had reckoned, in an aimless way, to head west to California, if for no other reason than to see the Pacific. But when Dan is murdered, Collings turns around and heads back east. 'I'm going home,' he tells Harris. 'How do you know you've got a home to go to, Harry?' asks his saddle pal. 'Well, I think I ought to go and see,' he replies. Home is the place Collings has left behind, but the return cannot fulfil all his needs and so he is fated to leave again. Back with Hannah (Verna Bloom), Collings does not take up the role of husband and father but works for her as a hired hand. He labours for his keep alongside Harris. Talking to Harris, Hannah bitterly tells him Collings will once more leave her and her daughter, it is 'just a matter of time'. 'Well, most things are,' he says in reply. But nothing is more certain than this time. The alliterative triad, Harris, Hannah and Harry, make for an eternal romantic triangle. Hannah wants Harry, he wants her, but he also wants the companionship of Harris, and the latter wants Hannah but not at the expense of his friendship with Harry.

Within the triad, who is the titular 'hired hand'? The front of the novel's jacket declares 'Peter Fonda as The Hired Hand', but in his *Playboy* interview Fonda calls Warren Oates's character, Harris, the hired hand, and in the story, in the novel and film, it is both. The hired hand is less a single figure than any man Hannah chooses to couple with, like those whom she let in her bed after Harry left and whom he now comes to replace. But Hannah too might be the hired hand, or at least that is her fear: 'Perhaps all he would require of her would be her body in bed and her performance in the kitchen. She envisaged a situation where she was only a kind of housekeeper to the two of them, where she was the hired hand.'[5]

The hired hand is a democratic figure forged in a country where all men are deemed to be equal. In the new Republic, the 'hired hand' replaced the role of the servant so as not to contradict the concept of self-determination. Server and served are predicated on a hierarchy, one step removed from master and slave. To be a hired hand is to claim autonomy as a citizen even if the terms of employment, the relationship, differ only in those used to describe wage labour. Yet crucially the role is not fixed, a citizen's present station in life might change, unlike a monarch's subject's. In the Republic, the hired hand can imagine being his own boss, owning her own labour.

Hannah's fear is that the autonomy she has as a landowner might be lost, that roles will be reversed and she will be subservient to the men's desires. As Harry moves to reclaim his role as her husband, to stop being her hired hand, he asks Hannah about those she has slept with in his absence. She refuses to give him the information he asks for: 'does it matter?' She tells him he was long gone before she took another man to her bed. She had needs and she chose the partner to fulfil her desire, but always, at the end of the season, when the work was done, her needs satisfied or not, she paid off the hired hand, 'because the man that's in a woman's bed thinks he's the boss and I didn't want another man'.

Female desire, female control of the bedroom and the land, opposed to a man's fecklessness and lack of responsibility, is at the story's core. Hannah's character does not cross into the role of the transgressive female protagonist, the type portrayed by Barbara Stanwyck in *Forty Guns* (1957) and *The Furies* (1950), a deviant, perverse figure who traduces gender boundaries in her refusal to accept the idea of submission to a patriarchal figure. Hannah stays within the historically prescribed role for her gender, but she pushes, almost to their breaking point, against those restrictions. Older, and more experienced, she had seduced Harry before he had yet turned twenty. She chose him because he did not present a threat to her as the dominant partner, and she survives even after he has left her and their daughter.

Though Hannah has been ostracized from the town's social circles, only invited back in when Collings announces his return by posting bills outside the sheriff's office and elsewhere, the film and novel are not much interested in the wider community. Instead they prefer to work on a contrast with the Del Norte thugs who killed Dan. McVey (Severn Darden) and his three underlings are a version of the Clanton clan in John Ford's *My Darling Clementine* (1946), which starred Peter's father Henry as Wyatt Earp. Led by Walter Brennan's violent patriarch, the clan, without any female influence, is utterly bestial.

McVey's gang are served by a 'Mexican Woman', played by Rita Rogers, who rarely earned a credit for her film appearances. For her earlier roles, IMDB lists her as 'Girl on Wiltshire Blvd', 'B Girl', 'Bit Girl', but she did make it as a cover girl for the nudie magazine *Knight* in 1967, where she was trailed as 'one of the most exciting movie finds in years'. The issue's lead story was on the 'Weird World of Psychedelic Music'. She is beautiful in a Claudia Cardinale mould and was cast to give the film some sex appeal. Her comeliness is incongruous in this setting. In the novel her character is shackled and repeatedly raped; she is a slave. (She is also, as one critic supposed, a Mary Magdalene figure, which rhymes with the film's ad hoc Christian symbolism – the stigmata implied in the scarring of McVey's feet and Collings dying with an outlaw and a thief on either side of him.[6])

Having left Collings and Hannah, Harris travels west. His journey takes him perilously close to Del Norte and he is caught by McVey's men. Crippled in both feet after being shot by Collings in revenge for the killing of Dan, McVey in turn retaliates. He sends one of his lackeys to find Collings and present him with one of Harris's fingers and the threat that he will cut off the rest of his digits unless he returns to Del Norte. In *Playboy*, Fonda worried that when the severed finger was unwrapped viewers would at first think it was Harris's penis. It is a throwaway line, a bit of a jest, but the truth is that the set-up is all about emasculation. If Collings stays with his wife he is as good as castrated, his relationship with Hannah will forever be deferential, while to go and rescue Harris means he once again plays out the part of the faithless and feckless male; conversely, he might prop up his masculinity by being steadfast in his commitment to his friend. But he cannot be both faithful husband and loyal friend.

Collings's impossible position is resolved by having him meet his death like a man. With the triad sundered, Harris returns to the farm to take Collings's place, not as Hannah's husband but as her hired hand:

When the horseman reached the edge of the yard, she saw that it was Harris. She rose and went indoors. Harris rode across to the shed and dismounted. In her room Hannah lit the lamp. Harris turned the gelding into the corral and carried his saddle into the shed. He lit the lamp and found himself a place to lie down.[7]

Which is how both film and novel conclude. When Harris takes his place with Hannah and her daughter, he is following a well-trodden path by replicating the ending of *The Oxbow Incident* (1942), where Henry Fonda's character plans to find the widow of the innocent man (Dana Andrew) whom the lynch mob has strung up, and *The Treasure of the Sierra Madre*, where Bob Curtin (Tim Holt) decides to find the wife of Cody (Bruce Bennett), a prospector killed by bandits. Films of wandering and returns.

As we enter the Seventies, the decade's first authentic cult hero has already emerged: Peter Fonda, who personifies – on screen and off – the radical lifestyle that has gained increasing currency among young Americans. Not since James Dean's *Rebel Without a Cause* and Marlon Brando's *The Wild One* has a movie actor so captured the imagination and admiration of a generation. In *Easy Rider*, Fonda projected the polarized mood of young America with such forcefulness that the film has become a requiem for the short-lived Aquarian Age.

Playboy, September 1970

This was how *Playboy* magazine introduced its intimate and candid 1970 interview with Peter Fonda. Topics discussed included how he lived with success and stardom, his love of sailing, his relationship with his father and sister, and the key political issues of the day: the environment, race, Nixon, Vietnam, education, drugs (marijuana and LSD), and his thoughts on the system and the counterculture – America, 1984. Today.

The piece assiduously constructed a narrative of Fonda as unaffected by stardom, shunning the glitz, glamour and frivolity of Hollywood-style showbiz. His house in the hills of Coldwater Canyon has an adjoining swimming pool and tennis court, but the latter is filled with his children's toys. The house itself is furnished in 'Goodwill Industries' moderne', thrift-store chic: 'it's about as far from movie-star ambience as one can imagine.'[8] *Playboy* covered his film career, including all the pablum prior to *Easy Rider* and his latest project, *The Hired Hand*. Of the latter, Fonda said, 'It's a very simple film. People may wonder why I'm doing it especially after *Easy Rider*, which seems to be such a contemporary statement of our problems. It's what I call a classical Western.'[9] *The Hired Hand* was a return to the genre's verities, but had he in fact gone anywhere? Westerns, Fonda told *Rolling Stone* the following year, 'are the way Americans tell our fairy tales and our parables. All our films are Westerns. *Easy Rider* was a Western . . . Absolutely.'[10]

May 1971, two months before the release of *The Hired Hand*: Peter Fonda is the cover star of *Rolling Stone*. Annie Leibovitz's photographic study shows him bare-chested, wearing his hair long; he is bearded, dressed in old Levi's and, sardonically, perched on his head is a tin hard-hat. Elsewhere in the same issue, Sam Peckinpah is interviewed on the set of *Straw Dogs* and the press junket for the Taos, New Mexico, premiere of the documentary *The American Dreamer*, featuring Dennis Hopper, is covered.

Fonda has his movie debut as director to promote, and, to make things interesting, *Rolling Stone*'s reporter is flown to Hawaii, where the star has moored his yacht. Told in eight scenes, the subplot of the story is that Fonda is escaping from LA, his parents' legacy and all that Hollywood fakery. The journey begun with *Easy Rider*, his search for America continues: it was a pseudo-psychological study of Fonda that promoted the image of an outlaw film-maker against the opposing and overwhelming evidence of the star's inherited Hollywood credentials and equally privileged present.

When not playing pirates on his yacht, Fonda was making an 8mm film, *The Deleted Portions of the Zapruder Film, Part II*, which may or may not be pure fantasy, the film's existence as much as its subject. As for *The Hired Hand*, it is a film located in the very real dilemma of what happens when an obligation to one person conflicts with that made to another.

John Weisman's *Rolling Stone* review of *The Hired Hand* opened by citing Richard W. B. Lewis's *The American Adam* (1955), a seminal work of literary criticism in which American exceptionalism is embodied in the figure of Adam. Cast out of the Garden of Eden, the American assumes the role of an anti-hero. He is, Weisman summarized, an outsider, who searches for 'a kind of honor that is uniquely American'.[11] This is the character type Fonda's cowboy is modelled on, but the film 'fails dismally' in its task, Weisman wrote.

> Basically the story of a lank, bone-tired saddle tramp who, after seven years on the road in search of himself and America, decides to leave his long-time trail buddy and head back to his wife and daughter, *The Hired Hand* should be the denouement of an American odyssey, in which Harry Collings, the hero, finds his honor and truth in what appears to be a senseless death.[12]

The only redeeming element, for Weisman, is the performance of Warren Oates, who, he argued, is also the only positive in Hellman's *Two-Lane Blacktop*, another film trying to resurrect an American Adam.

For Weisman, the essential problem with *The Hired Hand* is that the character's journey is rendered in a hokey and phoney manner and hampered by self-indulgent direction: 'Gilded with meaningful stares, endless close-ups of faces that say nothing, and travelogue-like montages, the film becomes a parody of its supposedly classic form – a kind of early west *Easy Rider* in which most justifiably at its close, Fonda could again say, "We blew it".'[13] He dismissed Fonda's overloaded symbolism – air, earth, fire and water from which comes life – as being 'laid on so thickly that it overpowers Alan Sharp's lightweight script right from the comatose, torpid opening sequence to the final, pastoral longshot and freeze-frame'.[14] Bruce Langhorne's 'up-to-date banjo score . . . adds nothing to the film but a saccharine coating to an already sucrose filling'.[15] Vilmos Zsigmond's cinematography, used 'masterfully' in *McCabe and Mrs Miller*, is here used carelessly, so that 'reality is hopelessly distorted.'[16] The symbolism and the reliance on hackneyed genre convention – the 'good guys wear white teeth' while the bad guys 'cause little Mexican boys to scurry for cover' – undermine the film's authenticity, which is further and irredeemably scarred by modern colloquialisms and zipper-fly Levi's.[17]

In fact, though Fonda does wear Levi's, they are button-fly with a cinch fastening on the waistline and fixings for suspenders. In these aspects, at least, his costume was not at all anachronistic, but that was not Weisman's point. *Newsweek* called *The Hired Hand* 'an antiquarian's "road" picture lost in the roadless isolation of 1880', which is a fair summation of the way the film pulls in two directions at once in its attempt to be historically authentic and of contemporary relevance.[18] Whatever authenticity, or lack thereof, Fonda's jeans might carry, his Levi's are cut whippet-slim to better emphasize his long, lean legs, as if he has stepped straight out of the shoot for Leibovitz and walked unchanged, except for the head-wear, in front of Zsigmond's camera, all the while maintaining his star aura of the authentic cult hero.

Not all contemporary reviews found the film to be blighted by Fonda's 'ponderous epic style'. Some, like the *New York Times* critic Roger Greenspun, found 'spiritual imminence' in its wandering.[19]

Its greatest glory is in the passing of the natural day, the coming of the evening light – in all those commonplace gifts of awareness that could be merely decorative effect but that here seem visionary insight . . . photographed by Vilmos Zsigmond with a perfect feeling for dramatic nature. Its music . . . is simple, directly appealing, and very beautiful.[20]

In the *Los Angeles Times*, Charles Champlin thought Langhorne's score to be 'austere to the point of being abrasive', which chimed well with the 'poetically spare story' Fonda was telling, but 'the undertaking demanded a particularly strong control, a rigorous paring away of inessentials, the sustaining of tone. Instead there are splendors in lieu of austerities and technique which forces attention upon itself.'[21] Like Champlin, other critics found fault with the film's declarative voice, stressing its formal properties and thereby drawing the viewer away from the story being told. The line between art and artifice was severed, leaving the body of the film to drift and spool in the current until it too fell apart as its audience tried to maintain its grasp of events.

He never wanted to be an actor, to live in his father's or sister's shadow. 'I wanted other things. A home, a family, security. Children,' the 22-year-old Fonda told *Seventeen* magazine in 1962.[22]

'All people seemed to be concerned with was what they could get out of me because my name was Fonda and Henry was my father.'[23] This is the story that would follow him throughout his career, the son of one of Hollywood's most respected and venerated actors and the brother to a much more celebrated sibling. And yet, 'finally I realized that I had to do the thing I enjoyed most: acting. Acting always makes me feel as if I have just put on a handsome new suit that fits me very well.'[24] So here he was, making his Broadway debut in a comedy called *Blood, Sweat and Stanley Poole*, in his first movie, *Tammy Takes Over*, and picked by Hollywood columnist Hedda Hopper as a 'new face'.[25]

A year later, in 1963, he had a bit part as a 'sensitive soldier' in Carl Foreman's Second World War drama *The Victors*, played a 'mental patient' in Robert Rossen's *Lilith* (released in 1964) and featured in *Seventeen* magazine.[26] The article's theme is that even though Fonda – presented as tall, slim and strikingly handsome – has a famous father and sister, and a significant inheritance from his mother, who died when he was ten years old, he is, despite his physical attributes and privileged background, a deeply thoughtful, complex and sympathetic character – a gentleman even. He has struggled with school, friendships and relationships with girls, who only seemed to want to date him because of who he is: 'Besides I made the big mistake; I would take girls to dinner. Nobody else did. They went to a dance or drank beer with the crowd. But I like to know about people, I wanted to *talk* to the girl. The only time you can do that is at dinner. You open up a little, she opens up a little. You get to know someone.'[27] His ambition? 'I want to be both a commercial and an artistic success, and I think I can be.'[28] In London with Jim Mitchum, son of Robert, a reporter asks whether their father's name and fame has been a help or a hindrance. Fonda doesn't 'think it has helped him at all professionally'. Mitchum contradicts him: 'It's been a help in that I know all the important people.'[29] Fonda's attempts to move away from his privilege and family always floundered.

After the publicity mill had closed on those two films, Fonda next appeared in *Seventeen* as a 'personality poster', which pictured him straddling his custom Harley in a scene from *The Wild Angels*: 'Anyplace you want to stir up a little excitement, hang a Peter Fonda poster. Or hang Steve McQueen, The Monkees, Bobby Dylan, The Rolling Stones, Marlon Brando. All larger than life, 30" by 40" . . . $1.00 at stores everywhere.' From a young woman's ideal, sensitive dinner date to a hoodlum biker sharing wall space with Dylan and the Stones.[30] His outlaw credentials had been raised a mite earlier, during post-production on *The Wild Angels* in 1966, when he and three others were charged with possession of marijuana.[31] And he was still mod enough to get passing mentions for his style choices in *Vogue*: 'Supposing you hankered after several kinds of sunglass frames. What colour lenses to fill them with? . . . Yellow, to see through the haze, define like a foglight; striking on motorcyclist Peter Fonda in the chilling film, *The Wild Angels*.'[32] *Vogue* used a candid photograph of Fonda looking louche and reported he was 'Currently at work on his second independently produced film, *Mardi Gras*. His way is his completely, takes in a quicksilver wit, easy charm along the way. His look draws heavily on the glamour of the West: his leather jeans from Mayfair Riding Shop in Los Angeles are worn regularly in the swimming pool to prevent sag.'[33]

The Wild Angels 'confirmed [Fonda's] status as a teen hero', doubling in a few weeks after its release 'the gross take of American-International's previous record holder, *Bikini Beach*'.[34] Fonda was a new star for a new film genre, the motorcycle outlaw picture:

'Teen-agers, Fonda says, perceive so much hypocrisy, so many outmoded values and so much blind authoritarianism among their elders that they are finding fewer and fewer reasons to respect them,' Kevin Thomas wrote in the *Los Angeles Times*.[35] Fonda had been involved in the recent riots on Sunset Strip, where young people had pushed back against repressive curfew and loitering laws: 'Man, the kids have had it. There's so much that's not real, and they can see it.'[36] He intended to make his own movies that 'reflect the new awareness'. He planned to make a 'Pop art musical comedy fantasy' with his friend Brandon de Wilde. He didn't want to be a teenage idol, 'I want them to think for themselves': 'Ultimately, Fonda is a man aware that "the map is not the territory", as the semanticists say, in hope of making us aware that reality and our

Peter Fonda (right), the son of actor Henry Fonda (left), speaks to reporters at the time of his trial on charges of marijuana possession, 12 December 1966.

description of it are not synonymous.'[37] Two days after this story in the *Times*, Fonda was pictured in the newspaper being arrested on the Strip. He told officers he was making a documentary.[38]

Meanwhile, the court case for marijuana possession got under way in December. The trial finished before the end of the month with the jury split and the case against Fonda dismissed when a key witness failed to appear. The judge, however, left Fonda in little doubt that he considered him to be guilty as charged.[39] When the story had first been reported, it seemed only a few plants had been found in a house in Tarzana that Fonda was said to have rented but which he claimed only to visit with friends. In fact, 'large quantities of marijuana were found all over the house', the judge admonished Fonda, 'and it is inconceivable that you were unaware of its presence in view of your repeated and prolonged visits there'.[40] Henry Fonda had testified on his son's behalf, which suggested there was still some familial loyalty and the generational rift could yet be bridged.[41] The divide continued to spasm and cramp in the increasing number of press reports that *The Wild Angels*, and then *The Trip*, Corman's LSD melodrama starring Fonda, elicited: 'Peter Fonda, 27, noncompliant son of Henry and simpatico brother of Jane, is left-handed, and it bugs him,' was the opening line of a *New York Times* profile of the actor.[42] He told the reporter about a recent run-in with a pettifogging policeman who had cited him for jaywalking, a story that followed his 'slight altercation' with the doorman at the Polo Lounge of the Beverly Hills Hotel, 'who chose to go cataleptic about Fonda's lack of a cravat'.[43] The issue was solved when a house tie was supplied. In case the police and the establishment took his recent film roles too literally and had half a memory for his recent marijuana bust, Fonda made it clear that these days he neither drinks nor smokes anything.

The piece was illustrated by a still from *The Trip* of a bug-eyed, hallucinating Fonda and two of his poems. 'Hash' repeats the title in graphic typewritten form, 'HASHHASHHAHSASHASH' with the interjection 'WHEW!' followed, after a few more examples of 'Hash', by 'love' stacked one on top of the other four times, before concluding with 'hash pipe love'. A final 'WHEW!' ends his Beatnik versification. The second poem is more trite, playing with news headlines about the Diggers feeding starving hippies in San Francisco, farmers wasting milk to artificially raise its price and a bus full of children killed by an anti-tank mine. It ends with the word 'love' repeated nine times. Fonda asked the reporter if she understood Marshall McLuhan, Ravi Shankar, Hugh Masekela, Jiddu Krishnamurti or even The Beatles. 'He does,' she wrote, 'they speak to his generation, which is not yours.'[44] Then, in keeping with her subject, she feigned a kind of hip confusion, speaking to herself as if to her readers: 'The generation gap is; trying to leap across it, you've tumbled into it, and it's dark and scary. Make lists. They're calming. Okay. But stop faking his argot. You can barely comprehend hang-up, let alone turn-on, freak-out, flip-out.'[45] In that moment of ersatz delirium, the reporter granted Fonda a gravitas his poetry did not warrant and which his philosophy did not merit.

Fonda did have a thesis to impart, one that stretched from *The Wild Angels* through *The Hired Hand*: he had an ethos that underpinned his method as a film-maker, to find a 'greater truth'. In one interview after another, he uttered that belief as if it were a mantra – 'he's addicted to telling the truth at all costs,' wrote the *Times*'s reporter, 'whether the truth hurts him or anybody else.' He sought, she implied, the truth about today, about parents, sex, drugs, violence, freedom, society's ills and its panaceas, whenever, wherever it was that a lie needed to be called out. It was never a particularly profound thesis, but it could support a tagline or two on the bottom of a movie poster.

The Hired Hand was first announced by *Variety* in February 1970, the movie part of a five-film portfolio of productions that belonged to the London independent Mitchell Lifton, who planned to fill a gap left by the majors' cutbacks. Fonda's film would be shot in Mexico with a budget of $600,000. Lifton would maintain 'complete control', it was reported, even though the film was being made for Universal.[46] Having a British producer partly explains how Scottish writer Sharp's script found its way to Fonda, though the actor's father, Henry, later told the journal that he had passed the story on to Peter.[47] Sharp had previously published two novels and had a number of television credits, but as far as Hollywood was concerned he was an unknown quantity. That would quickly change when his screenplay for the George C. Scott thriller *The Last Run* went into production around the same time as *The Hired Hand*,[48] and later with his scripts for Robert Aldrich's *Ulanza's Raid* (1972) and Arthur Penn's *Night Moves* (1975).

By May, still scheduled for release by Universal, who now were also providing financing under Ned Tanen's management, production had shifted to Pando Co. – which Fonda had set up with producer William Hayward to oversee *Easy Rider*. Lifton was listed as an associate producer on the film's credits. Locations were moved north of the border to New Mexico and the film's budget had risen to $800,000.[49] By June, Warren Oates and New York stage actor Verna Bloom, who had made her mark in *Medium Cool* (1969), were added as key cast members.[50]

Bloom had appeared in a May edition of *Life* magazine in a feature on the new Hollywood actresses 'who are real people':

Hollywood, the super colossal fantasy mill, once extruded starlets like link sausages, all perfect of feature, pneumatic of bust. Whatever God failed to give them, the studios gave . . . But now Hollywood has changed and so has stardom. Film makers intent on reality have created a whole generation of new movie actresses utterly uninterested in what anybody thinks they ought to look like. Their dream is to be themselves – that and to be first-class actresses. In their honesty they have the vulnerability, the spice of character, the sense of loveliness flawed which makes them especially believable and interesting, both on and off camera.[51]

Newsweek also ran a feature on Bloom as an upcoming star alongside other likely faces that included Barbara Hershey, Dorothy Tristan, Carrie Snodgrass and Sally Kellerman: 'The new American films want girls who look real, attainable, fallible. Here are five new faces who promise to fulfil that demand.'[52] In May 1970 further cast members were announced, including Severn Darden, Owen Orr and Robert Pratt.[53]

The Hired Hand was framed as belonging to Universal's autumn roster of fifteen forthcoming medium-budget films, which also included *Airport, The Beguiled, Diary of a Mad Housewife, They Might Be Giants, The Last Movie* and *Two-Lane Blacktop*. The latter two and *The Hired Hand* were scheduled by Universal for an August 1971 release.[54] Fonda had stipulated that his film should initially be shown only in houses with an eight hundred maximum capacity. The choice of venues was a compromise – he had originally wanted the film to play in even smaller cinemas. Such self-imposed limits on the film's exhibition called explicit attention to its art house pretensions, regardless of it being a Western. *Variety* reported in the same news piece, somewhat facetiously, that Fonda was presently shooting a Super 8 film in the Pacific Northwest, 'which should limit the size of theatres for this one'.[55] For Fonda, his auteur status was anything but a joke.

In its review, *Boxoffice* wrote that to call '*The Hired Hand* a western is comparable to labelling *Easy Rider* a motorcycle movie: it's in that vein but something much more than average . . . The Pando production won't necessarily appeal to the action crowd, nor is it intended to. Rather, art and specialty houses would be the best outlets.'[56] The review in effect confirmed the correctness of Fonda's stipulation that the film's first run be at more intimate venues. The *Variety* review supported the idea that it was an 'off-beat western' with 'some appeal to younger audiences'.[57] Yet, like Weisman, the reviewer thought the film a failure, having 'a disjointed story, a largely unsympathetic hero, and an obtrusive amount of cinematic gimmickry which renders inarticulate the confused story subtleties'.[58]

> Dramatically unmotivated violence and brutality alternate with dazzling montage to provide a literal trip for turned-on audiences; others may find the Universal release a heavy bummer . . . Film evidently is trying to show a truer picture of early western life, as opposed to formula plotting; but when one is trying to buck an entrenched cliché, extreme care and artfulness are required to persuade those few not already convinced.[59]

The proprietor of the Idle Hour Theatre in Hardwick, Vermont, submitted his thoughts on the movie to *Boxoffice*: 'Arty photography doesn't put any pep into this production. It is well made, but failed to produce business at the box office.'[60]

Before the round of promotional events began, and the lack of action at the ticket counter was apparent, Fonda had word sent out that he would not do any interview that required him 'to wear a suit, tie or jacket and he will also not discuss his actress-sister Jane Fonda or his actor-father Henry Fonda'.[61] His stance of noncon-formity, carried over from the AIP caricatures in *The Wild Angels* and *The Trip* through to *Easy Rider*, and performed to maximum excess by Hopper, was taken by *Variety*, when it reported on his New York junket, for what it self-evidently was, a routine: 'He also self-appreciates the incongruity of his standard sloppy appear-ance (long hair, beard, blue jeans, denim shirt) against the posh surroundings of his Regency Hotel suite.'[62]

To back up his rebel film-maker credentials he told his New York audience as much about his self-financed science-fiction movie *Idaho Transfer*, which he was directing, as he talked about *The Hired Hand*. Starring David Carradine, this largely non-union picture would not be submitted for a Motion Picture Production Code (MPAA) rating, even though Fonda thought it GP (all ages permitted) material. If that limited potential play dates, it didn't matter to him because he could always show it in Germany or Japan, 'where they love me'.[63] After New York, the promotional tour moved to Europe, where *Variety* was pleased to see Fonda's German popularity put to the test. His view somewhat modi-fied for the local crowd, he was reported as saying that the young Germans have 'categorized me as a junkie and that's the sort of film they expect'.[64] The report concluded that a mistake had been made in the dubbing and that the dying Fonda tells Oates, 'We are both criminals – I could see this coming.' The promoters, 'tongue-in-cheek, said this was an understandable error and would be rectified'.[65] Oates's revised line was not inappropriate, but his actual last words were, 'First time we was here had a feeling, then we rode out I thought it was all left behind . . . Hold me, Arch' – a final reiteration of the theme of return and circling back.

As trade press and their exhibitor correspondents suggested, *The Hired Hand* played poorly to the actioneer crowd, but neither did it capture the imaginations of the youth audience that *Rolling Stone* or *Creem* addressed. Despite the two scenes with gunplay and the perfunctory attempt to inject a little sex by casting Rita Rogers, the film lacked the prerequisites of a genre movie and yet was too formulaic to break out from its type to work as an art house film. Asked by a journalist what kind of film had he tried to make, Fonda answered: 'I wanted to make a tender film, subtle and slow, not flashy fast stuff . . . A classical poetic Western which was a ballad. Not just an epic or rock and roll like *Easy Rider*.'[66] Whether or not Fonda succeeded in his aim, the film failed to find an audience. Writing in the *New York Times*, Vincent Canby flippantly and irascibly paused to comment on this situation:

> When *Two-Lane Blacktop* didn't make it, I began to question my entire lifestyle. *Two-Lane Blacktop*, for God's sakes, with James Taylor! Then when the Fonda kid's picture collapsed – *The Hired Hand* – I knew we were all in trouble. I mean, what the hell good are cult idols if they bomb at the box office? It almost amounts to a conspiracy![67]

Dennis Hopper was about to discover he too had reason to be paranoid.

2

The Last Movie:
Dennis Hopper's
Three-Ring Circus

'**C**an the Cannes cowboy', Dennis Hopper, 'come back for the fifth time? Or sixth?' asked Tony Crawley in 1976 for the British soft porn magazine *Game*.[1] Seven years earlier the future had looked bright when *Easy Rider* was a nominee for the Palme d'Or and Hopper was awarded the Best First Work prize. Now, he was back in Cannes helping to promote the Australian movie *Mad Dog Morgan* and stir up some interest in Henry Jaglom's *Tracks*, in which he had the starring roles.

Crawley met Hopper in the crowded Carlton Hotel bar in Cannes, where the star greeted him with, 'You seen Dean?'[2] Hopper meant his friend Dean Stockwell, but the suggestion is he's still looking for James Dean, his mentor and idol – twenty years dead. When Hopper had played support to Dean in *Rebel Without a Cause* (1955) and *Giant* (1956), his future looked bright. He then fell out with director Henry Hathaway on *From Hell to Texas* (1958) and found himself 'blacklisted'. It was out of his relationships with Dean and with Hathaway that Hopper created his origin story. Affecting the mantle of being the dead star's chosen surrogate, 'He freely admits to having copied much of Dean's style in acting and in life,' wrote Crawley, which, back in his younger days, 'sure got me in a lot of trouble', said Hopper.[3] That unruly streak in him went up against the representative of Old Hollywood, Hathaway. The veteran director wanted a line reading from Hopper; the neophyte star gave him instead a performance that channelled lessons learned from Lee Strasberg. Eighty-six times Hopper is said to have delivered his piece before eventually giving Hathaway what he wanted – and then getting barred, for his contrariness, from any significant productions. From such repeated tales of appropriation and resistance, a rebel was born.

So, there it was, retold once more, the legend in print (again), in a British porn magazine. Unlike most contemporary, and subsequent, commentators, Crawley recognized the anecdote for what it was, personal myth-making:

> Can I finish by checking on your legendary run-in with Henry Hathaway, during *From Hell to Texas* in 1957. I've never heard the story, just the legend.
> I was blacklisted for eight years.
> But was there really as many re-takes as the story goes – or grows?
> Eighty-six takes!
> I don't believe it.
> Me, neither.
> What was the beef about?
> I was doing everything but what he wanted in the scene. Which for me was to give every line-reading the way he wanted it, you know, with every movement and gesture the way he wanted it. Remember, when I first went under contract at Warner Bros, I was eighteen. I'd come out of a school of Method acting, working through

our senses. I considered the directors old-fashioned – not really old-fashioned, but *older* people working in a certain way and even then I didn't put down what they had accomplished. There were others like me – we thought that acting and conveying emotion was the only thing. What I didn't realize was that you could convey emotion but that if you didn't hit your marks in front of the lights, it might be a great emotion but it wouldn't be on-screen. Directors of the time would tell you what inflection to use, whereas we, of the Strasberg school, believe that if we were emotionally prepared, the lines would come out right – *naturally*. I'm still of this persuasion, but now I realize that it has to be performed within the technical framework of picture making.

So what happened?

After eighty-five takes – three days! – I broke down, cracked, and did every gesture and every line-reading the way Hathaway wanted. And I didn't work again for eight years. Until he hired me again on *The Sons of Katie Elder* in 1964.

But what's the finish? That's what I never heard. When you saw *From Hell to Texas*, which version of the scene did Hathaway use – his or yours? Which take got in?

Shit, he only printed *his* take![4]

The number of takes Hopper routinely cited should always have given the game away as a bit of self-mythologization. Getting 'eighty-sixed' is drugstore slang for having run out of something, rejecting or refusing some service or being spurned – it rhymes with 'nixed'. The story had immense value for Hopper; in the way he retells it to Crawley, he used it to show respect for the elder generation, for their achievements and their craft, and at the same time make a claim for his artistry, his agency. He wanted to hit the mark Hollywood demanded of him, but he also wanted to make his mark, to leave his imprint. He admits too that his story is false, but then contrarily reaffirms its essential truth. His origin story is about personal and public truths: it may not be strictly true, certainly it is an exaggeration, but it contains an artistic truth, which for Hopper was the greater. Moreover, he implied, who would trust an actor anyway, whose craft is to play someone other than themselves?

Crawley's profile put Hopper back in the doldrums, as he was after the Hathaway incident. He had hardly worked at all since *The Last Movie* proved to be a bust. *Kid Blue* (1973), *Mad Dog Morgan* and *Tracks* are the sum, up and until 1977, of his movie appearances that Crawley lists (though he would also feature that year in Wim Wenders's *The American Friend*). Things had come to such a pass that Hopper suggested his next movie might be a pornographic art film.

In August 1965, American *Vogue* ran a multi-page profile of the Hopper family written by Terry Southern, author of the novels *Candy* (1958) and *The Magic Christian* (1959), co-writer of the screenplay for *Dr Strangelove* (1964) and one of Hopper's friends (he would also go on to be a key contributor on *Easy Rider*).[5] Accompanying Southern's text was a series of Hopper's photographs of home and family with commentary by an uncredited Joan Didion.[6] The piece began: 'The Den Hoppers are tops in their field. Precisely what their field is, is by no means certain – except that she is a Great Beauty, and he is a kind of Mad Person.'[7] Southern repeated, or put it in print for the first time, Hopper's origin story.

His work with James Dean was highlighted – 'He was the great one,' Hopper said, 'he never went to Actors Studio, but he had more natural talent than all the others. And he was a great teacher.'[8] Getting barred from working in Hollywood also featured: 'I was blacklisted for having super-talent – like the time Charlie Parker was kicked out of Howard McGhee's band.'[9] Hopper's ego aside, the cause, as always, was his quarrel with Hathaway, though in this telling he only did 78 of the mighty 86 takes.

Southern had first met Hopper at a New York Happening that was attended by Beat poets Allen Ginsberg and Peter Orlovsky. Luis Buñuel's *L'Age d'or* (1930) was being projected in reverse while 'a marvellous stark naked Negro girl' threw rose petals and dog hair into a fan that then filled the room like a snowstorm: 'It was pretty weird,' wrote Southern, 'now that I think about it.'[10] He ends this description of the Happening's racially inflected exoticism by attributing to Hopper's aesthetic an extreme complexity:

He revels in seeing an absurd, sometimes grotesque, beauty in objects which are generally least suspect of it. To walk down a city street with him is like being attached to a moving adrenaline pump. The sight of a new-style parking meter will elicit a super enthusiastic 'Wow, dig that! It's fantastic!' And, proper conditions prevailing, he will steal it.

I always try to control him. 'For chrissake, Hopper, you're outta your mind. I mean, that kind of "new-born babe impressionism" was old hat in the Village ten years ago!'

'Yeah, man,' he would say (pointing wildly), 'but dig!' And finally I began to believe him – not for me, of course, but for him – and then I could only nod and say: 'Yeah, *go*, Dennis *go!*'

And he did. And as far as I know he's still going – very strong indeed.[11]

Hopper elicited from Southern an overdose of exclamation marks; *you dig!* He is the beatnik hipster spilling into the 1960s Pop art scene, he is an actor, a photographer, a poet ('some six hundred manuscript pages of poetry' burned up in the 1961 Bel Air fire that overwhelmed his home), an artist working with 'collages, assemblages, and photo-abstractions', and he is a collector of contemporary art: 'works by Lichtenstein, Warhol, Jasper Johns, Rauschenberg, [Frank] Stella, [James] Rosenquist, Oliveira, [John] Altoon, [Claes] Oldenburg, Milton Avery, [Tom] Wesselmann, [Marcel] Raysse, Larry Poons – all acquired well before their prominence'.[12] Though the term is not used, he is being figured as a Hollywood renaissance man. Subsequent issues of *Vogue* add to his CV, pitching him as a mannequin for Swinging London psychedelic fashion – modelling a bespoke Granny Takes a Trip jacket made from Liberty fabric.[13] A year earlier, 1967, his photographs of the LA art scene were featured by the magazine across a six-page spread.[14] They were also used for a profile of David Hemmings, fresh from making Antonioni's *Blow-Up*. The location for the shoot was a Los Angeles billboard factory. Hemmings and Hopper, the profile noted, had a shared exhibition, 'Los Angeles Primer', then currently running at the Ferus/Pace Gallery, which featured their photographs 'of the city, and of objects and buildings which they simply signed where they found them, thus transmuting all of the Foster & Kleiser Billboard Company, for example, into found art by the single step of recognition'.[15]

To all of Hopper's talents and activities, the role of set designer must also be added. The photographs of his family home show a space more theatrical than domestic, a curated work of art, the living room a gallery:

> Up in the Hollywood Hills, above Sunset Strip, Mr and Mrs Dennis Hopper have a house of such gaiety and wit that it seems the result of some marvellous scavenger hunt, full of improvised treasures, the bizarre and the beautiful and the banal in wild juxtaposition, everything the *most* of its kind.[16]

Pop art mixes with Mexican folk art, Tiffany and Coca-Cola lamps share space and spill light on *fin de siècle* Parisian posters and on Ed Ruscha's painting *Standard*. A merry-go-round horse sits beneath a mirror ball hung from the ceiling, and the view from the kitchen window reveals a full-size fibreglass sedan that was once part of a street hoarding. The sum total is a beguiling, 'kaleidoscopically shifting assemblage of found objects, loved object, *objets d'art*. Everywhere in the Hopper house the point is to amuse, to delight.'[17]

Writing about his time spent on the set of *The Last Movie*, John C. Mahoney, in the *Los Angeles Times*, noted that Hopper had not wanted to make *Easy Rider*, quoting him as saying: 'I didn't want to do a motorcycle film at all. I just wanted to make the first American art film.'[18] The script for *The Last Movie* – story by Hopper, written by Stewart Stern (*Rebel Without a Cause*) – had been filed with the MPAA as long ago as 1965, back in the day when Hopper was accumulating his collection of American Pop art, being featured in the home and interiors spread in *Vogue* and dreaming of emulating

Godard. That year he wrote a short piece for *Vogue* on the need for American art house movies, though it went unpublished until 1969, when it was included in Signet's best-selling *Easy Rider* screenplay: 'Film is an art-form, an expensive art-form, it's the Sistine Chapel of the Twentieth Century. It's the best way to reach people. The artist, not the industry, must take responsibility for the entire work.'[19] Where are today's patrons for such endeavours? Hopper asked. Failing to find one, he needed to find other means to earn a living.

Hopper's 1960s beatnik shtick found a welcome home in a small number of low-budget exploitation films he made for AIP and Roger Corman between *The Sons of Katie Elder* (1965) and *Easy Rider* – *The Queen of Blood* (1966), *The Trip* and *The Glory Stompers* (1967) – as well as as part of the supporting cast in the mainstream movies *Cool Hand Luke* (1967), *Hang 'Em High* (1968) and *True Grit* (1969). The sum of these appearances was hardly a calling card for giving him the go-ahead to write, direct and act in *Easy Rider*, but a brief walk-on part in the Monkees' film *Head* (1968) suggests why he was given the opportunity. In a scene shot in a Hollywood canteen, *Head*'s co-screenwriter Jack Nicholson appears briefly before the cameras; gesticulating wildly, the film's director, Bob Rafelson, is also present. Before the moment ends, Hopper walks through the crowd, long-haired, wearing a handlebar moustache just as he would in *Easy Rider*, and looking like that other Laurel Canyon cocaine cowboy, ex-Byrd David Crosby (son of Floyd Crosby, blacklisted cinematographer and ace lensman on any number of Corman's exploitation pictures). Hopper may not have made many pictures in the 1960s, but he moved in the right circles and had friends who had access to those who could do him favours. He had finally found his patrons, with Bert Schneider, who produced the television show *The Monkees* and that band's feature film *Head*, being but the latest. Before Schneider, Phil Spector, the 'First Tycoon of Teen', had been Hopper's benefactor.

In July 1966 the *New York Times* called Spector a 'groovy kind of genius', 'a sort of American Beatle who has pulled down $5-million or so turning out such epics as "Da Doo Ron Ron" and "Oh Yeah, Maybe Baby"'. Now he had plans to make a movie, an 'art movie':

> 'Art is a game,' Spector explained in a soft, reedy voice. 'If you win that game too regularly it tends to lessen your motivation. That's why I've lost interest in the record business . . . That's why I must move on . . . My first movie will be called *The Last Movie*. It will be an art movie. I am an admirer of Truffaut, Stanley Kubrick, Fellini. It'll be in that tradition. Hollywood needs that kind of movie.'[20]

The film, he explained, would be a contemporary Western on the theme of guilt, set in a small Latin American town. With it scheduled to go before the cameras in Mexico in September, Stewart Stern had written the script and the director was set to be Dennis Hopper, a young actor who Spector believed could be an American Truffaut.[21] There was clearly some expectation that the production would go ahead. Promoting *The Wild Angels*, Fonda let it be known to *Variety* that he was 'committed to an independent Western, *The Last Movie*, which Dennis Hopper will direct from his own screenplay'.[22] Permission to shoot the film in Durango had also been sought because, when the project was resurrected in 1969, *Variety*'s Mexico-based correspondent reported that the 'Motion Picture Bureau turned thumbs down on Hopper's *The Last Movie* on grounds that no appreciable change had been made since the script was submitted four years ago and it "still damages Mexico's dignity"'.[23] Evidently the gamble of movie production was too great for Spector: he pulled out. But when *Easy Rider* showed just how much a good bet could return, *The Last Movie* was resurrected.

Post-*Easy Rider*, films with 'youth appeal' and 'art market product' were seen to be interchangeable, but as long as European films were the standard by which the latter was judged, American art films would always appear to be imitators. *The Last Movie* was seen as being true to this form. When, in the *New Yorker*, Pauline Kael reviewed Hopper's sophomore directorial effort, she wrote, 'This knockabout tragedy is not a vision of the chaos in the world – not a *Weekend* (1967), not a *Shame* (1968), but a reflection of his own confusion. It's hysterical to blame the violence in the world on American movies.'[24] Hopper could not compete with the Europeans, represented by Godard and Bergman. While the French auteur might indict American movies for all sorts of sins, he can do that because he sits outside Hollywood and is an acknowledged artist; Hopper cannot because, despite his reputation as a maverick, he is a pure *product* of Tinseltown, where art and commerce mix as well as champagne and Coca-Cola.

Variety recorded that after a faltering start, Universal was intent on bathing in the fountain of youth, from which it hoped streams of gold would gush forth. In December 1969 four films were announced that fitted the bill, including Hopper's *The Last Movie*, which had been secured on the 'basis of *Easy Rider*'s success. Ironic note is that *Rider*'s distrib, Columbia Pictures, nixed the *Movie* project prior to Hopper's arrangement with U.'[25] In retrospect, Columbia showed rather more commercial nous than Universal.

The film's finance deal was discussed by *Variety* in conversation with producer Paul Lewis. Universal's Ned Tanen, he said, had arranged a bank loan of $800,000, thus 'guaranteeing the negative pickup and distribution by Universal'.[26] The film-makers had 'been given absolute autonomy' and, on completion, the film would be turned over to Universal, who would pay the cost that then paid off the loan. 'The distributor takes 30% of the gross and certain costs off the top,' and then Alta Light, Hopper's production company, and Universal would 'split the remaining profits 50–50 after the original bank loan is paid off'.[27] The film had a '50% leeway in budget as far as the guarantee is concerned, but for every $10,000 it goes over the original $800,000 Lewis and Hopper lose percentage points in their participation in the profits'.[28]

Lewis explained that low-budget independent productions financed this way had specific hazards to manage when collecting any profit share:

> A film almost has to do what *Easy Rider* did to make money. It has to make a lot of money so that a lot of money can't be hidden. We have access to the books and have the right to challenge any expenses the distributor has. It's those extra charges where you can really get hurt. I was in an office and a guy is like calling New York and told the operator to get his wife. Asked who to charge it off to, he said charge it off to this picture. That's distribution.[29]

The success of *Easy Rider* gave Hopper a budget line and creative control over *The Last Movie* that he would never otherwise have achieved, one that included ultimate say on cast, script, final cut, advertising, and screening locations for the LA and New York openings. Another ace in the hole was that Hopper not only had final cut for the film but control of any revisions demanded by television, which 'has to be in conjunction with us', said Lewis.[30] This partly explains why, after the film was pulled from theatrical distribution, it was not sold on to television in a re-edited form. If you couldn't sell the film to theatres, how could you sell it for television syndication?

How, anyway, would Universal sell such a self-conscious American art film as *The Last Movie*? Would it use the techniques of exploitation film companies like AIP and Corman's New World? Hype the sensation – sex, violence, drugs – and let the art side of things take care of itself? Or would it promote the artist, the auteur, the director? Hopper made himself available to the broadsheets, teen magazines, film trades, mainstream magazines and counter-cultural tribunes. He would embody the duality of the artist as star, the star as artist.

While on location, Hopper was asked by *Rolling Stone* to explain his project:

'Can you tell me what the movie's about?'

'It's about reality and non-reality. It's about the respon-sibility you have making movies, like if you make violence, what are you into? It's about the paranoia of the United States and its vulgarity. It's about the beauty of some other people.'

'I think what I wanted was a plot outline.'

'. . . OK, let's be serious. What's the movie about? It's about this guy who falls in love with a donkey because he thinks the donkey is a Democrat but it turns out the donkey is a Republican. It's about the people who come down to Peru and fuck around. No, the movie is about . . . two hours long.'[31]

Others who were also intent on finding out what *The Last Movie* was all about joined *Rolling Stone*'s Michael Goodwin on location in Peru. Journalists from *Seventeen*, *Look*, *Esquire*, *New York Times Magazine*, *Show*, the *New York Times*, the London *Times*, *Twen*, *Life* and *Playboy*.[32] As with Goodwin, not being able to tell their readers what the film was about became the story of their trip; what replaced narrative summary was a set of star profiles of Hopper that had him getting 'heavy' and 'high' in the Peruvian mountains. Brad Darrach pitched 'the story' to readers of *Life* this way: 'Furor trails him like a pet anaconda. At 34, he is known in Hollywood as a sullen renegade who talks revolution, settles arguments with karate, goes to bed with groups and has taken trips on everything you can swallow or shoot.'[33] Violence, sex, drugs, politics and rebellion: Hopper had it all. The role of James Dean and Henry Hathaway in his fantasy biography was, once more, front and centre. This rebel persona might have been a good look for a rock star, maybe even for a certain sort of film star, but it was a cavalier image to sell when in charge of a million-dollar picture. Whatever the truth in all the stories of drugs, sex and violence on the film's set, muddying the line between fact and fiction was Hopper's project and it was an idea that would not be contained within the parameters of the film alone. For Hopper, everything to do with the film's production was to be included in his grand scheming.

Helping to maintain Hopper's high in the Andes was a mad coterie of Hollywood friends, many of whom would have as fleeting an appearance in *The Last Movie* as Hopper had in *Head*. The roll call included Peter Fonda, Dean Stockwell, James Mitchum, Russ Tamblyn, John Phillip Law, Michelle Phillips of The Mamas & the Papas (who would briefly marry Hopper after filming was completed), Robert Rothwell, Billy Gray, Owen Orr, Ted Markland,

Robert Rothwell, Owen Orr, James Mitchum, Dennis Hopper, Ted Markland,
John Phillip Law and Michael Greene on the set of *The Last Movie*
(dir. Dennis Hopper, 1971).

Michael Greene, Kris Kristofferson, Toni Basil, Severn Darden,
Sylvia Miles, Lynn Brown and John Buck Wilkin. The lead picture
illustrating the *Life* report showed a clean-shaven, short-haired
Hopper with cowboy hat and holstered pistol, wearing a Lee 101-J
jacket, denim shirt and jeans, standing in front of Rothwell, Orr,
Mitchum, Markland, Law and Greene. They are all dressed as
Western extras, looking like gin-mill cowboys from Laurel Canyon
or The Eagles on the sleeve of *Desperado*.

Whether or not Hopper was sober or high, he had orchestrated
and choreographed, with intent or by chance, the situation as if it
were an immersive theatrical experience with *The Last Movie* just
one of a number of material outcomes. Everyone, behind or in front
of the cameras, was considered to be a participant, the locals as much
as the American journalists, the film's stars as much as their friends.
'People generally think what Dennis wants them to think about

Dennis. "His best performance," a buddy of his remarked, "is his portrayal of himself".[34] On the set of *The Last Movie*, Hopper performed like he was both the carnival's ringmaster *and* the geek show:

> By mid-afternoon the games became more serious. Somebody made a cocaine connection and a number of actors laid in a large supply at bargain prices – $7 for a packet that cost $70 in the States. By 10 p.m. almost 30 members of the company were sniffing coke or had turned on with grass, acid or speed. By midnight much of the cast had drifted off to bed by twos and threes. At 2 a.m. I was wakened by screams. A young actress had taken LSD and was having a 'bummer'. At 3 a.m., I heard a rapping on the window beside my bed. A young woman I hadn't met was standing on a wide ledge that ran just below the windowsill. It was raining and her night gown was drenched. 'Do you mind if I come in?' she asked vaguely.[35]

'Hollywood figured he was playing the genius,' Darrach wrote in *Life*, 'but I remembered something Brooke Hayward had said, "Dennis is a demonic artist, like Rimbaud. Nothing matters but his work."'[36]

Goodwin's piece for *Rolling Stone* was presented as if it was a film script, an alternative *Last Movie*: 'MEDIUM SHOT. PRODUCER PAUL LEWIS SITS IN FRONT OF A DESK IN HIS HOTEL ROOM. THERE IS A PRODUCTION FLOW CHART LEANING AGAINST THE WALL.'[37] If Hopper was often cryptic in his explanations, Lewis was not:

> PAUL: . . . Our film company is the same as the United States – coming into an area, investing money, teaching

some kind of skills to, quote, backwards people and then splitting. And saying, 'Look at all the good we've done in the world.' And also saying, 'And now you owe us something.' Dennis is doing the same thing, personally and in the film. He wants to stay down. But then he leaves, the company leaves in the film, and *we leave* . . .

To get into the whole number, Dennis, who plays America, who feels like he does good for the people – he begins to realize that the people go back and do their *own* thing, create their own movie, their own history . . . when they shoot somebody they kill them. And when we come back, and we're aghast and we say, 'How dare you do a thing like this?' They say, 'This is what you've taught us.'[38]

Hopper's character, Kansas, is akin to Alden Pyle in Graham Greene's 1955 novel *The Quiet American*. Like the idealist Pyle, who naively causes havoc in French Indochina, Kansas represents a malevolent force that self-servingly and self-deceivingly devastates that which it claims to be saving, the Vietnamese as much as the Peruvian villagers. Hopper, however, takes the critique of American colonialism to another level by implicating himself and his film crew as being equally guilty in the process of destabilizing and despoiling an indigenous culture and society in the name of his art and the financiers who have bankrolled his movie.

This level of self-reflection, alongside calling attention to the film's materiality, the revealing of the means of the image's production – the film-within-a-film, 'scene missing' intercuts, the rattan cameras, lights and microphones, and all of its wilful discontinuities – are what make this picture (intended not for film society, college and gallery screenings but for the same commercial theatrical outlets, mainstream cinemas where *Easy Rider* played) that much more radical than any other of the films produced by Hopper's peers in this period. If Hopper's modernist aesthetic was second-hand, a set of borrowed elements from the avant-garde – Conner and Warhol in particular – in the context of a well-resourced Hollywood movie it was nevertheless utterly unique.

Talking on set to journalist Edwin Miller, whose piece would appear in *Seventeen* magazine, Hopper said:

> When I was a kid and went into Dodge City on a Saturday to go to the movies and saw John Wayne pick up an ax handle and smash somebody's head in, what he did was all right because he wore a white hat. There were good guys and the bad guys and whatever the good guys had to do to straighten things out – hit, shoot, whatever it was – it was okay. I was a good guy – nobody thinks of himself as a bad guy – there's no reason why I shouldn't take up an ax handle myself and beat someone if I thought it was the right thing to do. John Wayne has shown me the way.[39]

Hopper continued this theme with another anecdote, certainly apocryphal. Elvis Presley had visited to hear more from Hopper about his hero James Dean and to get advice about playing violent scenes, one where he has to hit a woman and another where he fights an actor. The problem, Elvis told Hopper, is that even though he is in 'pretty good shape' and can take care of himself in a fight, he can't bring himself to strike a woman. Hopper explained the scenes are not real, all is fake. Elvis got angry with him: 'He thought I was kidding him: he couldn't accept the fact that he had been deceived all these years by the movies.'[40] In *The Last Movie* the villagers play the Elvis role of the primitive naïf.

The villagers perceive the death of Kansas, played in front of the cameras, to be real so that his resurrection, when the film has stopped rolling, is a miracle. Hopper reinstated the idea of the moving image as a magic trick for sophisticates and a supernatural event for the innocent. A *Los Angeles Times* reporter, on location, described how 'Hopper, standing at 12,400 feet in a field of yellow flowers which flood the rocky outline of an Inca ruin, squeezed out that pinched, prefatory laugh that is equal parts Richard Widmark and Popeye the Sailor Man. "Oh man, it's all real. It's like, you know, we're using real life, real motion, real light, so many levels. You know?"'[41]

As with his other on-location interviews, Hopper played the idiot savant role to perfection. He tirelessly promoted the idea that the film was being made by a lunatic and a dope fiend: 'I know [Universal] are thinking, "A crazy man is directing the picture."'[42] 'Productive chaos', Mahoney called it in the *Los Angeles Times*, but he also noted that the core crew were those who had contributed to 'Richard Rush's AIP motorcycle trilogy, to which *Easy Rider* was indebted. Headed by cinematographer Laszlo Kovacs, his gaffer Richmond Aguilar, sound mixer LeRoy Robbins and script supervisor Joyce King, it is probably the best, tight, location unit in the business and often seems self-operative.'[43] The craziness and professionalism go hand in hand, but in journalists' accounts the former is always king. Mahoney witnessed the shooting of the Lenten carnival, which, as the participants get drunker, turns from merry-making to abrading the American interlopers. In Quechuan they chant 'Junkie go home'. Unsure if he had heard the translation correctly, Mahoney checked with two other Peruanas in the company. 'The pronunciation never varied. I'm sure, of course, that the word was and is "Yankee". But is it wise to underestimate native intelligence?'[44]

Getting high, high in the Andes as a promotional gambit certainly garnered the column inches, but it also backfired on Hopper. In a profile on five young directors in search of a renaissance, Dick Adler asked Hopper about the on-set excesses:

> During the filming, there were (or seemed to be) as many writers on the scene as actors, and as reports began to appear in the public journals it looked as if every variety of drug known to man was being smoked, swallowed, sniffed or shot by the cast and crew. Denials have since been issued, the most cogent being Hopper's: 'Making a movie is hard work – it would be impossible if I was using hard drugs.'[45]

When shooting finished in Peru, on budget and on time, the caravan moved to Taos, New Mexico, where Hopper summoned the spirit of D. H. Lawrence, who had stayed at the Mabel Dodge Luhan home that he now owned and which his family and friends now occupied.

The house's annexes were where Hopper and entourage edited the film from the forty hours of footage they had shot in Peru.[46] For the *Los Angeles Times*, Wayne Warga filed a report from Taos in March 1971: delays in the post-production process had put the picture seriously behind schedule. It had originally been promised for October the previous year. Despite the delay, Hopper appeared to be all business, working hard with his editors to get a working cut, though Warga reported it was still four and a half hours long. Hopper had bought the town's only movie theatre, ostensibly to run edits of his film, but commercial films were also screened for the area's predominantly Spanish-speaking audience. At first Hopper had programmed some of Buñuel's films, but turnout was 'rotten'. 'He then rented a Disney film and filled the theatre nightly. He tells about the experience with a head-shaking irony, sorry that customers walked away from great art.'[47] Universal, once Hopper had handed them *The Last Movie*, would also walk away from his art. Whether or not it was great art was another matter. Before the issue was decided, Hopper appeared on *The Johnny Cash Show* in September 1970, where he gave a recitation of Kipling's 'If' – the middle word in 'life', Dennis tells Cash's audience. The performance is kitsch personified.

Before filmgoers could make their own judgement on *The Last Movie*, Lawrence Schiller and L. M. Kit Carson's documentary *The American Dreamer*, with Hopper as its subject, was released in June 1971. Charles Champlin reported in the *Los Angeles Times* that it raised 'the same basic question as some other recent documentaries: how true is the "truth" we're being shown in the name of the truth'.[48] The film spends time with Hopper in Taos as he worked on the neverending edit of *The Last Movie*. Hopper strips naked for the film, struts down the town's residential streets – but is this the real man, unadorned without his Hollywood actor's mask? Is the portrayal of a nude Hopper any more truthful than one of him in costume? Is he really the obnoxious, self-centred, pretentious poseur shown here?

Variety's reviewer wrote that the documentary stripped away the 'phoney tinsel of Hopper's image, only to reveal what appears here to be the real tinsel underneath'.[49] The film was to be distributed exclusively to college campus film clubs, but the journal thought it might profit more by being played to high-school audiences, 'which have not yet tired of placard philosophy and playpen revolution'.[50] Hopper was criticized for mugging to the camera, mitigating the ideas of a candid portrait, and delivering 'deliberately outrageous verbiage . . . The only time Hopper seems to be expressing genuine emotion are scenes taken in his cutting room: he looks absolutely petrified.'[51] Like *The Last Movie*, *The American Dreamer* disappeared from distribution almost as soon as the roundly negative reviews had been published.

Hopper was under exclusive contract to Universal for theatrical releases. *The American Dreamer* was therefore sold to the college circuit, which was considered to be non-theatrical, usually with 16mm projection. Unbeknown to its makers, an off-campus cinema was hired for its run at UCLA and so Universal slapped an injunction on the film.[52] Subsequently unseen publicly until its release on Blu-Ray in 2015, it left behind only an indifferent soundtrack album to fill the gap. A brilliant, though rambling, carnivalesque portrait of Hopper, the documentary added to the mystique of *The Last Movie* as the great lost film of New Hollywood and to the image of Hopper, the artist, supressed by a monolithic, philistine industry.

Even as *The Last Movie* won the critics' prize at the Venice Film Festival and before a string of Italian and French critics were quoted on the ads running to promote the film's exclusive engagement at the Regent Theatre in Westwood Village, LA – 'a rebel of genius', 'a film of great and justified ambition', 'a fiery work of tortured romanticism' – things had started to go awry.[53] Though the *New York Times* correspondent sent in an upbeat report from Venice for the *Los Angeles Times* ('alive with the imagination of an exploring artist'), film critic Ian Cameron sent in a wholly downbeat assessment of *The Last Movie*, writing that it 'disappointed even the fans of *Easy Rider* . . . the overriding impression is of chaos'.[54] *Variety*'s review from the festival as good as agreed: it 'suffers from a multiplicity of themes, ideas and its fragmented style with flash-forwards and intertwined and only suggested plot structure'.[55] While in Venice, Hopper 'expressed dissatisfaction with Universal' to *Variety*'s reporter: 'Apparently U. is not interested in the pic, he said cheerfully, and may give it cursory handling.'[56] Still, the French wanted to see the film, and, after Venice, a special screening at the Cinémathèque Française in Paris was arranged.[57] In the USA, consensus was mounting against Hopper.

Champlin confirmed the dour impression from Venice with his review: 'a dismally disappointing and depressing experience. As a piece of film-making it is inchoate, amateurish, self-indulgent, tedious, superficial, unfocused and a precious waste not only of money but, more importantly, of a significant and conspicuous opportunity.'[58] Champlin was a discriminating critic: he did not just dismiss *The Last Movie* as incoherent and Hopper as an illdisciplined director and leave it at that – he spent time ironing out the kinks, as he put it, in Hopper's vain attempt to 'suggest that realism and surrealism coexist'.[59] Champlin recognized that the film was about the 'exploration of the nature of screen reality and the dangers of confusing reality', but, he thought, it needed a film-maker with an 'icy intellectual rage and control' to make sense of this dichotomy, which Hopper did not have. For Champlin, the problem was not simply a question of the film's formal properties, it was also its subject, which he described as a 'portentous aborted allegory'.[60]

If Champlin damned the film on the West Coast, Vincent Canby cursed it on the East Coast. He began by dismissing the

Venice award: 'someone must be kidding', because '*The Last Movie* is an extravagant mess.'[61] Suffering from 'inflated pretensions', Hopper was 'gifted with all of the insights of a weekend mystic who drives to and from his retreat in a Jaguar'.[62] *The Last Movie*, Canby concluded, was 'every bit as indulgent, cruel and thoughtless as the dream factory films it makes such ponderous fun of'.[63]

The promise of *The Last Movie* had sputtered like Hopper's marriage to Michelle Phillips, which lasted around a week. Publicizing the Mamas & the Papas' reunion album, Phillips's bandmates teased her about her brief appearance on film and in wedlock: '"I just read Champlin's review in *The Times* this morning: he really creamed it," said Denny [Doherty]. John [Phillips] added thoughtfully, "You'd think Hopper would have used you better in the advertising – something like 'And co-starring Mama Michelle, the Famous Six Day Wife'. Was it six days or seven?"'[64] The film and Hopper had become a joke.

One of the Italian critics quoted on the press advertisements proclaimed *The Last Movie* to be a 'really important film. A new era of the cinema . . . breaking with the usual traditional approach of film as entertainment!'[65] Universal, the film's financier and distributor, no doubt agreed that the film had little amusement value because, as Champlin noted, even before the film had received its debut public screening, the studio was letting it be known that it intended to withdraw it from distribution and maybe even 'reassemble it as other heads think best'.[66]

One trade press reviewer thought the film too complex for the same audience who had identified with *Easy Rider*'s protagonists; early scenes are praised, 'and the idea is so original, the viewer wants to see the film develop further', but 'instead of any development, it just starts to repeat itself, each repetition a more

Dennis Hopper with Michelle Phillips after finishing filming *The Last Movie* (1971).

simplistic rendition than the previous.'[67] The review's conclusion must have bruised Hopper's ego: 'His performance seems very imitative of Jack Nicholson and lacks a certain sincerity or belief in his own character.'[68] Nicholson joined Hopper and Henry Jaglom on a panel entitled 'Hollywood: The Establishment and the Challengers', organized for the New York Film Festival in October 1971. The establishment was represented by Otto Preminger, who thought Jaglom's *A Safe Place* 'was anything but new, because it had nothing new to say'.[69] He had not seen *The Last Movie*, but the audience for the panel, *Variety* stated, could agree that these two films and Nicholson's *Drive, He Said* 'did wreak havoc on customary cinematic plot structures, and did pose problems for that substantial segment of the audience which wants to know exactly what's happening all the time, and demands that the "meaning" be easily boiled down to a few terse sentences'.[70] Poor box office receipts, it was noted, confirmed that these films were a turn-off even for the young audience they were essentially aimed at.[71]

After its initial screenings, Universal's refusal to distribute *The Last Movie* is usually understood to have been a reaction to the scandalous stories that most of the on-location reports had carried, and Hopper's portrayal as an out-of-control, drug-addled paranoid in *The American Dreamer* only added to the company's anxiety about being seen as supportive of, if not actively promoting, such activities. In his detailed account of the film's conception, production and post-production travails, Alex Cox considers Hopper's rebel pose to be a big part of the film's problems, but he argues that it was Ned Tanen and, especially, Jules Stein and Lew Wasserman, Universal's bosses, who had decided to kill the film because essentially they did not like Hopper, what he stood for or his movie.[72]

Like Hathaway, Universal had hired a nonconformist and then tried to tame him; when they got nowhere, they simply blacklisted Hopper again and nixed his film for good measure – or at least that's the story that is most often told.[73] There is some truth in these explanations, but a more compelling reason is that Hopper's eighteen-month-long edit meant the film found itself in a very different commercial context from that which existed when the project was first greenlighted. That delay hurt the film's chances as much as, if not more than, any other reason. As Cox notes, Tanen and company knew exactly what they were getting when they agreed to finance and distribute *The Last Movie*, and Hopper's beatnik cant and hippie sex-and-drugs lifestyle were in good part what they were buying when they put him under contract. Dropping *The Last Movie* was a business decision: Universal decided to cut its losses rather than spend more on promoting a film it felt had little chance of returning its cost, let alone making a profit. Even before that commercial decision had been made, Tanen had outlined his business ethos to *Show* magazine:

> Someone once told me there's nothing as fragile as a motion picture, because once it's out and gone, it's all over. You can't say, 'Hey, we're remodelling and we'll bring it back next week . . .'. There is no middle ground. A picture is either successful or totally unsuccessful. And if it doesn't work it is a disaster. It's like there's a pipeline out that says 'Don't go see this film!' And not only in New York or Westwood Village – in Bangor, Maine![74]

Tanen's pipeline told him all he needed to know about the prospects for *The Last Movie*.

The Last Movie opened in New York in September 1971 and a month later in Los Angeles. *Variety* reported that the film did 'okay' in its opening week of release at Broadway's Twins theatre, taking 'near $25,000'.[75] However, it did not sustain interest, and receipts had dropped to just a little over $10,000 by the second week. To put these returns in perspective, *The French Connection* had takings of around $103,000 at two theatres in the same week, and *Kotch* made nearly twice that amount.[76] By *The Last Movie*'s fourth, and final, week, receipts were down to $5,000.[77] The extremely limited release schedule, which Universal was contractually obliged to fulfil, suggested just how few prints were struck, indicative of the company's resolve not to continue investing in Hopper's movie. Symptomatic of this fear of further investment in a dud was the decision by New American Library not to go ahead with publishing the script for *The Last Movie*, for which it had paid $15,000, ten times what was paid for *Easy Rider* with 365,000 books in print.[78] Neither was there an original soundtrack album released, despite the wealth of music used throughout the film.[79] *The Last Movie* opened in Los Angeles on 27 October, and finished its run twelve days later.

Writing for the *San Francisco Examiner*, Gene Handsaker introduced a 'defiant' Hopper: 'I think I'm the most advanced filmmaker in the country,' he said. 'I am a pioneer in film . . . I made a great movie. I don't think there's any question *The Last Movie* will live beyond my lifetime as a work of art.'[80] But the film had been 'panned unmercifully' and, Hopper told him, its one showing in New York had not made any money. While in LA he tried to drum up trade, using a little ballyhoo about agreeing to ride a motorcycle onstage for a television show: 'We've got a bomb on our hands. We've got to do anything we can to sell it . . . Most great movies are bombs', Hopper explained, 'because the audience has not been educated to receive them. Art lives beyond its own time.'[81]

> Seurat, Kandinski and Klee knew that when the camera was invented it would duplicate nature the way painting had done for centuries . . . And instead of drawing the usual apple or tree, they tried something new, created an extension of their talent; they revealed their brush strokes, pencil lines on raw pieces of canvas to show their structure.

Hopper told Todd Mason,

> And that's what I'm doing in *The Last Movie*, showing my structure with film, my underpainting, and also showing

that I can still make a tree, a little western, a 1940s movie;
I'm showing a palette of a young artist who wants to make
films and who wants people to look at films. It's no fluke
that *The Last Movie* is so disorienting to an audience. It was
intentionally made to be a new kind of film.[82]

The youth audience *Easy Rider* was thought to have unlocked
was proving to be an elusive and fickle demographic. In an early
November 1971 edition, *Variety* led with the headline 'Youth Shuns
Youth-Lure Films'.[83] The young were thought to comprise about
74 per cent of film-going patronage, but support was not being
given to *The Last Movie*, *The Hired Hand*, *Two-Lane Blacktop* or
Drive, He Said. Quite why these and other films had not sold well
escaped the journal's analysis, but what was selling was nostalgia
– *The Last Picture Show*, *Summer of '42* and *Carnal Knowledge* –
and 'slick, violence-packed actioneers like *Shaft* and *The French
Connection*. By the end of November, the story was more certain,
Variety reported, that 1971 was 'the year of the youth-market flop'.[84]
Two hits, *Easy Rider* and *Alice's Restaurant*, had sparked a cycle of
23 duds.

Writing towards the end of 1971, Beverly Walker echoed and
expanded on many of the points made by *Variety*. 'It is now a
cliché that the phenomenal success of *Easy Rider* in 1969 turned
the American film industry upside down. The Hollywood money
men suddenly began to look for new directors, with three key
priorities: youth, subject matter with youth appeal, and a low
budget.'[85] Alongside actors and producers turning to direction and
scriptwriting, 'rock stars turned from their frenzied audiences to
the relatively more serene occupation of movie-making.'[86] They
were joined by record companies (Fantasy Records with Daryl

Duke's *Payday* in 1972), other 'well-heeled American industries' (the Quaker Oats Company with *Willy Wonka and the Chocolate Factory*, 1971) and new companies (Cannon with *Joe* in 1970).[87] Hollywood, 'even on its knees', remained at the centre of the action.[88] Yet few of the productions had cut through to make a mark at the box office.

Walker surveyed a panoply of films either in distribution or in waiting. She moved from Alan Arkin's *Little Murders*; past Clint Eastwood's *Play Misty for Me*; Jack Lemmon's *Kotch*; Larry Turman's *The Marriage of a Young Stockbroker*; James Frawley's *Christian Liquorice Store*; the Terrence Malick-scripted *Deadhead Miles*, directed by Vernon Zimmerman; Jack Nicholson's *Drive, He Said*; Henry Jaglom's *A Safe Place*; Bill L. Norton's *Cisco Pike*; Douglas Trumbull's *Silent Running* and Fonda's *The Hired Hand*. All were part of the 'brief renaissance following *Easy Rider*' that was now over. Studios retrenched, and new directors could not find work unless, Walker wrote, it was in the exploitation field with 'porn-horror violence'.[89] While she found much that was problematic and much to celebrate with the films listed, she argued that the New York critical establishment must take some of the blame for the industry's retreat from supporting young talent.

After the few festival screenings and the short New York and LA runs, *The Last Movie* was not entirely locked deep in Universal's vaults. In May 1972 it was double-billed with Fonda's *The Hired Hand* for the West Coast drive-in and neighbourhood theatre circuits – an ignominious return for the films' directors to the venues where *The Wild Angels* and *The Glory Stompers*, biker exploitation movies they had starred in, once played.[90] In July, the two films played the San Francisco circuit. Soon after *The Last Movie*'s release, academic Foster Hirsch wrote a rare supportive critique of it (and *The Hired Hand*), but few others would get a chance to weigh up the merits of either film.[91] Hopper's didn't even make it to London until 1982, never mind Bangor, Maine.[92] Co-director of *The American Dreamer* L. M. Kit Carson was the 1972 director of the USA Film Festival in Dallas, where he along with *Time*'s Jay Cocks and Boston critic Deac Russell programmed *The Last Movie*, 'feeling it ha[d] been unjustly dismissed and unfairly neglected'.[93] Hopper was scheduled to attend the screening; he had little else in his diary to keep him away.

Though Walker felt that the quality of American film criticism had never been higher, the influence of auteur theory had moved from a positive to a negative, excusing, she wrote, 'vindictive, personal attacks' on film-makers.[94] With hindsight, the critical assaults on many of the films look to be particularly egregious, especially those levelled against *The Hired Hand* and *The Last Movie*. One film, by a young film-maker, that did emerge unscathed was *The Last Picture Show*. That it was directed by Peter Bogdanovich, a film critic and leading exponent of the auteur theory, was not missed by his peers.

3

The Last Picture Show,
Five Easy Pieces and *Payday*:
Cowboy Rhythm on KTRN

The *Independent Film Journal* opened its review of *The Last Picture Show* with, 'this is the best American film in a long, long time.'[1] It described director Peter Bogdanovich as a 'film historian who made a name for himself with his critiques on the works of Allan Dwan, Orson Welles, Alfred Hitchcock, Howard Hawks and John Ford'.[2] He is the 'first of the current breed of American archivists and film buffs to turn to making films, a la the French "New Wave's" Truffaut and Godard'.[3] This was not an isolated piece of hyperbole but part of a critical consensus that formed around the film and its director. Such acclaim, however, was by no means universal.

Feminist writer Rita Mae Brown, author in 1973 of the coming-of-age novel *Rubyfruit Jungle*, lambasted the film in the women's journal *Off Our Backs*:

> The shabby technical work collaborated with the shabby story line which is the archetypal American relationship: two male friends . . . They get drunk. They hurt a deaf-dumb friend. They screw girls. They fight each other. From these activities Sonny's 'manhood' emerges, an

understanding of life. No, I'm not making this up – if you've seen the movie you know it's true. Why do people make this shit? ... Why hasn't this sentimental slop about white, male, small town youth been rejected by critical male viewers? Worse, if it is a fairly honest portrayal of those youths then men are much worse off than I thought ... They have zero ability to empathize with a woman's life and only the tiniest ability to empathize with each other ... Unfeeling, unthinking, uncaring about anything except their concept of self, 'masculinity', these men are setups for any politician or military leader who can give them that 'butch' self they crave. If anyone doubts the severity of this collective male identity crisis and its potential for political manipulation remember that Hitler built a party out of that same psychological dynamic.[4]

Whether one takes this criticism as fair or false, considered or ill-conceived, Brown speaks eloquently to a culture riven by debates over race, class, sexuality and gender and how a film like *The Last Picture Show* deals with, or evades, that situation by sublimating it beneath a coating of nostalgia, retreating from the uncertain present to a known past.

Rather than interpreting the film-makers' decision to shoot in monochrome as a homage to Old Hollywood, Brown considered it to be a 'dishonest' representation: 'Human beings see in color, we don't need to be insulted by enduring a black and white movie which is to clue us in on the fact that it is "serious".'[5] She called the film 'artsy fartsy', which was not her way of saying movies should entertain above all (and that they are being pretentious if they have ambitions to be Art) but to call the film out for its false class-consciousness:

There's a class aspect to black and white movies in our times. Supposedly, the bleak screen will serve to heighten the viewer's sense of the drab, the working class, the impoverished. Those of us growing up impoverished were oppressed in living color and any deviation from that is a perversion of our lives justified in terms of "style". When our ceilings peeled they peeled from pea green to red to black to gray and all together it was more hideous than anything shot in black and white. The only possible excuse any film-maker can offer for shooting in black and white is money. Anything else is elevated crap.[6]

Brown's argument resonates because it calls into question the film's core idea that it is an honest depiction of the world – a little sentimental maybe, a little romantic perhaps, but essentially an authentic portrayal of small-town life in Texas in 1950. 'The movies may seem honest because the viewer can pick out parts of her/his experience which correspond to it. But to millions of us who are the "Other," those movies are white men's lies,' wrote Brown, 'lies we have to fight every day in our existence.'[7] Honesty, authenticity and the real are the currency *The Last Picture Show* deals in, but for Brown it trades in counterfeit bonds.

Before any dialogue or music in *The Last Picture Show* there is the sound of wind, a steady throb and howl that opens and closes the film, much as it does in Robert Altman's *McCabe and Mrs Miller*, which was released almost simultaneously in 1971. Overlapping with the wind is the grinding whirl of a starter-motor, a truck engine backfires, sputters and stalls before finally catching. Hank Williams's 1950 recording of 'Why Don't You Love Me (Like You Used to Do)?' is playing on the truck's radio. The young driver pulls his vehicle into the dust-blown road: it's a beat-up, rusty late 1930s Chevrolet. The hood panels are missing, and the driver's side fender has been replaced with one taken from another truck that was sprayed in an entirely different hue.

The small picture house the truck passes is playing the 1950 release *Father of the Bride*, starring Spencer Tracy. Out in the street, obscured by the dust storm, an adolescent boy sweeps the road with a broom. It is an image of gargantuan futility. The truck pulls over. Wearing a worn-out Lee 101-J denim jacket, Levi's jeans and cowboy boots, the driver, Sonny Crawford (Timothy Bottoms), takes the boy into a nearby poolroom. Following shortly behind them is an oil worker, who exchanges his hard hat for a Stetson. Inside and outside, the poolroom is as distressed as the truck, as dishevelled as the driver's clothing, as dust-blown as the young road sweeper and as beaten as Sam the Lion (Ben Johnson), its owner. The film's sets, by production designer Polly Platt, then married to Bogdanovich, are an impressive achievement, her American landscape pinned beneath cinematographer Robert Surtees's murky grey sky and obscured by gusting desert winds that penetrate the town's interiors and which have virtually obliterated the advertising and business names on the store fronts.

The Texas town of Anarene is one storm away from being returned to the desert out of which it was founded. Oil, not cattle, provides employment for some of the town's inhabitants, but not enough money flows through its streets and businesses to halt its retreat. The pool hall, diner and picture house sit out on the edge of town like a withered limb. Despite the ghost town appearance of the block of ramshackle buildings, Anarene has a thriving high school, which acts as a hub linking the generations and contradicts the idea that the town is falling apart. The disparity is evaded because the film barely concerns itself with the wider world and even less with the locations that link the communal with domestic or work areas. Movement between spaces, whether in the enclosed cab of a truck or in an open-top car, is just as removed from meaningful social context as the motel the teenagers visit for their sexual assignations. Social space is as fragmented as any relationship, each character isolated from their neighbour, a world beyond the immediate horizon unknown and unquestioned. The curious are nowhere to be found.

Poster for *The Last Picture Show* (dir. Peter Bogdanovich, 1971).

A rich boy, Lester Marlow (Randy Quaid), comes to town hoping to make it with Jacy Farrow (Cybill Shepherd), who is readily induced by an invitation to a naked pool party to duck out on her boyfriend, Duane Jackson (Jeff Bridges) – necking with Duane in the beat-up Chevrolet truck he shares with Sonny offers small competition. Time passes; the film starts in the autumn of 1951 and ends a little over a year later. Sonny and Charlene Duggs (Sharon Taggart) have been dating for twelve months, during which time Sonny has become adroit at taking off her bra but has got no further than kissing and fondling. It is passionless sex without a spark or a hint of frisson: he's bored, she's bored. Their relationship, like all others in Anarene, is over before it has even properly started.

Ennui is listlessly, barely displaced by a nostalgia for lost love, like Sam the Lion's for Jacy's mother, Lois Farrow (Ellen Burstyn), his reveries exacerbated by the unfulfilled promise of the town's youngsters, who hanker for something just out of reach, a little beyond their imagination. This entropy is perfectly encapsulated by Lois as she attempts to educate her daughter about sex and romance: 'Just remember, beautiful, everything gets old if you do it often enough. So if you want to find out about monotony real quick, marry Duane.' The wife of the school's football coach, Ruth Popper (Cloris Leachman), momentarily staves off a kind of soul death by her affair with Sonny, but he abandons her when Jacy turns her attention towards him. Ruth then no longer has the will to even bother to get dressed in the morning, their affair a brief respite as loveless as Lois's with Abilene (Clu Gulager), the poolroom cowboy.

The older generation are a combination of beat, broke, impotent, frustrated, inebriated, bored and melancholic; they are just counting down the days. The young circle around each other, waiting for something to happen, for someone to break loose. Radio, television, phonograph records, even cinema fail to import enticing images of otherness, of material plenitude, of the possibility of reinvention; Spencer Tracy and Elizabeth Taylor are mere momentary distractions, Hank Williams just the ever-present soundtrack to their quotidian days. No one is listening to him, he is not singing anyone's life story – or not one they are prepared to hear. Popular culture offers little promise of escape; if anything, it mocks their quality of life, but that would only matter if anyone were paying attention. In an English class, John Keats is being discussed: 'truth is beauty; beauty is truth', the teacher orates as the kids ignore him and pass around a copy of Mickey Spillane's detective novel *I, the Jury* (1947). On the blackboard is a quote from Julius Caesar, 'Men at some time are masters of their own fates', which, just as surely as Tracy's entitled patriarch worrying over the excessive cost of his daughter's marriage, derides the class of teenagers who will always be underlings to the fates, forever without agency. When Duane leaves town to fight in Korea, he tells Sonny he'll be back unless he gets killed.

Though the film's focus is on the town's youngsters, those who will soon graduate, they have not yet been remade by rock 'n' roll, James Dean and the ideal of the teenager as consumer. As they apathetically break up, Charlene faults Sonny for not having a ducktail, such is his lack of any attribute that might be considered teenage cool. Set in the first year of the 1950s, there is little that differentiates the young from the old. Everyone listens to the same music, country and western mostly (only a pop music historian can tell you why Tony Bennett's version of 'Cold Cold Heart' is heard on Jacy's bedroom radio when elsewhere it is Williams's original), and only life experience distinguishes Sonny from Sam. In its depiction of the young, the film could not be further removed from the type of nostalgia evoked by *American Graffiti* (1973), which is set ten years later and is steeped in the immediate aftermath of the first generation of rock 'n' roll – teen rituals now fully codified and commercialized. Everything seemingly falls apart after Sam dies. Joe Bob Blanton, the preacher's boy, turns out to be a paedophile; Duane smashes a bottle into Sonny's face when they fight over Jacy; the picture house is shuttered; and Billy, the mute boy who swept the town, is killed by a truck filled with cattle (a wry echo of the death of Kirk Douglas's character in *Lonely Are the Brave*, 1962, who is also run over by an eighteen-wheeler, though this one carried plumbing supplies to symbolize the West's end).

Three Hank Williams recordings are played throughout the film, offering a commentary of sorts on the proceedings; each might well be the film's theme tune: 'Why Don't You Love Me (Like You Used to Do)?', 'Cold Cold Heart' and 'Lovesick Blues'. Anarene is stuck in the past tense and without the myth of the Frontier to provide even momentary relief. The Texas-set film *Red River* (1948), starring John Wayne, which plays at the film's end was a 'good picture', Sonny and Duane thought, but they had seen it before, evoking for them nothing more than a twinge of ennui. Twice during the film, Sonny checks his reflection in the plastic dome of a jukebox, but all he sees is his own despair and all he hears is a honky-tonk lament.

Writing for *Sight and Sound* magazine, Jan Dawson thought the film displayed an 'elegiac wistfulness' and that 'it is one of the cardinal virtues of this brilliantly understated film that Bogdanovich never takes the easy option of mingling his characters' nostalgia with his own, never allows his evident regret for vanished worlds and wasted opportunities to intrude directly on his film's impeccably detailed surface realism.'[8] In *Rolling Stone*, John Weisman wrote that 'the film evokes images of the Fifties that make it almost overpowering to those who lived through the period.'[9] The movie's nostalgia an aching return, not a pleasurable reprise:

> Bogdanovich's vision of the rural American Southwest is painfully, drearily, true-to-life . . . Without being boring, the film brings to life the excruciatingly bleak future for small town boys like Sonny who chase dollar-and-a-quarter whores and seriously consider balling a heifer, and whose education in, say, music, comes from radio stations in Wichita Falls like KTRN, which beams Hank Williams, Hank Snow and Kay Starr to the fictional town of Anarene, as well as to real places in North Texas, towns like Joy, Deer Creek or Charlie.[10]

Besides the two-decade reverse look over the shoulder to Texas in the early 1950s from the viewpoint of contemporary Hollywood, which 'illuminates boredom from within and without and makes it entertaining', Dawson wrote, Bogdanovich also brought back an appreciation of 'craftsmanship' to American movies.[11] That is to say, the film not only conjured up a passing of the old order of Hollywood, its catalogue of film posters advertising past and forthcoming attractions at the Royal – *Wagon Master*, *White Heat*, *Sands of Iwo Jima*, *Winchester '73*, *The Steel Helmet* and with extracts from *Father of the Bride* and *Red River* (salutes to Bogdanovich's favoured auteurs John Ford, Raoul Walsh, Allan Dwan, Anthony Mann, Samuel Fuller, Vincente Minelli and Howard Hawks, respectively) – but it did so through a fidelity to continuity editing and in its use of black-and-white film stock.[12]

The Last Picture Show's key movie quotes, from *Father of the Bride* and *Red River*, underscore the theme of a lost film-making tradition; the latter reprises the frontier West's promise to Americans to provide the space and opportunity to reinvent themselves, to start over; the former provides its corollary: contemporary, suburban affluence – the promise delivered. *Father of the Bride* dramatizes a world of bourgeois security, material abundance and fealty to a patrilineal order. It is watched by Sonny as he fumbles through the ritualized make-out scene with his girlfriend in the back row, the beauty of Elizabeth Taylor seemingly taunting the utter ordinariness of Charlene Duggs, just as the cowboys in *Red River*, letting rip at the start of the trail drive, comment on the tedium and stasis of small-town life. Both throw up a challenge to contemporary film-makers to either follow their line or to break decisively from it.

Bogdanovich's respect for the past played in direct contrast to *Easy Rider* and Hopper's subsequent directorial effort: 'The title of *The Last Picture Show* is going to have ... indeed, already has ... plenty of confusion with Dennis Hopper's *The Last Movie*.'[13] While both films were highly self-conscious, Hopper's was essentially an exercise in modernism whereas Bogdanovich's was, at best, a conservative take on, if not a reactionary retreat from, the present in its play with mirrors. 'There seem to be more and more allusions to movies within movies,' wrote Champlin in his review of *The Last Picture Show* in the *Los Angeles Times*:

> In a time of hand-held footages, jump cuts, wipes, zooms, elisions and non sequiturs and of technique deliberately degraded for the sake of impact, *The Last Picture Show* has a stately, deliberate, well-joined control which celebrates

the immaculate surfaces of the great Hollywood movies
and their makers . . . Love dies, a boy dies, the Royal closes
(Bogdanovich gives us bits of early television, mostly vile,
leaving no doubt of his own contempt for the medicine
show which killed the palace of dreams) . . . We watch – I
watched – with cool admiration a very cool intelligence at
work. The events are hot but they have an icy remoteness
about them. Recreating not the reality but the vision of
small-town life.[14]

That drift from reality to an ideal is best signified by the change
in the film title used to mark the last night of the Royal between
Larry McMurtry's novel (1966) and Bogdanovich's adaptation. In
the former it is an Audie Murphy vehicle *The Kid from Texas* (1950),
in the film it is Hawks's *Red River*: a popular, formulaic Western
loved by small-town and neighbourhood audiences replaced by a
star-strewn, auteurist, big-budget epic loved by cinephiles.

The distinction between Hopper's and Bogdanovich's films
was underscored by Vincent Canby in the *New York Times*:

A film like Dennis Hopper's *The Last Movie*, which tries
to say a lot of fairly dumb-headed things about the effect
of movies, about innocence corrupted, about Christian
myth, and about six or seven other weighty things I hope
to forget, has the effect of an abstract expressionist painting by an artist who never bothered to learn about color
(and who, indeed, may well be color blind). *The Last
Picture Show*, however, isn't remarkable simply for the
mistakes Bogdanovich has avoided. It says a good deal
more about the movies, without trying very hard, than

Hopper's splintered, extravagantly over-produced film. *The Last Picture Show* rediscovers a time, a place, a film form – and a small but important part of the American experience.[15]

But *The Last Picture Show* was not simply an attempt at recreating a bygone age of small-town life and Hollywood's golden years, nor was it in all ways conservative; it also provided a decidedly contemporary take on things, which *Variety*, at least, found somewhat uncomfortable: 'where the film falters, is in taking ... passing incidents ... and treating them in a modern, "anything goes" manner.'[16] The reviewer is particularly irked by the film's casual approach to nudity, 'especially the inclusion of a very young boy in an overdone, tasteless nude bathing scene'.[17] With overt depictions of teenage sex, direct reference to child molestation, extramarital affairs and boys discussing the relative merits of doing it with a heifer, the film falls fully in line with its contemporary peers such as *Drive, He Said* (1971) and *Five Easy Pieces* (both 1970) by refusing the sexual taboos of an earlier Hollywood. The sexual licence of Bogdanovich's picture and its ilk does not escape a prurience, and his film's treatment of Jacy/Shepherd is creepily voyeuristic.

Jacy is the rich girl who should be beyond the reach of the town's poor boys; why she idles with them is not explained. On the other hand, the town's wealthy families are just as broken and dysfunctional as Sonny's and Duane's. Sonny looks to Sam the Lion as a male role model, learning during the film to roll cigarettes just like him. But, despite being played by Ben Johnson, a John Ford regular, the figure is a damaged man forever mourning a lost love. His death is a maudlin recall, an opportunity to grieve a little. The myth of the West hangs uneasily on his shoulders, diminishing him and the town's menfolk just as certainly as Tracy's patriarch does in *Father of the Bride*. In Anarene, the West is a reverberation heard in the wind that blows through the town, caught like yesterday's newspaper against the siding of the Cactus Motel or the Rig-Wam drive-in diner. It is signified by the cowboy boots the men wear and their common uniform of denim jeans and jackets. The day's popular music, especially Williams, underscores the film's historical verisimilitude, the social facts of the characters' lives, while the radio announcement that President Truman is visiting Dallas, heard in the first scene in the poolroom, confirms the film's spatial and temporal setting: 'This is Cowboy Rhythm on KTRN, Wichita Falls'. The frontier is no more than an echoed radio signal.

In Ross Macdonald's 1971 mystery novel *The Underground Man*, private investigator Lew Archer eats dinner in a southern Californian restaurant-bar that has a Western theme to its decor and a country and western band providing the musical accompaniment to the drinks and steaks:

> Behind the semi-elliptical bar four cowboys who had never been near a cow sang western songs which sounded as if they had originated in the far east. I ordered a second beer and looked around the place. It was a noisy mixture of the real west and the imitation west. The mixture included cowboys both dude and actual, off-duty servicemen with their wives and girls, tourists, oil-workers wearing high-heeled boots like the cowboys, a few men in business suits with wide ties and narrow sun-crinkled eyes.[18]

Anarene may be a dry town, and the diner serves hamburger not steak, but it is that same mix of the real and fake West. *The Last*

Picture Show promises an authenticity by positioning itself as a genuine undertaking to present the real, but it is a domestic melodrama, a romance, every bit as fixed in the formulaic as Minnelli's *Father of the Bride*. Despite its proletarian focus, Bogdanovich's film belongs to a group of movies that includes *Giant* (George Stevens, 1956), *Written on the Wind* (Douglas Sirk, 1956) and the earlier Larry McMurtry adaptation *Hud* (Martin Ritt, 1963) – dramas of Texas dynasties. Foot-and-mouth disease ends the ranching tradition in the latter; in the former two, as in *The Last Picture Show*, oil has replaced cattle.

John Huston's *The Life and Times of Judge Roy Bean* (1972) tells the story of the West's move from a frontier of derring-do, gunfighters, gamblers and big-hearted prostitutes to its despoliation by the oil industry. Stanley Kramer's *Oklahoma Crude* (1973), with its turn-of-the-century boom-time setting, picks up the story from that point and makes yet another romantic comedy from the material: the labour involved in extracting the oil is never part of that story. In *The Last Picture Show*, the wildcatters and roughnecks are seen only in the back of trucks, in the diner and in the poolroom. Both Duane and Sonny earn money on the rigs, but we never see them at work, because, like a good melodrama, the film is only really interested in the domestic. But BBS's companion piece to *The Last Picture Show*, *Five Easy Pieces*, in its early scenes, does show aspects of the work involved in oil drilling that Bogdanovich's film shied away from.

Five Easy Pieces was promoted with an image of a begrimed Jack Nicholson in work clothes sitting back on his haunches, two roughnecks silhouetted against an oil derrick behind him. The image

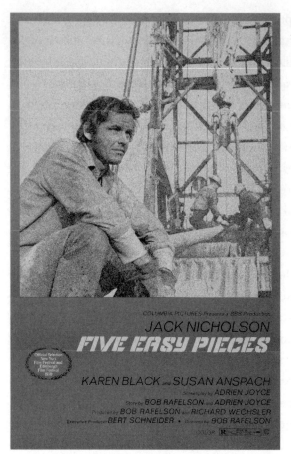

Poster for *Five Easy Pieces* (dir. Bob Rafelson, 1970).

is drawn from one of the three occasions, during the film's first thirty minutes, when Bobby (Nicholson) and Elton (Billy Green Bush) are shown toiling in the oil fields. The film begins with an expansive opening montage of men working together, moving dirt, running pipes and climbing rigs; it is shot in close-up and from a distance against a long horizon at sunset. Over the top of these images, Tammy Wynette's 1968 hit single 'Stand by Your Man' plays. The song continues on the soundtrack while Bobby, at day's end, drives home. The source of the recording is his girlfriend's record player. Singing along with Tammy, Rayette (Karen Black) is introduced in her waitress uniform, making up her face while sitting in the bathroom sink.

The depiction of physical labour, the dirt-encrusted denim jacket and jeans that Bobby wears (a match with those worn in *The Last Picture Show*), his work boots, hard hat, full sideburns, the country and western recording, Rayette's name, costume and tower of hair, their claustrophobic, shoddy house, the tacky pictures on its walls – all signify a proletarian bearing. The déclassé social milieu is confirmed by the following scene in a bowling alley, a blue-collar leisure activity with beers and a side-order of fries. The two gum-chewing women Bobby encounters there, and whom he and Elton will slip around with, are called Twinky and Betty. It is a plebeian world of hard-scrabble work, bawdy sex romps, trailer parks, pop music, hamburgers and television game shows that drown out all conversation.

The film's producer, Richard Wechsler, told *Variety* he was one of the 'new "revolutionary" young filmmakers that make today's scene . . . realism that conveys something to an audience is the object, including four-letter words'.[19] The film's 'story is the conflict of rebellious protest against artsie types. Scenario was written by Carole Eastman and is a character study draped around star. According to Wechsler it is not gimmicky, film trendy, and is an actor's pic, intrinsically entertainment. An odd slice of life.'[20] There is an unacknowledged contradiction in Wechsler's sales pitch of a film built on the notion of rejecting artistic pretension, made by film-makers who strike radical poses with an elevated aesthetic sensibility. Can the centre, between commerce – Hollywood – and art – 'revolutionary' auteurs – hold?

That Bobby is not at home in this working-class world, is not comfortable with its easy and cheap pleasures, is made immediately clear in his relationship with Rayette. He dismisses her taste, belittles and cheats on her. 'I'm not a piece of crap,' she tearfully tells him, but that is exactly how he treats her. However besotted, Rayette understands that Bobby will 'never be satisfied'; he doesn't even try to gratify her. As the first act of the film unfolds, Bobby is further delineated as someone apart from the world he is presently inhabiting, forever discontented. Driving home after a night shift, he and Elton are caught in a traffic jam. While barely tolerating his companion plucking away on a ukulele and singing a ribald song about a dog, Bobby berates the rush hour's conformist commuters. In an unspoken response to Elton's vulgar twang, Bobby gets out of the car and clambers onto the back of a truck with an upright piano lashed to its siding and plays a classical piece. High and low culture are pitched against each other in the democratic setting of a highway logjam. When the gridlock breaks up, Bobby, piano and truck get off the highway on a spur road, while Elton and the commuters carry on straight ahead. It is a bravura sequence, highly calculated in its effect and loaded in its meaning: Bobby unsteadily straddling the boorish and the refined.

The film's formal elements are just as precariously balanced. While the film is built around bold and virtuoso scenes, they are delivered by a set of techniques as conventional as those used in *The Last Picture Show*. As *Variety* noted, *Five Easy Pieces* shuns gimmicks, bizarre camera angles and the like to better 'tell a story and illumine character'.[21] Its theme of a 'search for identity' is 'timeless', the journal reported, its approach 'novelistic', and its actors are respected for their craft.[22] Such conventional values will confound fans of *Easy Rider* who, *Variety* explained, were hoping for more of the same from the many who were involved in its production.[23] The effect was to pitch *Five Easy Pieces* somewhat indeterminately between commercial melodrama and European art house.

As a hybrid, Rafelson's film echoed Jacques Demy's American movie *Model Shop* (1969), starring Gary Lockwood and Anouk Aimée (dialogue was by Adrien Joyce, aka Carole Eastman, who was responsible for *Five Easy Pieces* and *The Shooting*'s scripts). Set in Los Angeles, Lockwood plays George Matthews, a disaffected 26-year-old. He has quit his job as an architect, is estranged from his parents and is disenchanted with his wannabe-actress girlfriend. Unless he can raise what is owed before the end of the day, his vintage MG sports car is going to be repossessed. Furthermore, the imminent spectre of being conscripted into the army filters everything for him. Like Bobby in *Five Easy Pieces*, he is a middle-class dropout. He drifts around Los Angeles trying, without much effort, to drum up some funds. Listening to classical music on the car's radio, he calls in on old friends, one who leads the band Spirit (who provide the film's rock score) and others who run an underground newspaper. Following a chance encounter with a mysterious beautiful French woman, Lola (Aimée), she becomes his obsession, his grand distraction from all his middle-class travails. He follows her into the hills above the city and to a photographic studio where she poses for connoisseurs of female pulchritude – amateur photographers practising their *art*.

Before she flies back to France and he joins the army, the two have a brief liaison, an entanglement of high and low cultures, European and American, an exchange that involves all the points along the continuum of the vulgar and the sophisticated, from the high vistas from which George can overlook LA and chance to dream again, as he did when he studied architecture, to the back streets of Marina del Rey, where his weatherworn clap-board house has a nodding donkey pumpjack in the yard, just like his neighbours'. Oil wealth and impoverished housing lie side by side as uneasily (or maybe as readily) as Parisian refinement sits with downtown LA sleaze, or a rich patron's support for a bohemian artist.

During the final scene in the oil fields in *Five Easy Pieces*, Elton is arrested for an outstanding charge of robbing a gas station and Bobby snarkily quits, though his foreman doesn't give a damn what he does. Pathetically, Bobby is denied an audience for his wanton act of rebellion·- he fudges the climax to the great scene he thought he was creating. Moments previously, while he and Elton were on their lunch break, he had given a star's performance of indigna-tion: Elton had told him that Rayette was pregnant, and Bobby, in a deflected response to the news, took offence at Elton's homilies about family life. Bobby pushes back at the idea that his and Elton's lives are in any way comparable. In his concocted anger, Rayette is forgotten about. This, after all, is Bobby's stage upon which he struts beneath the oil derricks.

Elton's and Bobby's differences are starkly revealed at the beginning of the second act when Bobby visits his sister at a sound studio where she is recording a Bach fugue. Years have passed since Bobby skedaddled from his family's stifling hold, from his upbringing as a musician in a household full of musicians. On the film's end credits he is named 'Robert Eroica Dupea', his sister is Partita and his brother Carl Fidelio. The European-sounding sur-name and Latinate given names (*Eroica* and *Fidelio* are Beethoven compositions, a 'partita' a suite for solo or chamber ensemble) are as far removed from Rayette, Stoney, Elton and Twinky as Chopin is from Tammy Wynette, as a Lee 101-J denim jacket is from the corduroy sports coat Robert wears around the family home after returning to see his ailing, stroke-crippled father.

When Bobby travels north to Washington, the last vestiges of his proletarian persona are shucked off. His time working on the rigs, drinking, gambling and carousing with Elton, his life with Rayette – all masquerade. Middle-class rebellion, bourgeois slumming, the self-propelled downward trajectory of the privileged – his education and cultural capital were forsworn but never entirely lost. The denunciation of his own class maintains a semblance of authenticity, however, because it is played off against the comic refusal of social conformity enacted by the two women he gives a lift to on his way north with Rayette. Having driven their car off the road and into a ditch, Terry Grouse (Toni Basil) and Palm Apodaca (Helena Kallianiotes) fill out the back seat of Bobby's car. Palm is obsessed with cleanliness; she wants to go to Alaska, which is pure, away from people who are smutty. 'Dirt isn't bad,' she says, 'filth is bad.' She patronizes and belittles Rayette, just as she laughs at the waitress Bobby humiliates in his failed attempt to get a breakfast that is not on the menu.

Bobby and Palm treat Rayette as superficial, a scatterbrain with bleached hair, heavy make-up, a faux leopard-spot coat, a working-class accent and a love of pop records with trite messages and catchy tunes. Though Bobby twice defends Rayette, once against Palm and later in the face of the patronizing, pontificating woman at his family home, he still treats her like a piece of crap. But it is Bobby and Palm who are truly superficial; both are middle-class dropouts, both are fakes. He reveals as much to Catherine Van Oost (Susan Anspach), his brother Carl's fiancée and another refined American with a distinct European surname, when he concedes to the request to play something for her. She responds to his piece with sensitivity, but in turn he undercuts her, ridicules her empathy by revealing that his performance is a sham, a sleight of hand. He belittles her, as he has Rayette, his sister and the waitress.

Bobby may appear more virile than Carl with his neck sprain and restraining collar, beating him at ping-pong and sleeping with Catherine, but his masculinity is formed by the bullying and humiliation of others, especially women, including the sanctimonious lady who patronizes Rayette. When he does show his sensitive side to his father, out on the headland, talking to him about his 'auspicious beginnings', his need to get away from things that will go bad *if he stays* and his apology – 'I'm sorry it didn't work out' – they are all part of an act of epic self-delusion and exculpation, a confession given to someone who can neither comprehend nor respond. Bobby just zips up his windcheater a little higher, a little tighter, and wipes away a tear shed for himself alone.

It is not only the switching of the denim for the corduroy jacket that suggests Bobby/Robert's superficial play with identities, or the truly grotesque floral shirt he wears when visiting his father, which is a conformist's attempt to appear nonconformist, like a middle-aged man dancing with a woman half his age at a discotheque, or the putative figure in The Rolling Stones' '(I Can't Get No) Satisfaction'. That all this putting on and pulling off costumes has significance is confirmed at the film's end when Bobby climbs into the cab of a truck hauling lumber. He has left his jacket in the men's room, symbolically shedding his past. Like Palm, he is trying to get to Alaska to get clean – the last frontier available to middle-class bohemians, a place where cultural capital is not bankable. On filming in Victoria, British Columbia, cinematographer László Kovács said he liked this part of Canada, which 'offers texture, and the surrealism of a last frontier'.[24] Frontiers in the film are as much between the high and the low, between country and classical music, as they are between the farm and the wilderness, and they are not so much surreal as quotidian.

Country and western music is about consequences – what you do on Saturday night you'll pay for on Sunday morning. Rayette knows that, accepts it even. But that is not what makes her a tragic figure; she is that because of her love for Bobby. Her flaw, Bobby, is there for all to see. On the other hand, he wants to be like a character in a Little Richard number, the one who's just got paid, is a fool about his money and don't try to save. But his true face is that of a frustrated, unfulfilled man in an orange, red and yellow floral-print shirt, whose middle-class alienation is a cliché, not a flaw, and this makes him pathetic, not tragic.

When Bobby quits on his family again, he also leaves behind a pregnant Rayette, someone who *is* true to herself, does reach out to others, has feelings that are genuine. She may not have much of an education, but she is empathetic. By contrast, Bobby is emotionally stunted, refuses responsibility and has an adolescent attitude to life. His restlessness is not that of Huckleberry Finn romantically lighting out for the territory, escaping Aunt Sally and her civilizing ways. He is a man turning into his middle age and still running away from bad situations he himself has created. Abandoning Rayette at the gas station confirms, as if it were ever needed, that Bobby is not only in a permanent state of arrested development but is, at heart, an ugly misogynist – a piece of crap.

Bobby labours in the oil fields around Bakersfield, California, a town known for its displaced Oklahoma migrants who came west during the Depression, stayed where the Frontier had run out and formed a community from which the Bakersfield sound emerged – a rough-and-ready, amplified and electric response to the commercial sincerities of Nashville's countrypolitan blandishments. Wynn Stewart, Buck Owens and Merle Haggard are Bakersfield's best-known alumni, inspiring Gram Parsons (and through him the Flying Burrito Brothers, Emmylou Harris and The Rolling Stones).

With its colonial-like reach to the outer regions of its empire, Nashville had little trouble incorporating the music of Bakersfield under its imperial umbrella, certainly no more than it did other country outliers like Waylon Jennings, Willie Nelson and Kris Kristofferson – the 'outlaws' – who gave a contemporary turn to country *and* western. That conflation of the South with the West had long played out in popular culture with the figure of the Dixie cowboy, a mainstay of Hollywood oaters since the 1930s. In parallel with the movies, country singers from Jimmie Rodgers and Gene Autry onwards adopted Western costumes to present a less politicized, more acceptable image of themselves that would appeal on both sides of the Mason–Dixon line (and east and west of the Appalachians). For those watching *The Last Picture Show* from the viewpoint of the early 1970s, and having grown up on Saturday matinees of singing cowboy series and serials, country music was Western and the Western was country. Hank Williams was a hillbilly *and* a cowboy.

If the gift of the Western to country was that it provided an imaginative space for defeated Confederates to reincorporate themselves into the Union without submitting to a triumphant North, or to present a less culturally denigrated presentation of self than hillbilly, country, in return, provided a terrain where the Western could go when the Frontier closed in on itself and turned around – which is the route travelled by the protagonists in *Easy Rider* and *Two-Lane Blacktop*. It also defined the world of *The*

Last Picture Show with its characters circling back on themselves, like the newlyweds Sonny and Jacy, unable to escape beyond the city limits before being brought home by a policeman, and like Bobby in *Five Easy Pieces*, travelling first south and then north, still searching for his own personal frontier free of civilizing aunts and personal responsibility.

That sense of circling back, retracing steps, that all these films plot out is there in *Payday*, starring Rip Torn as a dysfunctional, alcoholic, pill-popping country and western star. Shot entirely in Alabama in the final months of 1971, but not distributed until January 1973, the film was a Fantasy Records production helmed by Ralph J. Gleason, jazz columnist and co-founder of *Rolling Stone*. The original script was by Don Carpenter, author of the cult beat novel *Hard Rain Falling* (1966), and four original songs were provided by Jewish Chicagoan poet and songwriter Shel Silverstein, who had written 'A Boy Named Sue' for Johnny Cash and other hits for Tompall Glaser and Loretta Lynn. He had also worked with Kristofferson and Jennings. He would later have a string of hits with Dr Hook, including 'Sylvia's Mother' and 'The Ballad of Lucy Jordan'. Rip Torn, who was from Texas, added a touch of the real to counter the hip metropolitan credentials of those others working on the film. *Payday* was a studied attempt at authenticity by some of Hollywood's self-defined outsiders, pushing for a truth about life on the road for a middling country and western star, Maury Dann.

The film records Dann's final 36 hours, his lifestyle echoing the excesses of Hank Williams, George Jones, Jerry Lee Lewis, Spade Cooley, Johnny Cash, Faron Young, Johnny Paycheck and Merle Haggard. Each of these stars are marked by alcoholism, barbiturate abuse, murder, petty larceny, or any combination of such sinful ways – and from which all were equally adept at seeking redemption in the most pious fashion imaginable. Author of the first hip history of country music, one aimed at *Rolling Stone* and *Creem* readers, Nick Tosches wrote in his review of *Payday* that Dann was a composite of Williams and Ernest Tubb, that it 'is a great fucking movie' and that, with a few more like it, 'the world of twang just might be coaxed into joining the present century.'[25] In *Rolling Stone*, Jon Landau joined the small chorus of rock critics who praised the film: he thought it more real and compelling than documentaries like *Groupies* and *Gimme Shelter* (both 1970), 'though no less sordid than either'.[26]

Most of the film takes place in the back of Dann's Cadillac as he and his entourage travel between gigs, with intermittent stops at motels, diners and gas stations along with a duck hunt, visits to see his mother, his estranged wife and a radio DJ. When it eventually arrives, payday for Dann is a heart attack while at the wheel of the Caddy. He fills his final hours engaging in rough sex with groupies in the car's back seat, necking whisky like it is Coca-Cola, swallowing handfuls of barbiturates, getting into fights, bagging some ducks and whooping it up with a pistol while hanging out of the car as it hits 85 miles per hour. Fun, fun, fun – except when it isn't. Dann's is a wretched, boring, narcissistic existence. He is so detached from reality he cannot even remember how old his youngest kid is, never mind when his birthday falls. He is a failure as a husband and father, and his idea of looking after his mother is to give her a handful of pep pills. Next time we see her she is as high as a kite trying to hang out the washing.

Dann had left his mother behind years ago; his home is the Cadillac, moving but going nowhere. His ostensible aim is to get to a gig in Birmingham, but it might just as well be any town. His driver dreams about being a chef, his manager about getting him a slot on *The Johnny Cash Show*. With his shit-eating grin and lascivious wink, Maury just wants to get stoned and fucked while he milks the adulation of fans, who see only a confident, successful performer, not the utter mess of a human being that he is, who treats everyone as dispensable. However bad their personal lives got, Jones, Williams and Lewis could always hang on to their music for sustenance, or at least believe that that was what sustained them, but Maury Dann doesn't even have that hand hold. When Jerry Weathermax and his band stop over at the motel where Dann is lodged, an impromptu jam gets going in his rooms. It is a joy to watch, but Dann doesn't take part, he just pops another pill, chases another bit of skirt and the next day gets back into his car, toots on his harmonica, and the road rolls on before him in all its awful emptiness.

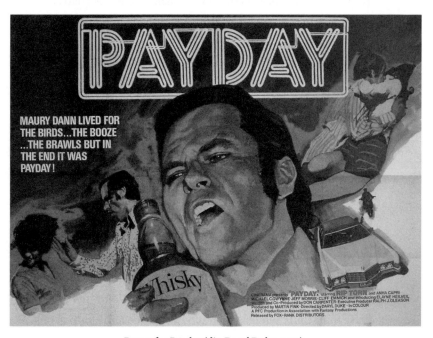

Poster for *Payday* (dir. Daryl Duke, 1972).

Variety called the film a 'topnotch melodrama' that could be sold two ways – 'as a slice of life to sophisticated audiences and as a bawdy, hell-raising entertainment in smaller situations'.[27] Roger Greenspun's lukewarm review of *Payday* for the *New York Times* dismissed, by implication, the dual appeal that *Variety* plugged. He began his critique with the observation that the

> pursuit of that ultimate all-American pop-culture arte-fact, the road movie, continues... To appreciate the road movie, or the spirit of the road movie, you must refine your sensibilities – until you become a connoisseur of main streets, motel rooms, roadhouse parking lots, and of the dawn rising warmly over superhighways in the Southeast. To such taste *Payday* offers some nourishment – perhaps too much. In other respects it is very thin.[28]

In his history of Wild West films, published in 1990, critic Kim Newman writes briefly about the movie world inherited by New Hollywood:

> The 1930s and 1940s children who admired the roaming heroes of 'B' Westerns became the adolescents who tuned in to the cult of Jack Kerouac's novel *On the Road*, which itself fuelled Dennis Hopper's *Easy Rider* and Monte Hellman's *Two-Lane Blacktop* and the whole 1970s cycle of 'road movies' [that concentrate] on the vastness and emptiness of the landscape through which their charac-ters obsessively drive. The most significant endings of these films find their lead characters – Fonda and Hopper in *Easy Rider*, traffic cop Robert Blake in *Electra Glide in*

Blue – dead on the road, while *Two-Lane Blacktop*, adapt-
ing the mood of Hellman's horseback road movie *The
Shooting*, finally recognises the futility of keeping on the
road by having the film itself burn to nothing.[29]

Torn's Maury Dann also ends up dead on the road, but the highway
he travels on is a narrow thoroughfare that goes nowhere but back
around behind him; it is a circuit of emptiness apropos of nothing
so much as the hole in his heart; a dead space. There is simply
nothing to romanticize in *Payday* – Dann's Cadillac is a hearse.
The film concludes with the Carter Family's 'Keep On the Sunny
Side' playing over the end credits, appropriate enough given their
status as country music's founding figures and the song's theme of
light against the dark, but it might just as well have been 'Can the
Circle Be Unbroken (By and By)' with its image of the life-and-
death cycle, from which Dann was never going to find an exit to
drive up and attempt a getaway.

Champlin's review in the *Los Angeles Times* went under the
headline 'Twang of Truth in *Payday*'. He wrote:

Amid a flotilla of pretentious flops and a clutch of cynical cop-outs, it is extremely reassuring to run into one of
those good, tough, economical, modest, thoroughly professional films which knows precisely where it is heading
and which gets there with power and grace . . . *Payday*
explores the Nashville-centered world with an easy
authenticity which makes this nothing like a repetition of
what has been before.[30]

Peter Schjeldahl's review, the second for the film in the *New York Times*, echoed Champlin's admiration for *Payday*'s realism: 'Its clarity is what makes it so extraordinary. It is a work of such dead-honest realism that it is hard to know how, except as a kind of literal truth, to take it.'[31] Whatever Rita Mae Brown would have made of the claimed realism of *Five Easy Pieces* and *Payday*, it would surely not have been any more favourable than her evisceration of *The Last Picture Show*, and she would no doubt have made the observation that not a single black face or figure, never mind a black character, appeared in these films. New Hollywood's social realism did not include the reality, or even fantasy, of black lives, but its film-makers did know that Williams, or even Wynette, could tell you things about life that escaped the blandishment provided by the financial security, moral piety and cultural capital enjoyed by America's educated middle classes, which was precisely its appeal for Bogdanovich, Rafelson and those who laboured behind *Payday*.

4

The Shooting, Ride in the Whirlwind and Two-Lane Blacktop: Who's Monte Hellman, You Ask?

Monte Hellman is about to surface. Who's Monte Hellman, you ask? He's the director of *The Shooting* and *Ride in the Whirlwind*, two melodramas that have enjoyed enormous underground success. Jack Nicholson starred in both films with Millie Perkins, and he wrote the screenplay for *Whirlwind*.

Now Hellman is set to direct *Two-Lane Blacktop* for the ultra-above ground Cinema Center Films. Michael Loughlin will produce Rudolph Wurlitzer's original script. What's it all about? Three crazy-for-kicks auto racers and one girl. Easy does it, riders.

A. H. Weiler, *New York Times*, May 1970

The *Times*'s piece was mostly hyperbole. Monte Hellman's brace of Westerns – *The Shooting* and *Ride in the Whirlwind* – produced back-to-back in 1965, were still not much more than hearsay in 1970. Four years earlier, a handful of French cinephiles, regulars at the Cinéma Mac-Mahon in Paris, might have been heard discussing the films' merits, but few others had seen or knew anything about them.[1] With the success of *Easy Rider* and the interest it promoted in Jack Nicholson, the two barely exhibited films were now being discussed as if they were some lost-and-found talisman, a harbinger of things that had now come to pass. As well as acting in them, Nicholson had written *Ride in the Whirlwind* and co-produced both films with Hellman. *The Shooting* had been scripted by Adrien Joyce, pseudonym of Carole Eastman (who later wrote *Five Easy Pieces*), and it starred the incomparable Warren Oates. Retrospectively, the two films had impeccable pedigrees and, as 1970 unfolded, echoes of the conversation begun in Paris were heard in amplified form as American critics turned to the films as indicators of their makers' once thwarted aspirations and the excitement felt over the promise they now held for a New Hollywood.

The story of the two Westerns had gone public when Kevin Thomas, film critic at the *Los Angeles Times*, declared Hellman to be Hollywood's 'Best-Kept Secret'.[2] He reported that *The Shooting* and *Ride in the Whirlwind* were 'extraordinary' movies, unaccountably hidden from filmgoers.[3] He thought Hellman's films needed to be seen by anyone who cared about cinema. Hellman's Westerns formed the backstory to Thomas's report on the production of *Two-Lane Blacktop*, scheduled for release in the late spring of 1971: still eight months away, but eagerly anticipated. Not having *Blacktop* to write about, Thomas focused on the Westerns, which 'are austere in the utmost; virtually devoid of exposition, they tell us no more about their characters than they can know about each other, which is not much – and which is very much the point'.[4] Both films evoke a 'profoundly disturbing sense of uncertainty and even intimations of paranoia', but especially *Ride in the Whirlwind*.[5]

He wrote that an 'existentialist philosophy' permeates the films, as he speculated would also be the case with *Two-Lane Blacktop*. Following Thomas, the characterization of the films as in some way philosophically profound quickly and inexorably became a default critical interpretation.[6]

Discussing with Thomas his choice of novelist Rudy Wurlitzer as screenwriter on *Two-Lane Blacktop*, Hellman said: 'He was interested in the same things I was. Man's relationship to society. The beauty and horror of existence – how's that! I guess "beauty and terror" is better. Anyway, the existential dilemma.'[7] Hellman also framed his work as Aristotelian, whose writings, he said, he was raised on: 'I always hope to achieve purgation by pity and fear. I really hope to disturb my audience, to move it to another place. Haunt it for a while, maybe.'[8] Thomas had no doubt that *Two-Lane Blacktop* could carry such intellectual baggage.

Hellman's background in exploitation cinema, as a director and editor, had been a creative apprenticeship, he said, that had left him alone to experiment, because 'you could try anything.'[9] With the two Westerns, 'Jack Nicholson and I both felt they were a chance to kind of throw away a lot of the traditional obligations of the western because of their low budgets and because nobody was breathing down our necks.'[10] The downside of such experimentation, he suggested, had ensured the films' obscurity, leaving them undistributed and unexhibited.

Prior to their late discovery, Hellman's Westerns left only a few traces in the trade press. Both had been shown to the committee of the critics' section at Cannes in 1966 but, though the films were said to have been positively received, there were no awards.[11] The French distribution rights, however, were promptly sold. Unfortunately, they were bought by a company that thereafter went bust, leaving the films in limbo and unscreened again in France until early in 1968. The occasion for their re-emergence was as part of a programme curated by *Positif*'s critics that highlighted movies not previously exhibited in Paris.[12] *The Shooting* subsequently played at the Avignon film festival in July–August 1968.[13] The following April, *Cahiers du cinéma* published its ten best films for 1968. Though neither Western made the top ten, *Whirlwind* and *Shooting* received a notable seven and six votes respectively.[14] The French interest caused *Variety* to describe the films as 'art house hits' in Paris, but, after their limited number of 1966 screenings, the two pictures remained unexploited in North America and, apart from in Paris, had only been seen on the festival circuit.[15]

Following Cannes, *The Shooting* was screened in Montreal's film festival in July 1966, where it was, *Boxoffice* reported, 'greeted by puzzlement and shock'.[16] Nicholson, 29, was there to help sell the film alongside Hellman, 'the picture's 37-year-old American director', who 'said at a press conference here that "ambiguity", if not puzzlement, was his intention'.[17] The journal called it a 'visually beautiful, mysteriously compelling feature film'.[18] Later in 1966, *Ride in the Whirlwind* was chosen to play the San Francisco festival in the New American Directors series. *Bonnie and Clyde* was the opening feature. Following the screening, *Variety* reviewed the film and derided its 'naturalistic style', which their critic felt could be apportioned to a lack of experience on Hellman's part: 'What unreels is a flat, woodenly acted western with mild suspense that never grabs.'[19] The problem, the critic thought, was in the script, which offered a 'promising plot line rather than a fully developed scenario'.[20] Concluding on a positive note, the 'malevolently barren Badlands of Utah', shot by Gregory Sandor, were 'impressive', and this despite the handicap of being filmed entirely on location for a 'rock low budget' (the cinematographer would work again with Hellman on *Two-Lane Blacktop*).[21]

American critic Beverly Walker added to the conversation around the two films in her lengthy interview with Hellman, given while he was shooting *Two-Lane Blacktop*. Walker was the film's publicist, a fact that was not mentioned in her piece, which ran in the Winter 1970 edition of *Sight and Sound*. Regardless of any conflict of interest, she gave by far the most detailed account of these Westerns' production and stalled distribution.[22] The two pictures were each budgeted at $75,000; to keep costs low on the six-week-long schedule, non-union crews were used. Equipment was limited, only two cameras and reflectors. Transport was equally basic, consisting of one beat-up utility truck and a station wagon. '*The Shooting* was made first and nobody could quite understand the bizarre script,' Walker wrote.[23] The crew and cast 'had been coaxed to Utah to make a quick, low-budget Western, but this one wasn't quite like anything they'd seen before'.[24] Hellman spent six months editing the pair; Corman then tried to sell the films to AIP, who declined. With no immediate buyer in hand, the films were promoted via the festival circuit.

The failed French distribution meant that both the duplicate negatives and rights were tied up for a year. Movie theatre and television company owner Walter Reade Jr then secured them for his West Coast television division, which resulted in the films once more being placed in an exhibition hiatus. Broadcasts of the films in the 1960s appear to have been as infrequent occurrences as any cinema screenings. Walker reported that Hellman and investors had recently bought back the rights to the films and were negotiating their imminent release. She thought the pair of films

>

remarkable, not only for production values which in view of how they were made make Hellman seem something of a wizard, but for an almost obsessive personal vision unusual in any American film and particularly a Western. Not really 'likeable', the films are startling and discomforting in their nihilism and oddly detached objectivity. Terse and pared to the bone, they offer none of the orthodox Western entertainment values. Action is minimal, rugged individualism is out, and nobody wins.[25]

Walker asked Hellman if he had consciously made the Westerns 'somewhat bizarre'. He responded: 'We thought they would be a couple more Roger Corman movies that would play on the second half of a double-bill somewhere. So any thoughts about doing something different were for our own personal satisfaction. We never thought that anybody would ever notice.'[26] As with his two films, mentions of Hellman in the trade press, prior to being contracted to make *Two-Lane Blacktop*, were few and far between. Most often he appeared in news items linked with productions that never quite came to fruition, first with Universal, then with a company he helped form before he returned to work for Corman.[27] The latter link partly explains why both Westerns played at the 1970 Edinburgh International Film Festival (EIFF), which, having previously showcased the producer's work with a retrospective, maintained a strong involvement with him and AIP in lieu of attracting films from the major studios.[28]

Hellman's earlier directorial efforts, *Beast from the Haunted Cave* (1959), *Back Door to Hell* (1964) and *Flight to Fury* (1964), were also screened in Edinburgh. In the programme notes Hellman acknowledged an Italian neo-realism influence on his work.

Searching for additional profundity, the writer of the notes added that Hellman had a 'very self-conscious camera style and montage, with the result that his films often appear schematic'.[29] This high-brow response to such pulp-ish exploitation material was fairly run-of-the-mill on the part of the festival's programmers, who wanted to sell tickets and their radical credentials. It was, however, the two cowboy pictures that were of real interest to their particular concerns: 'His Westerns have met with little approval in the States, where the nihilism and despair that they express questions the basis of American ideology, and undermines the fundamental elements of the Western as a genre.'[30] Besides the embrace of American movies that had been rejected in their home country (even if in the States no one much had even seen those films), the festival's organizers were also alive to the subversive potential of such B-movies to undermine their own formulaic concerns.

These intellectual approaches to American cinema had long been circulating internationally, especially in Paris, but the EIFF provided them with an anglophone and culturally legitimate platform, amplifying and further disseminating the critical practice of finding the seditious within popular culture. These were the high years of cinephilia in Britain: 'We caught the movie buff explosion, in the mid-sixties, and we were on the right wavelength,' said festival director Murray Grigor in 1970.[31] He, alongside Lynda Myles and David Wills, radically transformed what had been a conservative festival, without much ambition, into a true force in British and then international film culture. Such a passion for film as a transformative aspect of life was not just a passing affair; it was, Myles was later to reflect, 'as important as breathing'.[32]

The Hellman retrospective was linked to a gala screening of Roger Corman's *Bloody Mama* and *Gas! – Or – It Became Necessary to Destroy the World in Order to Save It* (both 1970), which in turn were links back to the previous year's 'History of AIP Thru Roger Corman', a retrospective that was inspired by the gala screening in 1968 of AIP's *Wild in the Streets*, directed by Barry Shear. Given the cultural current of cinephilia and the championing of illegitimate strands of American film-making, whether it was the New York underground (Warhol and Anger both had screenings of their films at the 1969 EIFF) or exploitation specialists like AIP and Corman, the programming of Hellman's juvenilia made sound ideological and economic sense. Like Corman with his low-budget grindhouse movies and the American underground with its iconoclastic shock tactics, the EIFF, with its shoestring funding, had to do whatever it could to grab the headlines and encourage patronage.

The association with Corman would continue over the next few years when the festival showed repeated interest in the early work of Jonathan Demme, screening *The Hot Box* (1972), *Caged Heat* (1974) and *Crazy Mama* (1975). The programme notes justified this attention when it claimed that the director, working 'within the limits of the softcore exploitation movie . . . has sought to subvert the traditional conservative values of the genre to examine the nature of revolution, and the limits of revolution through action'.[33] The EIFF deployed a similar tactic in its attempts to undermine traditional, conservative film festival programming to that which Demme, Corman and Samuel Fuller (who was the topic of Edinburgh's first retrospective) were said to have used while making their films on Hollywood's dollar. Hellman's two Westerns played their part in this intellectual drama and in doing so had their radical edge further honed.

After the renewed international attention, *The Shooting* was made available in March 1971 for screenings on the increasingly important college circuit.[34] Walter Reade had distributed these prints to university film societies, but by the start of 1972, *Variety* carried the news that both films were finally being released to the general public. Distribution was being undertaken by Jack H. Harris, with a double-billed opening in West Los Angeles in January and thereafter in thirteen western states. Reade, Hellman said, had originally 'figured that they might be too difficult to sell theatrically'. Even though they were made 'to satisfy audiences' they had 'been slightly ahead of their time . . . but now that audiences' film tastes have changed' they would, he hoped, 'be acceptable in small, select situations and might be compared to a "good dream"'.[35]

The critical response to the ambiguities and unresolved or uncertain story lines that baffled the films' original American reviewers is neatly explained by Hellman's suggestion that the pictures might be considered as dreams. Concurrently, critics like Kevin Thomas thought there was a more complex explanation for such moments of incoherence: he considered that they were the mark of self-conscious film artists who were deliberately aligning themselves with an existential philosophy. He thought the films had something to say about the human condition and about art.[36]

For Walker and the EIFF programmers, the films' merit lay in Hellman's subversion of genre conventions, his refusal to play to an audience's expectations. The status quo is negated by replacing optimism and conformity with nihilism and the flouting of convention. Later, when critics discovered more about Hellman's background in modern theatre, especially his production of the first West Coast staging of Samuel Beckett's *Waiting for Godot*, the Theatre of the Absurd would be added as an influence alongside existentialism and subversive intent. Hellman willingly played along with all of this.[37]

In a critical retrospective of Hellman's oeuvre, Kent Jones wrote about the two films as 'singularities in American cinema' that were symptomatic of a dread in American culture brought on by the Kennedy assassination.[38] Neither film was a polemic, but *Ride in the Whirlwind* did demonstrate 'the kind of nightmare scenario that would play out again and again in the America of J. Edgar Hoover and the impending law and order of Richard Nixon'.[39] Rather wildly, but beautifully in keeping with his thesis, Jones thought *The Shooting* akin to the 'luxuriant self-obliteration' of the Velvet Underground's music.[40] Both films, he argued, managed themes linked to urban alienation and suburban paranoia.

In an essay accompanying the films' Criterion Blu-Ray release, Michael Atkinson wrote that they share 'Antonioni's philosophical ambiguities – in being either out-and-out mysterious (*The Shooting*) or so run through with ellipses and known unknown and point-less struggle (*Whirlwind*) that the stress of the story has more to do with existence than circumstance'.[41] Such an insistence on the films' modernist aesthetic sensibility, their self-reflexivity, reframes incoherence as coherence, pulling them away from their lowbrow production context. The critical effort obscured the fact that, at least for some of the film-makers involved, these films were no more than an attempt at novelty, at providing a small twist on yet another example of popular, formulaic American culture. That truth gets lost in their over-alignment with European art house cinemas:

> Hellman's De Chirico-like compositions, unorthodox framing, abrupt contrasts between pregnant close-ups and vast, patient long shots sans dialogue (the thieves'

struggling capture and lynching in *Whirlwind* are virtually silent), the tactile relationship the characters have to the ominous topography around them – all told, it's a visionary strategy, and it's where the antiwestern, as a modernist commentary on and inversion of this most simplistic of all-American genres, was truly born.[42]

Whatever the veracity of such arguments, his final point is spurious. The Western is not 'simplistic': it may be simple, but the fact that it can carry the weight of such highbrow theories, regardless of merit or post hoc rationalizations, makes it one of the most adroit of popular American film forms.

The Shooting opens with Willet Gashade (Warren Oates) watering his horse. The reverie is disturbed when man and animal respond to some off-screen commotion, real or imagined. Riding on, Gashade turns in his saddle, checking the trail behind. Is his show of apprehension a fantastical flight of the imagination or does he have good reason to believe he is being followed? The film suggests an answer to the question by cutting, in close-up, to a rider on a white horse; only the top of a leg and gloved hands on the saddle's pommel are shown. Is this person pursuing Gashade? Halting, Gashade cuts open a flour sack that will leave a trail that implies he is aiding, not running from, his follower. But if that is the case, why is he so easily spooked and nervous? Ambiguity and uncertainty, apprehension and mystery are established in these initial moments, and from here on the film will work to compound this state of being by first offering and then undermining attempts to answer basic narrative questions.

Gashade's journey is seemingly at an end when he enters a mining camp that appears abandoned – at least, no one answers his calls. The camp is situated in a hollow that provides a view no further than the encircling ridge. The ambience is claustrophobic and eerie, an ominous foreboding prevails as Gashade reads the freshly carved inscription on a grave marker. A gunshot breaks the spell. The shooter is Coley (Will Hutchins), who along with Gashade is one of the four men working the mine. The man in the grave is Leland Drum, who was shot by an unseen assassin while drinking coffee. The missing fourth man is Gashade's brother, Coigne, who has hightailed it following his involvement in the death of a child. Left alone, Coley has gone a little crazy; his imagination is overheated, and he is fearful that the same fate that befell Drum will also claim him. The feeling of trepidation is now mixed with paranoia.

Still presented only in close-ups that continue to conceal as much as they reveal, the rider on the white horse follows the trail of flour left by Gashade. Something untoward then happens to the rider's mount; it is shown lying on the ground – a gun is drawn from a holster and pointed at the horse's head. Before that action is complete, the film cuts back to Gashade, who says to himself: 'Someone's coming.' His premonition is answered by the sound of a pistol shot. Awakened to the other's presence, Gashade and Coley nervously wait to see who will show themselves. In the interregnum, a buzzard circles overhead and strings are plucked and strummed on the soundtrack. Then, standing between ridge and sky, a woman is seen. She is petite, with black hair, matching hat, leather gloves and boots. Her eyes are rimmed with kohl that accentuates her pasty white, dirty face.

Coming into camp, she hires the two men as guides to take her to the town of Kingsley. Gashade is known to her; she, however,

Millie Perkins in *The Shooting* (dir. Monte Hellman, 1966).

is a stranger to him and won't give her name. Her attitude is antsy and aggressive. On a whim, it seems, she insists they make a detour to Cross Tree, which is not much more than a trading post, stables and a Chinese laundry. Quite where the laundry's owner, Sing Tan, gets his trade from in this godforsaken place is as much a mystery as whatever it is that motivates the woman and, maybe, no more significant.

While Gashade and Coley see to the horses and supplies it becomes apparent that the woman is using them to track Gashade's brother. She is not at all interested in getting to Kingsley, but the why of her pursuit remains unspoken. As they follow Coigne's trail she occasionally fires her pistol at uncertain targets. Responding to the apparent randomness of her actions, Gashade says. 'I don't see the point in it.' She replies, 'There isn't any.' But the shots do have a purpose: they are signals, but to whom and why?

As the threesome track Coigne, they too are being followed. Questions proliferate, only to be partially answered when their tracker finally appears. He's Billy Spear (Jack Nicholson), who looks and acts like a gun for hire. More significantly, his dress mirrors the woman's, clothed in black except for a white shirt. He too is in her employ, but the purpose of his work is unstated. As one puzzle is figured out, another takes its place.

Nicholson's character is a two-dimensional figure, a formulaic badman, unchanging. Millie Perkins's character, on the other hand, moves from being the archetypical woman of mystery, otherworldly, to become a much more earthly proposition. Dirt sticks to her. As the chase progresses, she becomes increasingly begrimed and dishevelled, her white blouse sweat-soaked and stained, her face soiled. Is her character reaching out for a kind of authenticity, a realness to contrast with the numinous elements, or is the dirt an Antonioni-like objective correlative to her inner turmoil, her madness?

The four continue to pursue Coigne, travelling across vast flat and empty spaces, sometimes viewed as insignificant specks in the landscape. At first, desert roses are seen in the foreground but they give out to an utterly barren, bone-dry landscape. Reading the traces left by Coigne, Gashade reasons that a rider has joined him. Eventually they encounter Coigne's travelling companion, who has been left alone to nurse a broken leg. It transpires that he is another man hired by the woman to trail Coigne. Leaving him to his fate, the woman pushes on until her horse becomes lame. She, it appears, is 'willin' to destruct everything', as Gashade says, including herself. When her horse finally gives out, she takes Coley's, who is left behind.

The distance between the riders and Coigne, now on foot, closes. Meanwhile Coley has recovered a pistol and rounded up a stray horse; at a gallop he chases after the riders as they hurry towards the foothills and Coigne. When Spear realizes that Coley is in pursuit, he and Gashade turn to face him. But the screen direction becomes muddled, intentionally or not, and the riders appear not to be meeting head-on but to be riding in the same direction. Perhaps they are going in circles, chasing their own tails? Coley's heedless attempt to rescue Gashade ends in his death, shot from his horse by Spear.

With his brother, scaling the rise of a foothill, now in plain sight, Gashade fights with Spear. Bettering the killer, he crushes the gunfighter's hand with a rock. Turning away from the two men, the woman continues after Coigne. With only a few feet between them, the pursued looks back at his pursuer. He is the living spit of Gashade. The three protagonists are then shown in granular slow motion, with the woman framed by the two identical men. Questions spill out, not the least of which is what motivates her, why does she want to kill Coigne? Is it for revenge? Is she the mother of the child Coigne is said to have ridden down? Just as importantly, is Coigne Gashade's twin or has Gashade been tracking himself all along? Is the whole story his death dream? The film refuses any definitive answers.

Vagueness and doubt, enigma and mystery, questions without answers run through the film as if they were a vein of pyrite, attractive in itself but still fool's gold. The film's puzzles, nonetheless, have traction and interest because they are creatively and imaginatively shaped and plotted. The film is alive to the seduction of doubling, it plays with parallels and repetition so that narrative progression is figured as a set of returns rather than arrivals – the end is in the beginning, the story is circular not linear. The hollow of the mining camp is a version of the slopes of the foothills where Gashade meets Coigne who is Gashade – the other side of the coin

– who is now surely fated to repeat the whole process by once again laying down a trail that the woman and he are destined to follow.

For Michael Atkinson, this is all reminiscent of Antonioni, a manifestation of the film's 'broader existential modernity' that further evokes Samuel Beckett, Albert Camus and, in its landscape, the 'American wasteland' occupied by the cartoon figure Wile E. Coyote.[43] In a career overview of Hellman, critic Chuck Stephens likens The Shooting to a Möbius strip and argues that though its director did not set out to make a psychedelic Western, that was the affect achieved as he 'wrenched the skullcap off the form anyway, rearranged the tumbleweeds' and 'left only what mattered'.[44]

Hellman appeared happy to confirm Atkinson's reading, especially the recurring theme in his films of circling back, even as he hesitates over its philosophical identity: 'A lot of people look at these films today and ask me if I was being existential. No, I was primarily aware that I was in trouble. I was shooting with hardly any money and less time.'[45] He explains that Corman had invested in his production of Waiting for Godot, which was staged as a Western, and having lost that $500 advance, he was attempting to pay him back with the two films; another return of sorts. Hellman said: 'I think I see a lot of things in terms of circles and circling back. It just seems that's what so much of human endeavour is.'[46]

Stephens ponders over whether this is an 'existential circle' or something a 'little looser; a little less like a noose, a little more like a hula hoop'.[47] Thomas Pynchon, Friedrich Nietzsche, Vladimir Nabokov are added to the highbrow cultural citations the film encourages critics to grab for, but so too is one of the titans of post-war comic books: 'Trussed inside a leather ensemble – vest, tethers, riding gloves too tight for a tiny toreador, and introduced with a closeup of his beady, Karen Black eyes so cut-to-shock that it might have been torn from a Jack Kirby comic book, comes Nicholson's lightning-draw gunfighter.'[48] Hellman's existentialism spins between the polarities of a Marvel comic and Beckett, just as his sense of life's absurdity sits inside a Road Runner cartoon and alongside Camus' Sisyphus. This construct between the high and the low is what New York film critic J. Hoberman has termed 'vulgar modernism' – an American mass-cultural response to the tensions inherent in modernity.[49]

Hoberman offers three exemplars of this conflation between the high and the low, the refined and the vulgar: film director Samuel Fuller, comic strip artist Chester Gould and photographer Weegee. These he calls 'abstract sensationalists' who practised a tabloid-inspired aesthetic of 'shock, raw sensation and immedi-ate impact, a prole expressionism of violent contrasts and blunt, "vulgar" stylization' that were necessary in any meaningful representation of the modern world.[50] Their work, however, is not mere exploitation but an 'active appreciation' of the 'mayhem' of modern existence that is as 'formally orchestrated' as that of any fine artist.[51] America's culture industries intermittently generated an analogue to 'local or European avant-gardism', Hoberman argues, that includes not only Fuller, Gould and Weegee but 'the Manet of vulgar modernism' Tex Avery and figures such as Spike Jones, with his 'primitive brand of *musique concrète* and disco's version of drone-seriality'; also 'the *Channel 11 Yule Log*'s anticipation of Jan Dibbets' *TV as Fireplace*, 1969, and the way that media coverage of the Kennedy assassination – from its historic instant replay of Lee Harvey Oswald's death to its later, microscopic analysis of the Zapruder footage – inexorably points toward Ken Jacobs' *Tom, Tom the Piper's Son* and the films of Ernie Gehr'.[52] 'Cinema', he writes, 'is rife with examples of such para-art.'[53]

The Shooting is just one such example of this vulgar modernism. Its self-conscious play with ambiguity, its refusal to answer all questions that are asked in the manner of classical Hollywood cinema, may evoke Antonioni, and terms like 'existential' and 'absurd' can all as such be readily applied, but the film cannot withstand the systematic analysis that the Italian auteur's films encourage, even demand, any more than Fuller's *Shock Corridor* (1963) might be seen as a serious examination of psychoanalysis. What *The Shooting* enacts is less the existential mystery of life, a philosophical disquisition on absurdity, than a thrilling story of mystery, suspense and the paranormal.

The Shooting's narrative ellipses, its doublings and returns belong to the realm of *The Twilight Zone* (1959–64). The film is closer to the 1962 French adaptation of Ambrose Bierce's 'An Occurrence at Owl Creek' that Rod Serling acquired and modified for an episode of *The Twilight Zone* than to *L'avventura*. At the close of the episode, Serling tells the viewer the story has 'two forms – as it was dreamed and as it was lived and died . . . This is the stuff of fantasy, the thread of imagination . . . the ingredients of the *Twilight Zone*.' 'Owl Creek' is the tale of a man who at the point of his death by hanging imagines the rope around his neck has broken and he has escaped his fate, but he hasn't. It is not hard to imagine Hellman referencing the programme and series as part of his pitch to Corman less than a year after the episode was broadcast.[54] *The Shooting*'s eeriness is in good part enhanced by the music of Richard Markowitz, who had scored numerous low-budget movies and television programmes. His arrangement is a series of formulaic aural punctuation points: a run of plucked, pulled and strummed strings, flutes and whistles, muted brass and rolling timpani, highly effective in underscoring the sense of apprehension and trepidation, shock and sensation. It is totally generic – a perfect fit with Marius Constant's theme music for *The Twilight Zone*.

All this takes the film away from the European art house cinema of Antonioni *and* from the genre conventions of a Budd Boetticher Western, leaving it in a state of cultural limbo. That liminality will be readily exploited by critics, some of whom will use such ambiguity as a licence to further interpret the film through the prism of a pop psychedelia, hence its much-touted reputation as the first of the 'acid Westerns'.[55] In such putative midnight movies, audiences (through drug ingestion or inclination) and the film's characters are placed into a hallucinatory state, senses disassembled and fixated on a repeating set of actions. In this scenario *The Shooting* is, post hoc, conceived as an earth-bound *2001: A Space Odyssey* (1968), or a pre-text for Antonioni's *Zabriskie Point*, Alejandro Jodorowsky's *El Topo* and Roland Klick's contemporary-set Spaghetti Western *Deadlock* (all 1970). However, the expansion of consciousness, a leap into the fifth dimension experienced when watching *The Shooting*, as with any episode of *The Twilight Zone*, is no more than the fever journey the viewer's imagination takes when it travels 'between the pit of man's fears and the summit of his knowledge', to quote Serling's voiceover. Conceived as formulaic, received as art – its conflation is pulp modernism.

Ride in the Whirlwind was a wholly different proposition, significantly more coherent in its adherence to classical continuity editing and narration. All questions asked during its story are answered; the film is anchored firmly in the tradition of the Westerns that Randolph Scott and Boetticher made in the 1950s. Like *Ride*

Lonesome (1959) and *The Tall T* (1957), *Whirlwind* is sparse, terse and economical, an apparently simple tale told efficiently and made with a small cast of characters, on location, and produced within a modest budget.

The film's hewing to convention is apparent in the naming of the characters. Caught between a band of outlaws and a bunch of vigilantes are three cowboys drifting towards Waco, Texas: square-jawed Otis (Tom Filer), range-bitten Vern (Cameron Mitchell) and the younger man Wes (Jack Nicholson). Their names simple and honest, nothing fancy. The outlaws are led by Blind Dick (Harry Dean Stanton), so called on account he has only one eye, and Indian Joe, played by Rupert Crosse, an African American actor who made his film debut in John Cassavetes's *Shadows* (1959) and looks even less like a Native American than Woody Strode. But then their characters are intended to be recognized not as authentic but as figures drawn from a dime novel's dramatis personae.

The film comfortably holds in play the seeming contradiction between rerunning formulaic generic attributes and its disavowal of romantic intrigue or heroic acts. The former is configured in the naming of the bad guys and in tropes like the stagecoach hold-up that repeatedly figured in nineteenth-century sensational pulp fictions and Wild West shows. The counter to these archaic elements is to provide a more authentic portrayal of frontier life, such as Blind Dick going behind a boulder to urinate. The film's dialogue was said to have been based on Nicholson's 'extensive research into diaries and records of the period', but you would be hard pressed to identify anything of the kind.[56] The dialogue is as unremarkable as the film's musical soundtrack, which is so completely generic it is all but subliminal. The film's authenticating bits of business are nothing more than attempts at novelty.

The costumes are, for the most part, dirty, worn and torn. They look lived-in, but for all the sweat stains, scuffs and rips, the hat styles, boots, chaps and shirts all pretty much conform to those worn on any number of contemporary television Westerns. Otis's costume provides some distinction between him and his travelling companions – he wears a heavy shirt with a flap over its placket like the kind worn by John Wayne. It suits his character and makes him seem a little more reserved, less given to idle chatter. Everyone wears a neckerchief, but Indian Joe's purple rag is the standout, complementing his green checked shirt and embroidered waistcoat which, combined, give him the air of a dandy when surrounded by his dowdy confederates.

The story has a concise three-part structure. The film opens with a stagecoach hold-up, proceeds to where the three cowboys encounter the outlaws in a robbers' roost, an isolated mountain cabin, and concludes with a shoot-out, a lynching and a chase. At the outlaws' eyrie, neither band of men want trouble, so they keep a respectful distance from each other, the cowboys bedding down a little way from the cabin. Planning to leave early in the morning, the trio's breakfast is interrupted by the arrival of vigilantes who set siege to the cabin. Faced with either getting shot or hanged by staying put, the three decide to make a break for it. Vern and Wes get away, but Otis is shot from his horse and then killed. Indian Joe and Blind Dick are caught and then lynched. Pursued by the vigilantes, Wes and Vern abandon their horses and climb higher into the mountain. Eventually the two men find temporary and uncertain shelter with a homesteader, his wife and daughter. When they try to take the man's horses, Vern is shot and wounded. He rides double behind Wes, but soon falls from the horse and can then ride no further. While Vern holds off the posse, Wes rides away.

As Wes disappears behind the dust cloud his horse's hooves have kicked up, the presumption is that he will outrun the vigilantes. The film refuses an easy sentimentality just as it did the possibility that Wes might have a fleeting romance with the homesteader's daughter, played by Millie Perkins. She performs her role as a taciturn, sulky adolescent with no choice but to be obedient and respectful towards her parents, her father especially. But unlike her equivalent, played by Mariette Hartley, in Sam Peckinpah's *Ride the High Country* (1962), she makes not the slightest effort to use the men's arrival as the means to escape her oppressive existence. In fact she does nothing at all except watch. That she is an attractive proposition is not in doubt: vigilante outriders who visit the homestead comment on her comeliness, and though her dress is drab, her eyelashes, incongruously, are thick with mascara. The potential for the threat of sexual violence is there but like any notion of romance is no sooner raised then quashed when Wes makes it clear to the girl's mother he has no intentions of any kind whatsoever towards her daughter.

Perkins was 29 when she appeared in the two films. She had had a short marriage to Dean Stockwell and then to screenwriter Robert Thom. Her résumé included playing the titular figure in *The Diary of Anne Frank* (1959) and the ingénue in Elvis Presley's *Wild in the Country* (1961). Casting her as a withdrawn adolescent in *Whirlwind* was in type, but she was given too little to work with in the role. In *The Shooting* her aggravated petulance made her the perfect contrast to the bewildered Oates, Hutchins's doltish man-child and the cool disposition of Nicholson's cartoon badman. Putting her at the centre of the drama is one reason that *The Shooting* continues to fascinate, and her marginalization in *Ride in the Whirlwind* is but another formulaic aspect that film is content to play along with.

Whirlwind is a good enough Western in and of itself not to need any artificial veneer of critical respect and reverence, but because it holds so resolutely to generic archetypes it would be a forgotten film if not for its pairing with *The Shooting*. The existential dynamic of cult film appreciation is always less about the film than it is about the critical discourse in which it circulates.

While his two Westerns were all but hidden from view, Hellman's next effort burst into the light as the April 1971 cover story for *Esquire*, 'The Magazine for Men' – 'Read it first! Our nomination for the movie of the year: *Two-Lane Blacktop*' – which published the whole of Rudolph Wurlitzer and Will Corry's screenplay across thirteen pages. 'Where the road is and where it is going: the first movie worth reading', the magazine announced. Anticipating continued interest in the film after that issue of *Esquire* was no longer available, Universal, the film's production and distribution company, had Award Books, their publishing subsidiary, couple the screenplay with Walker's *Sight and Sound* article, some production notes, eight pages of photographs and a splash tag from *Esquire* on the paperback's front and quotes from the *New York Times* on the rear: 'it is a tragedy about street racers which stars enormously popular soft rock singer James Taylor … an *existential* story of four nameless people, outlaws of the night performing their reason for existence on a quarter-mile stretch of any two-lane blacktop at any hour between midnight and dawn.'[57]

The 'existential' philosophical tag that critics applied to the Westerns is here front and centre – as a marketing slogan.[58] Like an academic donning a gown and mortarboard, *Two-Lane Blacktop* wears its pretensions openly. Conscious of both art house antecedents and genre convention, *Two-Lane Blacktop* is a *détourné* Western refracted in the light generated by Godard's *Bande à part* and Truffaut's *Jules et Jim* and then sucked through the lens filter of *Bonnie and Clyde* and *Easy Rider* for a quick sell to the new youth audience.

As in *Easy Rider*, the journey undertaken in the film moves in a southeasterly direction, from California through Arizona, New Mexico, Oklahoma, Arkansas and, finally, into Tennessee. Unlike Hopper and Fonda's film, Hellman's movie eschews pictorial scenes, tourist-eye photographic snaps of America's natural splendours like Monument Valley; instead the viewpoint barely

Poster for *Two-Lane Blacktop* (dir. Monte Hellman, 1971).

shifts from the road in front of the travellers, and the world of the movie extends no further than the interiors of the Chevy and the GTO. Space is foreshortened and restricted; outside the cars the environment is mostly gas stations and diners, motels and bars. The road is generally empty, the race meetings presented as temporary congregations, affiliates with the Western movie towns of Tombstone or Deadwood – waystations used to break up the monotony of the road or the cattle trail.

Only once does the film provide a point-of-view shot of a far-away horizon: as he readies himself for the final race, The Driver (James Taylor) looks out of his side window and takes in the distant image of a farm. It's a momentary visual repast, a view into another world that has otherwise been beyond his vision. Almost as soon as it is seen it is lost as he turns away and refocuses on the race ahead, his only reason for existing.

Both the Hellman Westerns were shot by Gregory Sandor. His cinematography is a major part of the films' attraction, whether that is catching a still twilight in *The Shooting* with Gashade, Spear and the woman in silhouette or when running a camera alongside Nicholson and his mount at a full gallop in *Ride in the Whirlwind*. Sandor's lighting and compositions are precise in the dialogue scenes, elastic and expansive when shooting desert landscapes, and dynamic and kinetic for the action sequences. For Hellman, as director and editor, Sandor must have been the perfect creative partner, so much so the two were back together for *Two-Lane Blacktop*, where they fashioned both an aesthetic that rejected the picturesque and a kineticism able to evoke the thrill of a chase or race – the precise opposite of what they achieved with the Westerns.

Each character in the film is defined and named by what they do, not by who they are. They exist only in the moment in which they appear on-screen. No one has a backstory, at least one that can be trusted; their histories are compiled out of their filmic antecedents. Wanting to attract the attention of The Driver and The Girl (Laurie Bird), a waitress calls them 'Romeo and Juliet'. When they continue to ignore her, a truck driver suggests she try 'Bonnie and Clyde'. The film is hyperconscious of their status as archetypes, consistently highlighting the dramatic potential of the romantic triad, formed by The Driver, The Mechanic (Dennis Wilson) and The Girl, which is pitched as being in keeping with Godard's and Truffaut's outlaw lovers and the trios in *Bonnie and Clyde* and *Butch Cassidy and the Sundance Kid* (1969). But *Two-Lane Blacktop* only evokes the trope, it does not enact it.

The published screenplay, an amalgam of a shooting script and a transcription of a near-final assembly of the film that has been adapted to be read, has several small scenes and dialogue lines that were cut from the film, most of which deal explicitly with developing the relationship between the two men and the girl. Early in her travels The Girl climbs into The Driver's sleeping bag and they make love. Left in place, the scene would have added a more piquant frisson to the moment when he pauses outside a motel room listening to her and The Mechanic have sex. It would have suggested a competition between the two friends for her attention and better explained The Driver's motivation to bring The Girl back, picking her up hitching on the edge of town after she has walked off while he was racing. Towards the end of the movie it would have helped explain why The Driver is so determined to catch up with her and G.T.O. (Warren Oates). But the film wants to tease its audience, not fulfil its expectations, and so the scene was cut.

Pulling the scene also meant that the relationship between the two men is left open in that moment when The Driver slumps down outside the motel room and draws his knees into his chest: a melancholic gesture. Is he jealous of The Girl or The Mechanic? Has she come between him and his friend? Because the homoerotic charge remains barely suppressed, the film-makers provide a distraction by casting Stanton as a queer hitchhiker. His cowboy's fey attempt to court G.T.O. is played for laughs, the stereotype deflecting attention away from questioning the sexual nature of the pairing of The Driver and The Mechanic. Typically, a girl's function in such a scenario is to act as a disruptor – an alien element to test their friendship – and to confirm their heterosexuality, but, in the end, The Girl seems barely to bother the pair any more then she is bothered by them. The film's only interest in such intrigue is to raise it in order to then shut it down.

Two-Lane Blacktop is littered with self-referential motifs, not only in its play with archetypes and the film's endnote with the celluloid strip burning as it is caught in the projector's gate, but also in the dialogue. 'Performance and image, that's what it is all about,' says G.T.O. 'I dig you and all,' says The Girl, 'but you're not letting me into your movie.' A little later she confesses to 'have lost the thread' of the story she's telling (but probably also of the one she's in). G.T.O. makes few, if any, attempts to hold true to a narrative line. In one of his fantastical constructions he explains he is on a scouting trip for movie locations, which is more plausible than his story of being a test pilot looking for kicks, but not much. The stories he tells of himself change with the colour of the cashmere sweaters he wears. He is defined by the surface values of the consumer culture he moves within, forever searching for gratification and satisfactions that are permanent.

Just how flirtatious the film is in its refusal to satisfy audience expectations can be gauged in the passages that were not filmed or were left on the cutting-room floor. In one major scene The Girl strips out of her clothes and swims in the river as the two men watch her. She calls for them to join her in the water, but they remain on the bank talking about their favourite cars. It is a dialogue exchange overripe with sexual innuendo: 'I sorely miss the feel of that automobile. I polished that crankshaft so fine the cylinders whispered my name. That was more r.p.m. without bursting than any machine I ever knew . . . it slipped right in and increased the stroke . . . That was a nice little body made for surprises.' Maybe the scene didn't play well, its innuendos unintentionally too humorous, pardoning rather than heightening the pair's sexual dysfunction or alienation. Hellman, it was reported, simply felt it held up the action.[59] But what action?

A further cut has The Driver fondling and kissing The Girl's breasts as The Mechanic works on the car, G.T.O. sleeps and a farm boy watches the couple get it on. It is another moment of loveless lovemaking, as blank as the amateur actors' expressions throughout the film. Perhaps the film-makers thought this set-up a little too prurient, but its removal, when added to the other omissions, meant that there is no nudity and that whatever sex does take place is done off-screen – a perverse ploy given cinema's contemporary fixation with making capital out of the naked female form.[60] The skinny-dipping scene had been shot and was exploited by *Show* magazine, which ran a series of stills featuring a nude Laurie Bird to accompany Shelley Benoit's feature on the film in its March 1971 edition. Its absence from the final cut was likely not because it too stalled the action but because it was in keeping with the film-makers' desire to close out one filmic convention after another.

After G.T.O. has picked up a hitcher, the film's avoidance of convention is mordantly stated by showing a New Mexico State

Hospital sign on the side of the road that warns against stopping for hikers, but there are no escaped psychopaths to pose a threat. *Two-Lane Blacktop* is not Ida Lupino's *The Hitch-Hiker* (1953), Jim Thompson's novel *The Killer Inside Me* (1952) or Donald E. Westlake's *Pity Him Afterwards* (1964), pulp thrillers based on, or evoking, the trope of the lunatic at large preying on unsuspecting travellers, but it is self-aware enough to pose such expectations before dashing them.

Hellman's casting of musicians James Taylor and Dennis Wilson as the central characters, both without any acting experience, suggested he was intent to make a connection between the worlds of street racers and rock stars, exploiting their mutual investment in outlaw poses. Both tendered revolts into style that presented a set of stances about going faster and further out. The casting undoubtedly played a role in helping to get financing for the film and in marketing the movie, but at the point Taylor and Wilson were put under contract neither name would have been considered a significant draw on the scale of Mick Jagger or Jim Morrison. But they were at least affordable, obtainable and credible. When he signed up for the film Taylor was not yet a household name, but he was fast gaining commercial traction.

It was the billboard advertising for Taylor's second record, *Sweet Baby James*, released in February 1970, that had caught Hellman's attention and made him think he had found the face to match his conception of The Driver. Though Hellman never mentioned it, the album's title track worked as a pop equivalent of the story he and Wurlitzer were intent on telling. The song's protagonist is a young cowboy who is working the range, fantasying about the time to come when he can again chase women and drink beer. But he has just 10 miles behind him and 10,000 more to go, so he

Cover of James Taylor's *Sweet Baby James* LP (1970).

is left to sing to himself. By the final chorus, the Old West has collapsed into the contemporary and the cowboy is joined by a driver on a highway, a sailor at sea and a pilot in the sky, each plotting a lonely path on a journey to nowhere in particular.

In one of the finest accounts of the film, Ian Penman recommends that you watch the film with 'western music in your head'.[61] Hellman's two protagonists are 'nothing if not modern-day gunslingers'.[62] Wilson and Taylor represent the entropic end of the 1960s' promises for Penman: 'A whole dark stain of mission creep, under the nerveless mainstream smile. The Stones' woozy, crackling *Exile on Main St* (1972) could serve as an apt subtitle for *Two-Lane Blacktop*.'[63] The film is a precursor, Penman writes, to Neil Young's 'so-called "Ditch trilogy" (1973–5): *Time Fades Away, On the Beach, Tonight's the Night*', all carrying 'a sense of lost direction'.[64]

While the film was being shot, a track from *Sweet Baby James*, 'Fire and Rain', became a hit single, and in March 1971, a month before the *Esquire* spread and four months before the film's Los Angeles premier, Taylor was on the front of *Time*. The magazine's profile began by explaining that the over-amplified rock music of the 1960s was now giving way to a more introverted, acoustic, individual form of expression, one led by James Taylor:

> Offering a kind of Americana rock, they are likely to cele-
> brate such things as country comfort, Carolina sunshine,
> morning frost in the Berkshires. What all of them seem to
> want most is an intimate mixture of lyricism and personal
> expression – the often exquisitely melodic reflections of
> a private 'I'.[65]

Taylor sings, he says, because 'he doesn't know how to talk', and in *Two-Lane Blacktop* his character drives because it is his only effective form of communication.[66]

Most of the film's pre-release publicity inevitably focused on Taylor (and Joni Mitchell, his then paramour and companion during parts of the shoot). The shades of male intimacy and vulnerability, his proclivity towards melancholic introspection that Taylor transudes through his music is hinted at in his performance as The Driver, but that side of his character is dependent on his fans' willingness to project such emotional colour onto his blank face and flaccid physicality. Hellman thought such readings were 'detrimental empathy' and ran in opposition to his conception of his main characters.[67] Penman writes:

> Before he became the model 1970s singer/songwriter, 'Sweet Baby James' was solid junkie through and through – Chet Baker with a Gibson acoustic and workhouse denim; the public image of hokey introspection belied a private life of some turmoil and slide. Here he has a look in his eyes that can't be taught – both sleepwalk and switchblade.[68]

Wilson was a late addition to the cast; as the drummer in The Beach Boys, he had little or no counterculture profile nor much name recognition, but he had a face that mirrored Taylor's gibbus brow and deep-set eyes and he projected a similar aura of sullen disaffection. *Variety* picked up on the general vibe the pair generated and reported the film had a 'strong poptune personality pre-sell'.[69] The paperback of the screenplay featured Taylor alone on its cover, but there things ended for promotional tie-ins. Despite the best efforts of the studio, Hellman could not be persuaded to use his stars on the soundtrack, not even for an opening or closing credit song. Like *Easy Rider, Two-Lane Blacktop* threw aside the convention of using a musical underscore, but unlike its predecessor it made little use of pre-existing recordings to serve its narrative and thematic needs. The published screenplay cites four songs by The Rolling Stones, two by Chuck Berry, and one each from The Doors, Ray Charles, Tina Turner and Hank Snow.

Writing for *Show* magazine, Shelley Benoit spent a week on location with crew and actors in Tucumcari, New Mexico. One of those days was spent filming in a diner: 'The jukebox in this forlorn spot affords one Beatles, no Stones and a whole lot of Merle Haggard.'[70] *Two-Lane Blacktop* seemed to have become stuck with that jukebox selection. Not getting, or being unable to afford, the Stones' recordings 'Honky Tonk Woman', 'I'm Free' and 'Time Is On My Side', the film-makers made do with having The Girl sing 'Satisfaction', flat and off-key, as she plays pinball. All the performances by the Stones would have matched the film's dedicated sense of ennui and estrangement, yet, with one notable exception, none of the songs that made it into the release print have anything other than a minor ambient role. There are no grand showcase moments, time-outs from narrative progression as in *Easy Rider*, to put together the protagonists with a rock soundtrack. Staging another 'Born to Be Wild' audio-visual spectacle was never on Hellman's agenda; instead The Doors' 'Moonlight Drive' is concealed beneath the sound of revving engines and tyre squeals. The one musical performance that is emphasized, that sits on top of the action rather than beneath it, is Kris Kristofferson's 'Me and Bobby McGee'.

Covers of Kristofferson's song had been hits on the Country and Pop charts for Roger Miller, Gordon Lightfoot, Charley Pride and a posthumous number one for Janis Joplin. Even Jerry Lee Lewis took it into *Billboard*'s Hot 100 before the end of 1971. Much of this interest in the song took place in the latter stages of post-production on *Two-Lane Blacktop*, which meant its use had a contemporaneity and an immediacy that would have connected with the film's original audience. On the other hand, 'Bobby McGee' is the very thing Hellman had elsewhere avoided: cliché. But there it is, all but asking the audience to make a connection with its romantic sentiments – detrimental empathy – even as the film refused to be drawn in the same direction. Besides, the song was also featured in Hopper's *The Last Movie*.

Because it too was a cliché, one other excised scene from the screenplay is notable. In order to outrun a cop car, The Driver and The Mechanic pull into a suburban driveway. Peering through the window of a middle-class ranch house they see a man watching the news on a television and a pretty woman preparing to serve dinner while looking after a baby: 'the atmosphere is serene and ritualized.' After taking it all in, the pair return to their car and 'glide out of the driveway and into the night'.[71] The scene that follows has the two men rolled up in their sleeping bags next to a dirt road and their car. The contrast of domestic bliss, as peddled out of Madison Avenue, and the two latter-day cowboys bedded down beside their steed with the night sky for a roof, could not be more obvious. Overly suggestive, the domestic symbolism would have attached itself to the point-of-view shot of the farm at the film's end, giving the idea of alternative worlds too much significance.

The film's anti-domesticity, its rejection of everyday convention, of middle-class rituals, does not need such overstatement, it is there in every scene. It is the basis on which the film was sold, like *Easy Rider*, offering the freedom of the road as the counter to the prison of suburbia. Like Hopper and Fonda's protagonists, The Driver and The Mechanic are heading west to east, the frontier having finally run out. Though the pair's *raison d'être* is to race, to compete with others and themselves to go ever faster, the fact of their existence is to labour in order to scrape together enough to get by, to deal with the demands of the moment, to eat, sleep and love as things dictate without thought for tomorrow or memory of yesterday. The point of it all is that filmic moment of existence, the passing of the strip of images through the projector.

Two-Lane Blacktop is *only* a film; it certainly wasn't *Easy Rider* (part two), the cultural event its financial backers thought they were buying.

Not having yet seen the finished film, one contemporary commentator said of the screenplay, 'it is nonviolent, non-political and all but nonsexual' but it has a 'stark, more low-key-than-thou script that happens to be so compelling you can't finish it fast enough. Like a fall from a skyscraper, you can't get your breath. Speed is what this film is about. Speed that overrides temporal sex, violence and politics. Speed that is sport to some, necessity to others.'[72] Discussing *Two-Lane Blacktop* on the set of *Pat Garrett and Billy the Kid* (173), Wurlitzer told a British reporter that Taylor was not given any direction, no support, and Hellman forgot about two essentials, 'the road and speed'.[73] *Rolling Stone* called *Two-Lane Blacktop* 'an uninspired, mediocre film . . . a bore'.[74]

By producing a movie that delivered the things critics had identified and admired in his Westerns, not the least of which was an adherence to the idea of characters defined in terms of an existential dilemma, Hellman inadvertently removed the agency of those who had championed him and disappointed this group as much as he did the film's financiers. On its initial release he didn't receive their applause because he gave them on a plate that which previously *they* had been active in ascribing. He had given them not another example of 'vulgar modernism', something with which they could conjure and fool around, perform a little alchemy and make gold from pulp, but a movie that was unambiguously modernist – an art film by a film artist. *Two-Lane Blacktop* critiqued itself; it would now be buried and ignored long enough to allow later generations of critics to discover it for themselves, extol its virtues and thereby re-establish a correct division of labour.

In that moment before the film crashed into the scorn of the nation's film critics (and its own scriptwriter), things had looked positive. Benoit noted that for 'the first time in his life, [Monte Hellman] knows what his next project will be – *Pat Garrett and Billy the Kid* (another Rudy Wurlitzer screenplay)'.[75] But as Hellman was soon to learn, it is best not to take anything for granted, and as he already knew, satisfaction is never permanent, it is not even attainable.

5

Cisco Pike: Kris Kristofferson Has Got a Great Future Behind Him

He is, everyone agrees, the hottest thing in Nashville right
now – and if you're hot in Nashville, man, you're hot
everywhere. He's just been in Peru with Dennis Hopper,
writing and singing his songs for Hopper's *The Last
Movie*. Johnny Cash, Roger Miller and Ray Stevens have
been recording his numbers. He sings three songs on the
soundtrack of *Ned Kelly*, the Tony Richardson movie in which
Mick Jagger plays the title role of a notorious Australian
outlaw. And though he started off as a songwriter, he's just cut
an album of his own.

New York Times, July 1970

In 1970, Kris Kristofferson was a known-unknown. Throughout that year he was presented to readers of an eclectic
range of newspapers and magazines.[1] *Rolling Stone* introduced him
in a multi-page on-set report by Michael Goodwin on the filming
of Hopper's *The Last Movie*. Wearing a white shirt, Levi's jacket
and beat-up cowboy hat, Kristofferson is pictured on one page of
the spread sitting between Hopper and Toni Basil. But he was far
from being the star of the show; that was Hopper's moment.

Goodwin's piece began and finished with a set of lyrics from Kristofferson's 'Screaming Metaphysical Blues', a salute to 'Mr Hopper'. About halfway through the article, the songwriter's 'The Pilgrim – Chapter 33' is quoted at length, though here it is titled 'Hang In Hopper'. 'Pilgrim' was one of Kristofferson's compositions that took on a second life, when it featured in *Taxi Driver* in 1976, quoted by Betsy to Travis. But by that time, even if Robert De Niro's character didn't have a clue who Kristofferson was – which said a whole lot about him – most readers of *Rolling Stone* would have little trouble identifying the singer and any one of a half-dozen songs of his that had by then been covered by everyone from Johnny Cash to Janis Joplin.

Kristofferson had travelled to Peru with a party of actors, singers and hangers-on to join the media circus that surrounded the filming of *The Last Movie*. They all ended up in the picture's opening section, which featured the wrap party of the film within *The Last Movie*. Hopper had invited Kristofferson to perform 'Me and Bobby McGee', but when the others went home the singer stayed; he was appointed 'minstrel-in-residence' and ended up playing the part of a wrangler and, according to some reports, writing twelve songs for the soundtrack. No album emerged from his efforts, just his musical cameo, which went barely noticed owing to the film's summary withdrawal from distribution. Hopper's career thereafter went into a spectacular nosedive, while Kristofferson's reputation soared.[2]

Kristofferson was part of the Nashville 'underground', a loosely aligned group of musicians who were positioned as a counter to the glitz, pomp, shellacked hair and bejewelled cowboy suits that then formed country music's conservative mainstream.[3] In this context he was, as the *Sunday Times* described him, 'unperfumed and unbuttoned'.[4] For a new figure on the scene, Kristofferson's bona fides hung less on him having paid his dues in bar bands and honky-tonk performances, like Maury Dann, than on a series of highly arresting anecdotes that suggested a much storied past and a man, as the saying went, 'with a great future behind him'. These tales included his prowess in boxing and football; his postgraduate education at Oxford University as a Rhodes scholar; his service as an army captain and helicopter pilot; his work as a gofer in a recording studio in Nashville when Bob Dylan was recording *Blonde on Blonde*; and the time he had sought Johnny Cash's attention by landing a chopper on the star's lawn. All of which would have counted for little if his songs were no more than grist for Music City's mill. Not only did his own records sell but his songs were as eagerly covered as those by Lennon and McCartney, and he made spotlight appearances on the Johnny Cash, Porter Wagoner and Glen Campbell TV shows, among others.

As was the Nashville norm for the time, Kristofferson's compositions tended to tell a story, but rather than linger on the consequences of a Saturday night or an illicit assignation at the dark end of the street, his songs dealt in the moment before guilt gained a hold or a price had to be paid. The best of them were honest, adult and without cheap sentiment.

During *The Last Movie*'s eighteen-month-long editing saga, Hopper announced that his next picture would be based on Kristofferson's song 'Me and Bobby McGee'. *Boxoffice* reported the film would 'roll later this year' in 1970, while *Billboard* added that, according to Hopper, it was set to star Michelle Phillips.[5] Sung by himself, Kristofferson's songs were used on the soundtracks of *Two-Lane Blacktop* ('Me and Bobby McGee'), *Clay Pigeon* (aka *Trip to Kill*, 'The Law is for Protection of the People'), *Cisco Pike*, in which he also starred ('Loving Her Was Easier', 'I'd Rather Be Sorry', 'The Pilgrim – Chapter 33' and 'Breakdown'), all in 1971, and 'Help Me Make It Through the Night' was effectively the theme tune of John Huston's *Fat City*, released in the following year.[6] These were all films that their producers considered would appeal to a target audience of young, educated, hip movie lovers who shunned the blandishments of Hollywood glamour just as Kristofferson shunned Nashville's fakery.

To help promote his debut album in 1970, Kristofferson put together a band of like-minded musicians, Nashville outliers mostly: Billy Swan, Donnie Fritts, Norman Blake and ex-Lovin' Spoonful guitarist Zal Yanovsky. His showcase appearances in Los Angeles and Manhattan clubs attracted the patronage of those he had travelled and worked with on *The Last Movie*, such as Phillips (who joined him onstage at the Troubadour to sing, what else, 'Me and Bobby McGee'), as well as other Hollywood and recording stars who made the most of being seen in his audience.[7] The *New York Times* reported on his New York residency that year:

> Kris Kristofferson projects casualness the way it should be projected – effortlessly. And yet, as he stands on the tiny stage of the Bitter End, picking his guitar and rambling through his songs in a low, husky voice, the discipline behind the casualness becomes increasingly evident . . . He keeps touching on life on the borderline, any kind of borderline that can be crossed and re-crossed . . . His approach is that of the storyteller rather than a singer. There is such a naturalness and ease in his delivery that one is scarcely aware that these are carefully crafted songs.[8]

In August, the band flew to the UK to take part in the Isle of Wight Festival, which linked him with rock's aristocracy in a line-up that featured The Doors, The Who and Jimi Hendrix. That he was able to move as easily in the rock sphere as among Nashville songwriters was confirmed with the posthumous, January 1971 release of Janis Joplin's 'Me and Bobby McGee'. The singer and the songwriter had once been lovers, if but for a short while.[9]

Uniquely viewed, and valued, by two distinct markets, Kristofferson was accepted as Nashville's token hippy, who tempered the city's countrypolitan, glitzy extremes; he sat easily alongside Cash, Haggard, Jennings and Nelson and was valued as a performer who moved in the same circles as Dylan, The Band, The Byrds, Parsons, Grateful Dead and Crosby, Stills, Nash & Young, all of whom were then deep-mining a seam of authentic Americana to challenge the shibboleths of pop. Acknowledged by both rock and country audiences, Kristofferson was a genuine crossover artist, an accomplishment few, if any, others of his generation could claim and which was never achieved even by the likes of Dylan or Cash.

In December 1970, the *New York Times* published a major profile on Kristofferson that labelled him the 'New Nashville Sound', a performer writing 'bluntly sensual protest songs that are sometimes only a shade away from being underground . . . Once word gets around, he could become a hero to these hordes of kids trying to find their own truths.'[10] The country music establishment may have shunned much that he stood for – best summed up as the Beat values of a middle-class dropout with a *nostalgie de la boue* – but he was presently the 'hottest country songwriter going', so he was accommodated if not exactly accepted.[11] Besides, he was friends with Merle 'Okie from Muskogee' Haggard and a protégé of Johnny Cash, who had penned the sleeve notes on Kristofferson's debut album, so he could not be denied. Things had moved too on the film front. A film producer 'spotted him at Janis Joplin's funeral and signed him on the spot for the lead in a movie about a luckless musician-turned-junkie', an event that made Kristofferson out to be his generation's Lana Turner, though the truth of how he won the part in *Cisco Pike* (1972) (working titles 'Silver Tongued Devil' and 'Dealer') was certainly not because of a chance encounter.[12]

Seeing the year out, Kristofferson appeared at Carnegie Hall, sharing the bill with Canadian folk duo Ian & Sylvia: 'There was some fumbling as Mr Kristofferson and his four back-up men – his "Band of Thieves" – tried to get into a song. And Mr Kristofferson often looked as if he'd rather be anywhere than where he was. But somehow the uncertainty, the fumbling, the artlessness provided just the right setting for his songs of drifters, losers and fumbling relationships,' the *New York Times* wrote.[13]

Kristofferson was never particularly publicity-shy, or rather he had little trouble attracting it. He first appeared in the *Los Angeles Times* in 1955, where it was noted the nineteen-year-old was unlikely to play in Saturday's football game.[14] A little over two years later, the football hero of Pomona College was being cheered for his boxing ability; he fought as a welterweight.[15] Three weeks after that notice, he was given a four-column write-up as boxing's 'smartest'. Alongside a photograph of the 21-year-old, it was reported he was a straight-A student and four of his short stories had been given awards by the *Atlantic Monthly*. He achieved the highest score in physical tests held among 2,000 cadets, and was a commander of his Reserve Officers' Training Corps battalion to boot.[16] Yet, not everything went his way: this gifted son of an Air Force major general was knocked out in the third round of his second boxing bout.[17]

Before taking up his scholarship in England, and no longer harbouring any pugilistic ambition, Kristofferson killed time by teaming up with a college roommate, Tony Lynds, with whom he formed a folk duo. They recorded two of Kristofferson's songs, which were released in autumn 1958 on the independent Manor label. Continuing to follow his career, the *Los Angeles Times* covered his new distraction with a two-column article and a photograph of the troubadours.[18] While at Oxford, the performance bug still held him in its thrall, and he was briefly signed to the Top Rank record company as 'Kris Carson'; he also made his screen debut, alongside Anthony Newley, in J. Arthur Rank's magazine-styled film series *Focus on Youth*. *Time* described him as an 'Idol Apparent', even though he sang folk music with a blues tinge, not rock 'n' roll. In a manner that would be echoed by Dylan, Kristofferson deployed, despite all his newsworthy exploits to date, a good dose of self-invention and told *Time* he had picked up his style while 'working on Wake Island, labouring with railroad crews and fire-fighting gangs in Alaska'.[19]

A short news stub in a 1959 edition of *Disc* noted Kristofferson's otherwise barely documented tenure with Top Rank and put his age as 22.[20] This was true, but after his postgraduate study had ended and he had returned to the USA and served a five-year term in the military, he had, by 1965, aged but a single year when *Billboard* reported that a 23-year-old Rhodes scholar and ex-army captain had signed with Bill Justis and Marijohn Wilkin's publishing company, Buckhorn Music. His first notable composition for them was a talking blues in a 'patriotic vein', recorded by Jack Sanders on Dot Records, 'Viet Nam Blues'. Wilkin's son, John 'Bucky' Wilkin, had been a member of the Nashville-based surf and hot-rod band Ronny & the Daytonas. With his new group,

The American Eagles, Wilkin would be among the first to record a version of 'Me and Bobby McGee', released as a 45 in July 1969, a few weeks after the Roger Miller version that would become a top-ten hit in the country music charts. Wilkin may have missed out with his cover, but he appeared, and sang, alongside Kristofferson in Hopper's movie.[21]

Kristofferson's name registers only periodically in the trade press between 1965 and 1969, usually listed alongside other Nashville songwriters, but as the hits emerged and his solo career took off, that changed. After the Tony and Kris piece, there are no more mentions in the *Los Angeles Times* until October 1969, when his writing credit for Ray Stevens's new release, 'Sunday Mornin' Comin' Down', is noted. Early in 1970, that song and 'Me and Bobby McGee' won awards as outstanding compositions in the country field for the year just ended.[22] By April, the *New York Times* reported Kristofferson was 'one of the most talked about songwriters in Nashville' and was part of a trend in 'social commentary' that was then taking place in country music.[23] In June, the *Los Angeles Times* had finally pulled the now familiar backstory together and announced 'A Rhodes Scholar Finds Song Niche' as the headline for its wholly positive review of his debut LP.[24]

Kristofferson's role in *Cisco Pike* was casting to type insomuch as it 'coincides with real life', as one trade journal reported.[25] The backdrop to this tale of a dope dealer trying to go straight, but pulled back into the trade by a crooked policeman, is the story of a one-hit wonder and a music industry as equally unsure of its direction as the film industry. Not so long ago, four or five years back, Cisco had his taste of fame and fortune, but that soured when his partner,

Jesse Dupree (Harry Dean Stanton), got hopelessly addicted to drugs. Now, with girlfriend Sue (Karen Black), he has given up dealing and is trying, none too successfully, to get his career back on the tracks. The couple live together in Venice Beach, a location that exudes a suitably beat-up atmosphere of good times long gone. In a series of vignettes of his encounters with the city's subcultures, the film follows Cisco hustling his demo tape and trying to offload a large stash of grade A marijuana as he drives up and down Sunset Boulevard and around and about Hollywood.

Poster for *Cisco Pike* (dir. Bill L. Norton, 1972).

Seymour Cassel, a key figure in John Cassavetes's troupe (*Faces* and *Minnie and Moskowitz*, 1968 and 1971 respectively), was originally cast to play Cisco, but he walked off the production shortly before shooting was scheduled to start. Casting director Fred Roos brought Kristofferson to producer Gerald Ayres's and director Bill L. Norton's attention. Written with Cassel in mind, the lead character was a glib, fast talker, but, as Ayres explained, Kristofferson's 'charm is slow to arrive and more apt to stay; his flavour is down home . . . the wanderer, the hung-over loner', and so the script was changed.[26] For some, the changes enhanced the film's integrity:

> Cisco is a man *Cisco Pike*'s audience knows well; there's no room for theatricality. Norton was lucky in securing Kristofferson for the role. If nothing else, he looks the part. There's no problem believing Kris is a songwriter with a soul. He's convinced the audience of that for the last two years, through his music.[27]

Kristofferson was coached by Jaclyn Hellman (then estranged wife of director Monte Hellman), who had previously worked with musicians and non-actors James Taylor and Dennis Wilson on *Two-Lane Blacktop*.

The pronounced effect of casting Kristofferson is that he appears to have literally walked off the street with his guitar and into the film. The clothes he wears in the movie's opening sequence, jeans over cowboy boots, denim shirt under a Levi's-style suede jacket, are what he would choose to wear every day – a point underscored by his sophomore album, *The Silver Tongued Devil and I* (1971), which uses a portrait of him drawn from the film on its cover and features the three songs used on the soundtrack.[28]

The slippage between real and reel life is beautifully crafted and convincing, accentuated by minor scenes where he drives past the Troubadour, where Waylon Jennings is in residency; when he is reminiscing with Jesse about their old bandmates, Swan and Fritz (aka Kristofferson's confederates Billy Swan and Donnie Fritts); or where we see the magazine cuttings stuck on the wall above the table in his kitchen, which feature The Charlatans' Dan Hicks giving the photographer the bird and the MC5 in their *Back in the USA* leathers – all so suggestive of the moment's pop and rock milieu that he works in.

The *New York Times* reviewer wrote that

> it is Kristofferson who holds the film together. Whether he has much range as an actor is not yet clear, but he has extraordinary screen presence, a classic mixture of strength and vulnerability, plus an original sardonic wit. This is as perfect a union of actor and character as one can expect to see in movies. Cisco Pike and Kris Kristofferson seem to draw life from each other.[29]

The *Los Angeles Times* film critic concurred with his East Coast colleague: 'Kristofferson, a natural actor and a figure of rough-hewn grace, is perfect.'[30]

The casting of the support roles in *Cisco Pike* was done to match Kristofferson's lack of affectation and to achieve the same effect as *Two-Lane Blacktop*'s true-to-type characters, which mixed professional actors with non-actors. Fresh from the box office success of *The French Connection*, Gene Hackman played the corrupt lawman Leo Holland, who has scored a large consignment of marijuana he wants Cisco to distribute. Hackman needs the money in short order, giving the story a race-against-the-clock dimension: can Cisco offload $10,000 worth of dope in one wild weekend? Following her appearance in *Easy Rider*, Black had established herself as the working-class girlfriend of Nicholson's character in the previous year's *Five Easy Pieces*, which *Variety* now considered to be a fixed performance style: 'Karen Black in another Karen Black role as Pike's amiable but confused girl'.[31] Stanton had a long CV of bit-parts and character roles in film and television that went back to the mid-1950s, so his face would have been well known to filmgoers even if they could not put a name to it (though 'H. D. Stanton' appears as graffiti on the wall of the jail cell that Fonda, Hopper and Nicholson's characters share in *Easy Rider*). His appearance in the same year's *Two-Lane Blacktop* no doubt helped him gain some further recognition, but it was the familiarity of his beat-up face, dour expression and general demeanour of being one of life's eternal losers that counted. Other supporting roles and small parts, including Warhol star Viva, blaxploitation regular Antonio Vargas and Severn Darden (*The Last Movie*, *The Hired Hand* and *Werewolves on Wheels*, all 1971), would have been known to various degrees by the film's intended audience, as would Wavy Gravy, the infamous hippy scenester, and Doug Sahm of Sir Douglas Quintet fame, who plays Rex, a musician and speed freak with whom Cisco tries to offload some dope.

Cisco Pike was 27-year-old recent UCLA film school graduate Bill L. Norton's first directing job on a feature film. He had been eking out a living by making promotional short films for rock performers. *Cisco Pike* was based on his original screenplay (an uncredited Robert Towne helped give it shape, especially Hackman's dialogue) and was also the first film Ayres had produced (he would later work the same role on Hal Ashby's *The Last*

Detail, which had a Towne screenplay). Fred Roos, with credits for *Five Easy Pieces* and *Two-Lane Blacktop*, was casting director, and he would work on *The Godfather, Fat City, The King of Marvin Gardens, Dillinger* and *American Graffiti*. Cinematography was directed by Vilis Lapenieks, a documentarist by trade but who had also lensed the Venice Beach-set *Night Tide* (1960), Curtis Harrington's phantasmagorical remake of *Cat People* starring Dennis Hopper in a one-size-too-small sailor outfit.

The predominance of neophyte film-makers in key roles was undoubtedly a result of the presumption that catching a huge youth audience had been achieved by novices with *Easy Rider*, so why not with *Cisco Pike*? Besides, this was a relatively cheap film in terms of production cost and salaries. But as happened with *Dirty Little Billy* that same year, Columbia made little effort to promote and distribute its property. The fate of these two films, as well as what happened to *The Last Movie, The Hired Hand* and *Two-Lane Blacktop*, is suggestive of a film industry that momentarily took a risk with inexperienced film-makers, bankrolling a number of relatively inexpensive films, but then baulked at the investment needed to strike sufficient prints, to actively market and promote their properties and then to meaningfully distribute the pictures when they seemed unsure, following less-than-enthusiastic reviews, that an audience would turn out.

Ayres, *Cisco Pike*'s producer, writing about the Hollywood he worked in, called it an industry without a sense of its own traditions, hence it was constantly in flux and, right now, in 1971, it found

itself on a periodic quest for integrity. Boss Buck is asked to hide his face and the front men get younger, dress quasi-hip, and say they're on the lookout for art. Although this is for the most part Hollywood's spastic recoil to a street event called the youth movement, it has given some young filmmakers a chance to make their films, many of their first efforts coming out the year of this writing.[32]

'Integrity' was a key term for Ayres: he worried that his film might be 'taken to be a teen exploitation film', which was not his intention. 'Dealing in the world of dope and rock . . . you are always in danger of seeming to exploit ever-shifting idioms on which too many consider themselves expert,' he wrote.[33] The tendency has been for film historians to look back and see this moment in time, immediately post-*Easy Rider*, as in good part the industry's pursuit of the youth market, but, as Ayres's remarks showed, that target audience was never homogeneous.

Would the film be attractive to drive-in kids who enjoyed motorcycle outlaw pictures? The inner-city cinema patrons who watched blaxploitation? The university film club members who rated Godard and Cassavetes? Beyond being bracketed as 'youth', was there much that these audiences shared? Would *Cisco Pike*, described by one commentator as 'the first suspense thriller of the "New Culture"', cut through and cross over?[34] The selling points for *Cisco Pike* were all fairly self-promoting: Kristofferson's rising reputation; his songs on the soundtrack; Hackman's and Black's billings, albeit limited; the counterculture milieu and bohemian setting; the anti-authoritarian, paranoid, crooked-cop drug story. All suggested a post-*Easy Rider* exploitation set-up. *Variety* predicted that 'Kristofferson's musical reputation is the immediate marquee bait, but there's good drama in the Columbia release to warrant a respectable b.o. response in general youth-oriented dual situations.'[35] But the company's lack of faith in the picture was clear

Cover of Kris
Kristofferson's
Cisco Pike EP
(1972).

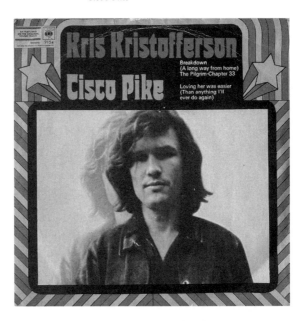

when they double-billed it on the East Coast with Italian mobster
movie *Machine Gun McCain*. That picture may have starred John
Cassavetes, but it was little more than a formulaic gangster pic –
everything that *Cisco Pike* was trying not to be.

At this point in time, Kristofferson's box office clout was limited, and certainly less powerful than Mick Jagger's, who had
recently been cast in *Ned Kelly* and *Performance*. Jagger had a
more certain attraction for the youth audience, but neither of his
films fared well. Nevertheless, film producers were enamoured
with the idea that rock stars could help animate and pre-sell properties with a counterculture setting to the same audience who had
bought tickets to see *Easy Rider*, went to Woodstock (or watched
the movie) and bought Dylan and Stones albums. What director
Norton attempted to explore in *Cisco Pike* was the idea of the breakdown, or flux, in any absolute between the law and lawlessness,

between policeman and criminal. The Rolling Stones personified the idea of rock stars as outlaws, and Kristofferson intimated
something similar in his relationship with Nashville's custodians.
Explaining his film, no doubt with Dylan's maxim echoing in his
head that to be honest one has to live outside the law, Norton said:
'nowadays we are all criminals. I mean it's hard to do anything
without breaking laws. We are all criminals. We are felons.'[36]

From the moment The Beatles made waves with *A Hard Day's
Night*, the Stones' manager, Andrew Loog Oldham, had wanted
his charges to appear on the silver screen. He first imagined them
in an adaptation of Anthony Burgess's *A Clockwork Orange*, but
the film rights had already been sold. He then sought to turn Dave
Wallis's novel *Only Lovers Left Alive* into a vehicle for the band, but
the story of rogue teenagers in a world without adults was never
quite fashioned to his satisfaction into a screenplay. Oldham and
Keith Richards at one point met with Nicholas '*Rebel Without a
Cause*' Ray to discuss his participation, but it was not a meeting
of like minds. Though Oldham continued to dream his life as if it
were a movie, he gave up on the idea of a Rolling Stones film, before
eventually giving up on the Stones themselves.

With hindsight, Oldham felt the problem that could not be
overcome was that rock stars were rarely able to make a successful
transition to acting:

> There are not many examples of music personalities who
> have shifted their creative spark over to the silver screen.
> Rock stars seem for the most part to lose the very essence
> of their sensual being the moment they hit their mark and
> attempt to act – they lose rhythm, they lose the swing and
> they end up contorted, unsexed and stiff.[37]

Oldham didn't sit down to watch *Performance* until the close of the 1970s, and even then he didn't make it to the end of the film. As he wrote in his autobiography *2Stoned* in 2001: 'Mick Jagger was playing my biggest nightmare and James Fox was playing me. *Performance* remains symptomatic of the late 60s ennui. Part of its sinister appeal is that it is an ode to excess, drugs, sloth and an inability to produce.'[38] *Cisco Pike* was playing out the same dystopian set-pieces, as one contemporary reviewer noted:

What the film is really about is what has happened to the 'love, get high, brotherhood' scene that existed in the late sixties. Its aftermath is very much a sad disaster and the psychic scars left on the people who took part in it are deep and harder to relieve than any physical wounds caught in war or riot. As Kristofferson's character says late in the film when told that he has dealing to fall back on if he doesn't make it again in the music business, 'But it ain't fun no more selling it.' Even dope has become a commercialized establishment enterprise involving sick money games.[39]

Both films were fashioned on an understanding that rock 'n' roll and criminal activities inevitably intersected, and, as the 1960s turned into the 1970s, what had been hidden was now in plain sight. Everyone was an outlaw.

6

Dirty Little Billy: Scuffling on Madison Ave

BILLY THE KID WAS A PUNK
'Dirty Little Billy' is a different kind of movie.
It's not about the Billy the Kid you've known and loved.
It's about the real William H. Bonney.
And the real William H. Bonney was a loser.
'Dirty Little Billy' is the end of his legend.

Advertising copy, *Dirty Little Billy* (1972)

The location for this American tale is Coffeyville, Kansas, which is little more than a row of clapboard buildings set on a rise with a dirt road running down its centre. The town's prospects, however, are looking good: the Galveston Railroad has laid track to its outskirts, and its citizens are encouraged by the news that an epidemic has broken out in a neighbouring community – all being well, the survivors will likely make Coffeyville their home. Another's misfortune, as the saying goes. The potential boost in population would mean the town will become big enough to qualify as a 'third-class city' and can then elect a mayor and a peacekeeper. But right now, prospects are all they've got, and circumstances are so straitened that a dead man's coat and footwear are removed before interment. You don't bury material goods with a resale value.

The film opens with a close-up of a muddy puddle into which steps a pair of boots. Above the primal sludge, seen in a window-pane's distorted reflection, the Stars and Stripes is raised. The boots belong to young Billy, played by Michael J. Pollard, recently arrived from New York with his Irish mother and stepfather. They have bought a broken-down farmstead. But Billy is no farmer – he is lazy, feckless and given to bellyaching.

Looking for a distraction, but unimpressed by Coffeyville's gang of motley adolescents led by Basil Crabtree (Gary Busey), Billy throws in his lot with card sharp and pimp Goldie (played by Richard Evans) and the town's prostitute, Berle (Lee Purcell). The pair's gambling and whoring is carried out in a small store-front drinking hole, out the back of which is a room with a bed where Berle entertains the town's menfolk. Her room is filled with knick-knacks and photographs, reminders of other times, other homes. On one wall there is a Pears' soap advertisement, its idealized image a stark contrast to Goldie and Berle's world. The spaces the pair inhabit are the antithesis of bourgeois domesticity; sepia-lit, not as filtered by nostalgia but as if piss-stained. Theirs is a whiskysoaked, dissolute existence.

When Billy's stepfather dies, the town's leader, Ben Antrim (Charles Aidman), wastes little time in filling the dead man's place in Billy's mother's bed. Showing some parental respons-ibility, Antrim asks the boy what he would like to do. He offers him all sorts of easy work, but Billy doesn't want to do anything apart from spend time with Goldie and Berle. She will take Billy to her bed and Goldie will teach him to shoot, which is but the same thing. When a game of cards with three male drifters and

Lobby card for *Dirty Little Billy* (1972).

a woman ends in violence, Billy is drawn deeper into the pair's world.

Goldie is not a roving dandy gambler figure – a Doc Holliday type; a man without a future looking to escape his past and drink away his present. He is an errant son of Coffeyville – a town his parents helped build and died in – another exile on Main Street covered in the pitch that defileth. Goldie's negation of the world they left him puts him at odds with the town's progressive agenda. Told by Antrim to leave or be killed, Goldie spits back that he has rights and that he'll do the killing. But Antrim is unperturbed; Goldie's privileges are non-existent, and his threats are hollow.

The mud of Main Street having turned to dust, Goldie and Berle pull out in the morning. Holding Billy back, Antrim watches as the ambush he has organized unfolds. The world is all around a dishonest place. Berle is killed defending Goldie, who, with a dust storm as cover, slips away. Cutting loose from Antrim, Billy hightails it behind the gambler. Together the pair wander through the Kansas Badlands and into its hills, where they encounter three bandits. The highwaymen think them easy spoils, with Billy's body the prized bounty. Playing the part of a half-wit, Billy takes the robbers by surprise. Showing no hesitation or fear, he slays them all. Billy and Goldie pick over the bodies, taking anything of value, especially their boots. With their new footwear the pair drift into legend.[1]

Dirty Little Billy was industry veteran Jack L. Warner's first independent production; the eighty-year-old had moved on from the family firm after it had been bought by parking lot and rental sales conglomerate Kinney National. His principal role in the film's production, it could be safely assumed, was to act as a front for his co-producers, movie neophytes the Wells, Rich, Greene (WRG) advertising agency.[2] The six-year-old agency, led by Mary Wells Lawrence, whose clients included Benson & Hedges, Volkswagen, Braniff Airways, Trans World Airlines (TWA) and Alka-Seltzer, was expanding into movie production. Lawrence told the *Los Angeles Times* that their advertising ethos translated effortlessly into the kind of small-budget, intimate pictures they were planning: 'Most westerns are big, panoramic objective stories you don't get very caught up in except for the chase. *Dirty Little Billy* will be about the people.'[3] The film's hook, she said, was that it would be the 'real story of Billy the Kid' – what made him become an outlaw. For instance, 'we found he was born in the Lower East Side and his parents decided to move west because they thought it would be a better environment. Isn't that ironic?' she concluded.[4]

Equally new to film production was Stan Dragoti, the agency's top television commercials director. He had written the screenplay with Charles Moss, president of the firm, and would direct the picture. At the time of the film's production, Dragoti was married to *Sports Illustrated* swimwear model Cheryl Tiegs; his Madison Avenue CV and penthouse lifestyle hardly suggested a director with a keen eye for the Western's tellurian qualities, its muddy boots.[5] But perhaps that was why he was the project's ideal director: the production would work on the play between fantasy and reality, finding glamour in the dirt, which suited WRG's advertising ethos, which itself was built on the principle of nonconformity.

Tightly controlled production values, however, were very much part of WRG's plans when it came to making movies. 'We're not indulgent,' said Lawrence, 'we aim to make movies simply, with a minimum of nonsense.'[6] Founded in 1966, WRG quickly amassed a significant portfolio of blue-chip accounts, all eager to benefit from what Thomas Frank in *The Conquest of Cool* (1997) dubbed the 'new hip advertising'.[7] By 1971 the agency had pocketed $100,000,000 in billings. Frank writes:

> No company in America was hipper than Wells, Rich, Greene. It brought together in a dynamic, explosive combination the two great themes of advertising in the 1960s: creativity and the new system of values being ushered in by youth culture. In campaign after campaign, WRG produced memorable, often hilarious ads that combined hip sensibilities with uncompromising sales messages and high production values.[8]

WRG sold itself on youth, creativity and talent above organization, which underpinned its concept of nonconformity – of going against convention. Frank continues:

> The consumer was no longer merely skeptical of mass society, but positively *hip*, young-minded, wise to television's tricks, drawn to the alienated filmmaking of the era, and only reachable through the coolest of advertising agencies . . . WRG simply upped the ante on the decade's violence against advertising convention: it would discover whatever was the usual way of pitching a given product category and then seek to do just the opposite.[9]

These creative principles can be seen in the decision to develop and produce what in essence was an anti-Western but which, like the campaign WRG ran for Love cosmetics (sold as 'makeup for a time – and a generation – at war with the pretence and falsehood of makeup'), was also transparently the very thing it denied.[10] As much as *Dirty Little Billy* invited its audience to query and doubt the conventions of the Western, it also put back into play the very tropes that it questioned. WRG conceived and sold the film by confirming an audience's cynicism rather than evading it, endorsing their apostasy. The concept is deeply contradictory – a hip conservatism – but it worked, at least it did when selling cigarettes and cosmetics.

A youth audience was deemed key to the film's success, and its 1972 American premiere, as part of October's San Francisco Film Festival, emphasized this point. Press agents worked four of the Bay Area's university campuses, organizing screenings for student opinion makers and handing out promotional tie-ins, including

T-shirts, buttons, posters and derby (bowler) hats, like the one worn in the film by Pollard. All printed materials and gewgaws featured the campaign slogan 'Billy the Kid was a Punk'.[11] Vincent Canby's *New York Times* review amplified the significance of the slogan in setting the terms for how the film should be received: 'It winds up substituting for the heroic Billy of earlier movies a Billy who is so witless that he becomes a new kind of hero, the sort of legend that any kid who's ever knocked over a subway candy dispenser can identify with.'[12] The effect, he thought, was that the film was 'in tune' with younger audiences, more accessible than *Pat Garrett and Billy the Kid* with Peckinpah's middle-aged visions 'that worry about questions of personal freedom, choice and compromise'.[13]

Despite having long since left their teens behind, Pollard, Purcell and Evans escaped the ignominy of appearing too old for their parts. At 33, Pollard was eight years older than Purcell and two years Evans's junior. With some suspension of disbelief, he could still pass muster as a teenager. Though, truth be told, in 1971, with hair thinning at the front, he looked less like a punk Dead End Kid than his contemporary Elton John. Beneath the grime, Purcell, 25 years old and in only her second feature role, still had a youthful glow, but Evans, at 37, with a portfolio of television roles behind him, countered his advanced age by giving the appearance of a pinched-faced alcoholic who had too quickly put on the years.

Pollard had made his name in Arthur Penn's *Bonnie and Clyde*, where his supporting role as C. W. Moss confirmed his runty, witless, juvenile punk persona that had been rehearsed in the biker film *The Wild Angels* and, also in 1966, in an episode of *Star Trek* as the leader of a gang of kids who attack Captain Kirk. He would continue to play the character type in *Hannibal Brooks* (1969) and

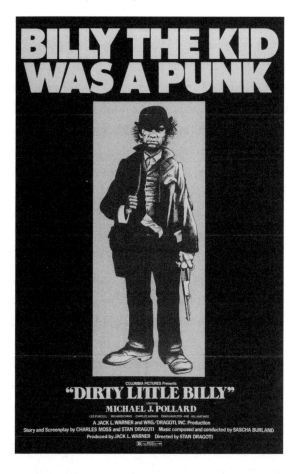

Poster for *Dirty Little Billy* (dir. Stan Dragoti, 1972).

Little Fauss and Big Halsy (1970) before bringing it to a mannered peak with *Dirty Little Billy*. Pollard's Billy assumed the same place in relation to the malodorous pair as his C. W. Moss had taken with the outlaw couple in *Bonnie and Clyde*. The latter triad had parodied the idea of the respectable family unit, and *Dirty Little Billy* degrades it further.

Three times in *Billy* he is called a 'punk', an insult that was at once sexual and demeaning. The slur was also an endorsement of the film's casting to type and confirmation of its marketing hook, 'Billy the Kid was a Punk'. In the pre-punk-rock world in which *Dirty Little Billy* was marketed, 'punk' was used as a pejorative term aimed at someone who had assumed an unentitled position. In Billy's case, calling him a punk undercut his claim to heroic or mythic status. The slur belittles, pulling Billy back down to size; it infantilizes and emasculates him. In North American prison slang, 'punk' was used to designate the weaker, passive, often coerced partner in homosexual acts, so that for many, the term carried a heavy suggestion of deviancy, both sexual and criminal.[14]

Helping sell the movie to a British audience for whom 'punk' was not necessarily a familiar or even understood term, Pollard's personal manager took time to explain to *Daily Mail* readers that 'If Billy were alive today, he would be a skinhead.'[15] By whatever name, Billy was a hoodlum. Even as punk's catamite allusions resonated across the film, the term's core premise was to make Billy a more recognizably human figure, to bring him down from a mythical, unearthly sphere to occupy a more worldly, muddy space.

The play between the extraordinary and the ordinary, between star and anti-star, had been rehearsed and performed to eventual perfection by The Rolling Stones. Their personas depended upon a neverending oscillation between states of being – attainable yet distant, knowable yet unknown, dumb yet erudite, ugly yet beautiful. They were inarticulate wits, gutter gods, youth's saviours in leather jackets – hoodlum poets. That the film-makers sought to capture some of this in how Billy would be portrayed was suggested by having Terry O'Neill shoot the production stills. He was ostensibly a fashion photographer, but also an early chronicler of the Stones and a contemporary of Swinging London lensmen David Bailey, Terence Donovan and Brian Duffy. Most importantly, O'Neill was a man capable of making grime stylish. If *Bonnie and Clyde* was its obvious filmic predecessor, The Rolling Stones were the model for selling Billy the Kid as a punk hero.

Boxoffice considered *Dirty Little Billy* to be 'by far the most authentic version of the usually glamorized picture of the young killer'.[16] *Variety*'s review led with, 'Incisive look at the way the West might have really been. Directed and played with vigor. One of the grittiest of the "new" oaters.'[17] The Italians had made the Western 'campy' and 'horse operatic', the review continued, and in turn, with films like *Doc* (1971) and *Little Big Man* (1970), 'u.s. Oatmakers are stripping them of their myth, romanticism and glory', with *Dirty Little Billy* the 'grittiest of them'.[18] The film was not a 'didactic' look at the West but rather a picture with 'probing flair for the period . . . No spurs, Stetsons or dry streets, but a forceful recreation of a time that has resonances'.[19]

Contemporary reviews emphasized, and then restated more to make sure their point was driven home, that *Dirty Little Billy* was part of a trend in Western film's new authenticity. At the end of 1973, for the *Chicago Tribune*, Gene Siskel summed up the state of play:

> Except for John Wayne's annual memoir to the good old days, the Westerns of the last two years have been grubby little pieces of history. Before Julie Christie arrives to lend a feminine hand, Warren Beatty's whorehouse in *McCabe and Mrs Miller* is just a row of tents amid mud. In *The Great Northfield, Minnesota Raid*, the Jesse James–Cole Younger gang is a collection of rag-tags with knots in their hair and snot running out of their noses. *Kid Blue* and *The Culpepper Cattle Company* are similarly designed in various shades of

brown. The West was a dirty and dreary place, these films seem to say.[20]

The idea of 'dirt' was at the core of the latest trend in Westerns, but dirt was everywhere in post-1967 movies.

The film's exploitation of *Bonnie and Clyde* was a given with the casting of Pollard, his character's relationship with Berle and Goldie and its tale of outlaws, but *Dirty Little Billy* was also part of a slew of films with similar titles: 'Billy's no kin to Dirty Dingus or Dirty Harry', wrote the *Los Angeles Times* gossip columnist and film critic Joyce Haber.[21] This particular fad effectively began with Robert Aldrich's box office success with *The Dirty Dozen* (1967), which begat imitation movies such as *Dirty Heroes* (1968). Frank Sinatra's *Dirty Dingus Magee* (1970) took the adjective out west, while Clint Eastwood's *Dirty Harry* (1971) gave it a contemporary urban aspect. Sex films worked on the illicit side of its equation with *Dirty Weekend* (1973), *The Dirty Dolls* (1973) and *Mama's Dirty Girls* (1974). *Dirty Mary, Crazy Larry* (1974) with Peter Fonda and Susan George mashed all the aspects together, put the stars in denim, and headed off down the road.

A dirty object is not itself dirt, reasons the philosopher of dirt Olli Lagerspetz: 'On the contrary, the implication is that the object needs cleaning precisely because it is something different from dirt.'[22] The idea presupposes an object has become degraded by contact with a foreign substance; dirt suggests a state of being prior to contamination, emphasizing the purity of thing that has been despoiled. Dirt is defined by its ability to alter an ideal, which is not necessarily a negative process. If the ideal is neither sought nor desired, then dirt can have a positive value. For those wishing to push back against the strictures of society – rebellious middle-class youth, for instance – cleanliness and order can seem like regulation and sterility: everything in its rightful place, where real-life experience, the dirt beneath the fingernails, is scrubbed away, excluded.

The modern poet, as Arthur Rimbaud declared, must make themselves 'scummy' if they are to become artists or seers. On The Stooges' track 'Dirt', from their 1970 album *Fun House*, Iggy Pop followed Rimbaud's calling and wallowed in the mire, but, as he sang, he don't care, because he's just dirt. 'The music [The Stooges] play has been described as stupid rock at its best,' wrote Mike Gormley in 1969 for the *Detroit Free Press*, 'Iggy calls it dirty music and the group's manager, Jimmy Silver, says "it's dance music, fun music for kids."'[23] Which was why, seven years on, 'punk' could be seen as a badge of honour, worn willingly by young people as an act of wanton negation. WRG planned that their dirty Billy, the punk kid, would be just such an anti-figure. Dirt, then, was not just a case of pushing the historically authentic but a way of communicating with the film's target audience by aligning the protagonist with their own desire to spoil their bourgeois inheritance and besmirch the image of John Wayne and all that he and his peers might represent. But for WRG, selling dirt proved to be a harder act than hawking Love cosmetics.

Writing in the *New York Times*, A. H. Weiler noted the film's ability to capture 'the look of an authentic period and place', but he thought the characters 'vague' and motivation 'confused'.[24] The following month, his colleague at the *Times* Vincent Canby wrote of *Dirty Little Billy* that 'debunking is an especially appreciated American art' but that film, even as it exposed lies and shibboleths, would, owing to the scale and mystique of its form, in turn replace them with an equally dishonest representation.[25] At the beginning

Billy, Iggy, Rimbaud.

of the film Billy, mired in mud, walks out of myth; by the film's end, covered in dust and with a second pair of boots strung over his shoulder, he walks back into myth. Art and the authentic are not separable but in dialogue with each other. The *Boxoffice* reviewer heard the authentic part of the exchange and connected with it, the *Los Angeles Times* reviewer ignored or dismissed that side of the chatter and responded only to the line about fabrication. Most critical respondents fell somewhere in between the two polarities. Jay Cocks for *Time* magazine wrote:

> The actors wear worn clothes coated with dirt, as if they had all been wrestling in an anthracite pit. Their faces are ever so carefully caked with filth. Reality is swallowed up in such elaborately misplaced attention to detail; the movie looks quite as fussy and phony in its ramshackle posturings as *Shane* did in its opulent mythologizing. What is remarkable about *Dirty Little Billy* is the fervor with which its director has seized upon each thumping bromide of the anti-western and put them all on review, like a rodeo parade.[26]

It was reported that Pollard had been so taken with the film's idea of authenticity he spent trips to Manhattan searching for a vintage 1844 Navy revolver and for 'suitable tattered clothing'.[27] Perhaps he felt the quest would better help him inhabit the concept of the film's dialectic between truth and myth, but in reality it was probably only a planted story to help pre-sell the film. Two months later, in March 1971, Pollard was featured in some costuming shots, which, like the news squib about his Gotham ramblings, were run in the *Los Angeles Times*. The bearded actor is shown modelling a floor-length duster and a fetching derby hat, being appraised by seated director Dragoti, fist to chin.

Alongside one of Dragoti's design sketches for the film, the photograph of director and star illustrates an article on the 'costume design revolution'. Theadora Van Runkle, 'who unwittingly turned *Bonnie and Clyde* into a Technicolor fashion show and simultaneously turned the whole world on to Depression dressing', is the feature's main attraction. She has happily 'retired' from the business.[28] Hollywood is changing and, along with those shifts, costume design is having to adjust to the new economic reality of low-budget, under-a-million-dollar movies like *Dirty Little Billy* and a star's power to set their own style criteria.

As the grande dame of designers, Edith Head, reasoned, 'We're in a period of intense realism. You can't fool the public. And we're on low-budget pictures. If everything is real and you have no money, who needs a costume designer?'[29] Pollard, it was reported, was working with Dragoti and they were 'personally selecting the costumes'.[30] Which meant that not only was the Madison Avenue man writing, directing and producing the film, he was also its costume designer: 'It's the whole Orson Welles trip,' wrote the *Los Angeles Times* journalist. Dragoti had originally wanted Van Runkle, but his budget would not stretch and so he had been 'combing Western Costume Co. for clothes that don't look cowboyish – "Go to any ghetto and you'll find out what the West was like," he said.'[31] That Hollywood company, despite its name, provided costumes, props and supplies for all types of films, and had been doing so since 1912. The lesson? Search hard enough and the truth can be found on a hanger in the props department just a few racks down from the historical anachronism of the worn and tattered Levi's and Wrangler jackets that once suggested the real and which *Dirty*

Little Billy renounced in its bid for the authentic – the now look of a historical ghetto West.

The film's music underscores this idea of the West as part of an American modernity, not as some pre-modern arcadia. The soundtrack for *Bonnie and Clyde* had used Flatt & Scruggs's 'Foggy Mountain Breakdown' (1949) to enhance its setting as belonging to a pre-rock 'n' roll America, but the choice was an anachronism. Bluegrass did not exist until the 1940s: it was a thoroughly modern expression of an old-time music. Yet the fact that it was historically inappropriate went unquestioned by most filmgoers. For many, unamplified, fast-picked stringed instruments unambiguously signified the past – the technicality of when that musical form first appeared and whether it was contemporary with the film's setting was irrelevant. The banjo was also the most prominent instrument on *Dirty Little Billy*'s soundtrack, but here it was backed by a tuba and a harpsichord. The latter too implied the past, but in combination with the brass instrument it was a rejection of the Western's conventional soundtrack of orchestral arrangements of Stephen Foster minstrel tunes and theme songs sung by pop singers – Frankie Laine or Ricky Nelson once upon a time, B. J. Thomas and Leonard Cohen more recently – and it hinted not at the rural but at an urban sensibility.

Sascha Burland's short sketches for *Dirty Little Billy* evoke a bygone form of musical entertainment, the sort provided for a parade by enthusiastic amateur musicians that hints at ragtime and jazz to come, the sounds of the metropolis. It was Burland's only film credit; he had made his name with novelty records for animated cartoons like Yogi Bear and Huckleberry Hound and as the vocalist on The Nutty Squirrels' recordings, a band that worked the same side of the street as Alvin & the Chipmunks. Burland was a jazz musician with rent to pay. The producers, nevertheless, thought there was something in his compositions, perhaps buoyed by the success Flatt & Scruggs had enjoyed in the wake of *Bonnie and Clyde*, and reportedly sent out a promotional disc featuring 'Billy's Theme' and 'Berle's Theme' to radio stations. But if it was ever pressed, the record has sunk without a trace.[32]

The true value of the soundtrack was that it, among other elements, worked on the basis that authenticity was best achieved when it was understood to be jettisoning existing genre conventions – the film's lack of spurs, horses, Stetsons and cowboys in Wrangler jeans, for instance, and their replacement with rough wool suits, derby hats and lace-up work boots. Like others, the *Independent Film Journal* thought *Dirty Little Billy* could be the 'ultimate in Old West authenticity': no cowboys, 'only mud and rotting shacks'.[33] For this reviewer, however, the dirt was all too transparent, too readily revealing the sham it was trying to conceal. He argued that the film-makers' creative background in advertising worked against the film's bid for a certain verisimilitude: the movie 'looks most like a 93-minute sell for visiting the gritty colourful Old West. Superficiality passes for realism with the added touch of real brutality.'[34] Pollard's performance is in an 'affected style', conjuring a 'one-dimensional persona' that blurs 'the difference between his cowering cowboy and the kooky teenager from his past work'.[35] The *Los Angeles Times*'s reviewer also found the film more 'arty' and 'mannered' than authentic.[36] Revealing the tension between the film's avowed realism and the means used to achieve the effect was a fairly consistent trope in critiques of the movie: intent and affect were too often at odds with each other.

Writing for the bimonthly magazine *Rock Scene*, Donald Lyons provided an overview of Hollywood's depiction of Billy the Kid and the changing face of the Western, which in its latest iteration represented the West as 'evil and life so pointless that the hero can barely get up enough energy to be killed'.[37] A trend that had 'reached rock bottom' with *Dirty Little Billy*, its hero a 'dribbling, scratching, vomiting, verminous blob. He makes Kris Kristofferson's Billy look like Fred Astaire ... Anyone can tear down a Myth; who can build one? Now how about Candy Darling as Billy the Kid in a musical ...'[38]

While *Variety* thought *Dirty Little Billy* would capture a youthful audience, *Boxoffice* and the *Independent Film Journal* were less assured of its potential. The latter thought there was too much competition among other films taking part in the 'new vogue for realistic westerns' with an emphasis 'on grit and dirty faces', which included *Bad Company* (1972).[39] A double-page advertisement for the film in an end-of-year edition of *Variety*, headlined 'PAYDIRT', played on such uncertainty around the film's box office prospects (and an ambivalence around the value of 'dirt'): 'When we set out to make *Dirty Little Billy*, we knew it wasn't the kind of Western people were used to. And to be frank, we weren't really sure how they'd react to it. But now the pre-release results are in.' Ballyhoo followed, with packed houses listed for St Louis, Dallas, Houston and Midwest screenings. The ad proclaimed it as 'The movie that shows up the Old West for what it really was. Now available for January bookings.'[40]

But in truth the film fairly tanked. Distribution by Columbia followed the pattern usually reserved for exploitation films: costs were saved by having a limited number of prints struck, these were then circulated on a regional basis, moving on to other areas when runs had been concluded. This meant that though the film was first screened in autumn 1972 on the West Coast, it was not shown on the East Coast until May 1973. *Dirty Little Billy* took two years from its first press screening in Paris before it turned up on 42nd Street, and seven months to get from LA to NYC. National media interest generated on its initial release had long since been forgotten by the time it arrived in Manhattan cinemas. The cost of *Billy* was listed as $1.3 million.[41] A year after its initial West Coast release, in October 1973 the company reported it expected to write off as losses half that investment, $652,000.[42]

Following *Dirty Little Billy*, its production company, still looking to exploit the revisionist Western, had planned an adaptation of Dee Brown's *Bury My Heart at Wounded Knee* (1970), but the modest box office returns for *Billy* forced the company to withdraw from the movie business.[43] Success on Madison Ave was not, then, replicated in Hollywood by WRG. Though the advertising company had a viable product and marketing campaign, it did not have the reach or the resources to put the film into enough cinemas to find its audience. But it did leave a record that indicates just how complex the play is between artifice and the real, commerce and art, myth and history. The Western film cycle *Dirty Little Billy* was part of was sold on the novelty of a new authenticity that posed as a dirty challenge to the veracity of Hollywood's earlier idealized depictions of cowboys. But, truth be told, the dirt was never anything other than a new form of greasepaint, its scummy aspect just another line of cosmetics to be worn by those who professed not to wear make-up.

Payday's scriptwriter, Don Carpenter, in 1965 published a short story, 'Hollywood Whore', about a neophyte screenwriter's meeting with a producer. The writer is poorly attired, wearing sports socks with a suit, which prompts a lecture on costume and authenticity:

One thing I learned in this business is to treat clothes like costumes. If it's a pirate picture, we dress our people like they were pirates. We have men who look up in books what the old pirates used to wear, and they tell us, and then we dress our pirates like we saw them dressed in another picture. The public has not looked in the books, but they have seen the other pirate movies. Get it? He laughed and waggled a plump finger at me. 'Authentic is what looks right.'[44]

The authentic that looks right in *Dirty Little Billy* is predicated on a refraction of this convention. The film's producers have refigured the familiar, twisted it a turn or two to give the appearance of novelty, providing enough of a distinction on which to hang a marketing campaign but not going so far that it no longer signifies a West that audiences would recognize. The film's costumes have not been chosen as the antithesis of Gene Autry's dandy raiment or John Wayne's Stetson, placket shirt, denim dungarees held up by wide suspenders and belt; rather, it is the more recent costuming found in *Butch Cassidy and the Sundance Kid* (1969) that it works with and against.

George Roy Hill's Western starring Paul Newman and Robert Redford was one of the most successful films of the 1969–70 season, turning a profit of $11 million for 20th Century-Fox after production costs of $5.5 million.[45] It won four Oscars, including Best Original Screenplay by William Goldman. It was a charming, light-hearted romp that did as much to cement the idea of the buddy movie as it did to help rejuvenate the Western.

To the same effect as the slideshow of Depression-era photographs interspersed with images of the film's characters at the start

of *Bonnie and Clyde, Butch Cassidy* uses turn-of-the-century footage from period Western melodramas interspersed with scenes of
the film's stars that then merge into an opening sequence processed
in monochrome. The sepia tint and the old reels indicate a historic
and mythic confluence, which is reverberated in the costuming. In
the opening scenes, the two principals are each dressed in a three-
piece woollen suit with white shirt and tie, topped with a derby hat.
The urban, modern appearance of the costuming is doubled by the
bicycle that Newman's character rides and fools around with in the
company of Katharine Ross. That sequence is given a time-out-of-
joint aura as B. J. Thomas's rendering of 'Raindrops Keep Fallin'
on My Head', by Burt Bacharach and Hal David, romantically, and
anachronistically, plays.

Any disjunction caused by the shift from business attire to a
more generic Western costume, which the pair don when robbing
trains and attempting to stay ahead of their trackers, is eased by
maintaining continuity in the characters' silhouettes. When riding,
both men wear less formal suit jackets – tan corduroy by Newman
and a lightweight black jacket with matching pants by Redford – set
off by small-rimmed Stetson-style hats with flattened crowns and
riding boots. No denim, fancy chaps, paisley neckerchiefs or shirts
with darted pockets, the like of which might be seen at a rodeo or
in earlier Westerns. As with the opening montage of found and new
footage that seeps into the monochrome beginning, the effect is
to simultaneously suggest the old and the modern – history in the
now of the present. In his review, John Simon fully understood
this play with time:

> The attempt is to be both very attentive to period flavour,
> and wildly 'now'. Thus we get the quasi-imperceptible

switch from Conrad Hall's photography from the sepia
tones of yesteryear to the artfully understated colors
of just yesterday; the continual dependence of William
Goldman's script on standing every possible western convention on its brainless head; the endless wisecracking
of Paul Newman and Robert Redford in a language and
humor that are half a century too early and half a continent
too easterly for their historic time and place.[46]

The film's pretensions, as identified by Simon, are precisely the
targets at which *Dirty Little Billy* aimed its cynical barbs. Where
Butch Cassidy is overbearingly adorable and 'calculatedly puckish',
Billy is unlovable and emphatically squalid.[47] This is particularly
visible in the way both films overtly refigure and exaggerate distinct elements of the dramatization of the *ménage à trois* in *Jules
et Jim*, either exaggerating the comic and sentimental or piquing
the desperation and anti-romance that Truffaut had executed with
perfect balance. To all of this, Robert Altman thought he too might
have something to add to the conversation.

7

McCabe and Mrs Miller: Pipe Dreams – Lows and Highs

In 'The Evolution of the Western', André Bazin, the most influential film critic of his generation and father figure to the French New Wave, laid out a set of propositions that scholars of the genre have since regularly used as a starting point for sketching out their own concerns. He began by noting that on the eve of the Second World War the genre had reached a 'definitive stage of perfection', exemplified by John Ford's *Stagecoach* (1939). It then entered a 'baroque' or 'decadent' period in the post-war years when outside themes were imposed, turning the humble cowboy picture into the 'Superwestern'. This was 'a Western that would be ashamed to be just itself, and looks for some additional interest to justify its existence – an aesthetic, sociological, moral, psychological, political, or erotic existence, in short some quality extrinsic to the genre and which is supposed to enrich it'.[1]

The culmination of this shift was the move towards a self-reflexivity whereby a film's theme is the myth of the Western, an idea Bazin thought best represented by George Stevens's *Shane* (1953). This investigation along a hall of mirrors was tempered by the more talented film-makers Raoul Walsh, Howard Hawks, Nicholas Ray and, above all, Anthony Mann. These auteurs were 'sincere' in the attitude they held towards the material they worked with, which meant, wrote Bazin, 'that the directors play fair with the genre even when they are conscious of "making a western"'.[2]

Bazin's 1950s essays on the Western were first published in translation in 1971, too late to suggest they had any influence on American film-makers of that time but early enough to help explain what Hollywood's auteurs were doing with the genre. Whatever the shifting shape of the Western or its mythic dimensions (of most interest to academics), Bazin was also exploring through the genre the 'evolution of cinema taste – or indeed taste, period'.[3] He developed his ideas in a short essay based around Mann's *The Naked Spur* (1953). The 'true Western', he wrote, 'does defy criticism. Its qualities or its weaknesses are evident but not demonstrable.'[4] Critical approaches to the Western tended towards a bluntness and a set of preconditioned responses when what was needed, he urged, was a more respectful, nuanced and sensitive interaction. Engaging positively with the Western, he argued, called for critical discrimination based on the application of a refined and studied taste: 'But try to make taste the subject of criticism! After all, an appreciation of its vulgarity or refinement presupposes love and familiarity.'[5] To fully appreciate the Western, the filmgoer must be a connoisseur of the genre, someone who has the capacity to distinguish between *Shane* and Boetticher's *Seven Men from Now* (1956), the former by general consensus a 'masterpiece', the latter, according to Bazin, 'much superior to Stevens's film'.[6]

Those sensitive to a Western's qualities, wrote Bazin, can expect to achieve a 'virile and tender serenity that is indisputably superior to the more explicit moral lessons of those films for which the critics reserve their favours because they are "better than a Western"'.[7] Bazin was no doubt aware he was playing with the apparently irreconcilable idea that a critical position can be both 'virile' and 'tender'. Yet his approach to critical appreciation meant that a film like *Seven Men from Now* could be described as 'one of the most intelligent Westerns . . . but also the least intellectual; the most refined and least aesthetic; the simplest and most beautiful'.[8] These paradoxes defined the contemporary Western for Bazin: 'The intelligence we demand today may serve to refine the primitive structures of the Western and not to meditate upon them or to divert them to the advantage of interests remote from the essence of the genre.'[9] Those anglophone critics who followed in the slipstream of Bazin, Jim Kitses, Ed Buscombe, Philip French and Steve Neale among them, practised just such a refined sensitivity in their acts of discrimination.[10] Their critical stance was shaped by a Bazinian virile and tender serenity that embraced the puzzle of that approach and of the Western itself.

In Bazin's terms, the 1950s Superwestern asked that it be taken seriously, that it no longer be patronized as a lowbrow dumbshow. The genre had opened itself up and made explicit its exploration of gender issues (*Westward the Women*, 1951), sex (*Duel in the Sun*, 1946), character psychology (*Pursued*, 1947), racism (*The Searchers*, 1956), violence (*The Gunfighter*, 1950) and its own myths (*Shane*). In turn, critical appreciation of the Western also turned serious. New Hollywood's film-makers were the inheritors of these shifts in form and meaning and continued to push at the boundaries of what a Western was and might yet be, even as others, as film historian Andrew Patrick Nelson has argued, reacted against the more earnest, provocative and questioning run of anti-Westerns.[11] It was as if the new generation of cineastes – Fonda, Hopper, Nicholson, Hellman, Altman, Peckinpah et al. – were now involved in a game of poker with the old order, Wayne, Hawks, Andrew V. McLaglen and Hathaway. Cards shuffled, cut,

McCabe and Mrs Miller

dealt, opening bid made. A high-stakes game being played out within the films themselves.

Like the gunfight, poker is a mainstay of the genre and a trope that can be replayed and refigured to suit the needs of story and storyteller. The game here between the new and older generations moves around the table, between those betting on the myth of the Western to trump their opponent and those playing the bluff that the anti-Western can win the pot. If the analogy becomes strained, then it is no less so in the films themselves. 'Poker in the Western is at once a deeply serious activity and a marginal one,' wrote the film critic and Western connoisseur Philip French,

> Success is defined more by character than by skill, and personalities are determined more by character than by their attitude to the game and the way they play it. Those who devote themselves solely to poker as professionals, whether they be winners or losers, can never be accorded the centre of the stage, though they may have a certain superficial attraction for the audience and for women within the film.[12]

The reason the gambler cannot be the hero is a matter of character: his labours are essentially dishonest, he is an idler and a dandy. He is responsible to himself alone, committed only to his own cause. He therefore cannot be trusted, and his ethics are questionable. The possibility that a game has been fixed, that the gambler is a cheat, is always in play. Yet the card sharp is inexorably linked to the hero, who 'must be capable of acquitting himself well at the gambling table as proof of his manhood. Yet he should view the game philosophically and with detachment.'[13] This construct has

its embodied ideal in the matched characters of Doc Holliday and
Wyatt Earp in John Ford's *My Darling Clementine* (1946). An audience's acceptance of the distinction between gambler and hero,
a ready recognition of the formula, freed film-makers to use the
convention as the basis for establishing an anti-hero in the post-
Superwestern era. French identifies a small set of contemporary
films that did just this: *Doc, McCabe and Mrs Miller* and *The Life
and Times of Judge Roy Bean*.

The film critic for *Playboy* confirmed French's take on these
films in his review of *Doc*:

> [*New York Times*] columnist Pete Hamill wrote the scen-
> ario for *Doc*, a myth-debunking Western shot in Spain by
> director Frank Perry as if he wanted to make sure the myth
> was dead . . . [the] theme seems to be that all our mythic
> heroes were sick, dirty, violent, decadent and otherwise
> far from perfect creatures. So that's why the nation's values
> are screwed up.[14]

The marketing of the film echoed the critique. Publicity materials
used distorted portraits of the three protagonists – Doc Holliday
(Stacy Keach), Kate Elder (Faye Dunaway) and Wyatt Earp (Harris
Yulin) – with the tag: 'For the past 90 years these three people
have been heroes. Until now!' Alternative posters used 'There has
never been a Western like *Doc*' and 'Heroes aren't always beautiful'. The trailer employed these lines to introduce the three main
characters, beginning with Holliday: 'He gambled for a living and
killed for a hobby. He's spent seven years dying and he made damn
sure he didn't go alone.' That these were not the clean-cut heroes
of yesteryear was emphasized by first presenting Doc and Kate

Poster for *The Presbyterian Church Wager* (dir. Robert Altman, 1971),
later titled *McCabe and Mrs Miller*.

beneath a layer of grime so thickly laid on they looked as if they'd been shovelling coal on a tramp steamer. *The Life and Times of Judge Roy Bean* (John Huston, 1972) also began in the company of filthy and foul characters, grotesquely obese prostitutes and alcohol-puddled cowboys. *McCabe and Mrs Miller* similarly traded in dirt, but mud rather than soot was its considerably more artful way of besmirching its stars.

In the Fall 1972 edition of the then recently established academic *Journal of Popular Film*, PhD candidate Gary Engle argued that Altman's film was an 'anti-Western' that used the 'forms and themes of the conventional Western to systematically undercut the meanings traditionally associated with them'.[15] Like other scholars to follow, he based his analysis on John Cawelti's *Six Gun Mystique* (1971), published a year or so earlier and fast establishing itself as a cornerstone text in the new discipline of film studies. That book joined Jim Kitses's auteurist study of the Westerns of Mann, Boetticher and Peckinpah, *Horizons West*, published in 1969. Both books were focused on the structural issue of how shifting oppositions defined the form – wilderness versus civilization, individual versus community, nature versus culture, West versus East – with the hero acting as a mediating figure. These studies did not anticipate the more self-conscious Westerns of the period; rather they are part of the same cultural mix as the film-makers, like Altman, who were aware of the conventions of the formulas they were working with and who had imbibed enough of the modernist sensibility of European art house cinema and its critics (such as Bazin) to want to explore the history of those forms. Moreover, the cineaste was just as sensitive to the countercultural concern with colonial wars in East Asia, and the racial, sexual and gender dynamics of contemporary society as any academic cinephile. The countercultural and the anti-hero were well paired, producing echoes that emanated from scholar and film-maker alike.

Both parties were moving together towards a more committed and critically engaged form of working practice – one that did not shy away from the popular arts any more than from the day's politics. As a leading representative of this inchoate movement, Altman's intention with *McCabe*, wrote the *Los Angeles Times*'s critic, 'seems to have been to prove that you could de-mythologize a certain hunk of the Western past and still entertain – still sketch in the beginnings of a romance, in fact'.[16] The town of Presbyterian Church is 'hell upside down', bleak and miserable. Life is 'crude, raw, dumb, forlorn and hopeless. And Miss Christie's co-workers are a far cry from the dance hall girls of the mythic (Hollywood) past with the topless tutus of gold brocade and their peaches and cream complexions.'[17] The film's anti-hero and anti-heroine he considered to be contemporary constructs of a cynical society, though this is qualified by the picture being a 'star vehicle' in which 'the charm of its principals obscures the sardonic and corrective view of the past which, if I'm right, the movie had been intended to take'.[18]

The Life and Times of Judge Roy Bean also takes a carnivalesque turn and puts the world on its head. Paul Newman's Roy Bean is a hanging judge who dispenses summary justice, but he does so without fear or favour; all are equal who stand on his scaffold. Even when wrapped in the flag of Texas, he is without guile or cupidity. He may be an outlaw with a twisted neck masquerading as a judge, yet he is more honest and truer than any straight-backed magistrate who represents those who hide their hypocrisy behind a veil of respectability. Civilized and cultivated sensibilities destroy Roy Bean, not a faster gun or a more ruthless rival. The discovery of oil transforms his small town, yet it is not industry that vanquishes the frontier but universal suffrage. Women have the vote and drink-ing, gambling and whoring is declared illegal. The new times are owned by a generation of vipers, gangsters rule the streets and cops have become pimps. 'Beanism' is dead, but the myth lives on, and, for Texas and his fetish, Miss Lily Langtry, the spirit of Judge Roy Bean returns in the form of a vengeful angel. Like William S. Hart's character in *Hell's Hinges* (1916), he burns down the modern Sodom and Gomorrah. The town of Vinegaroon is reclaimed by the desert, all that remains is the train station and the saloon, now, fittingly for these modern, effeminized times, transformed into a museum dedicated to the judge's memory.

Judge Roy Bean is broad comedy, a bawdy comic-book tale. John Milius's script is an explicit homage to the frontier as the testing place of modern masculinity as expounded by the Eastern Establishment of Theodore Roosevelt, Owen Wister and Frederic Remington. The film might flirt with the contemporary appeal of the figure of the anti-hero, and push back a little against formu-laic tropes, but in the end it returns things to their proper place. *McCabe and Mrs Miller* is a very different proposition. *Playboy* enjoyed the film's setting and premise – a story based on gambling and prostitution – and considered Vilmos Zsigmond's cinematog-raphy 'superb, making the movie a feast for the eye in its images of a frontier town that gradually takes shape through a haze of kerosene fumes and cheap whiskey'.[19] But what was good about the film was lost when Altman decided to get serious about ideas: 'Before he is finished, Altman is up to his ears in allegory.'[20]

Like Altman, Philip French was also looking for such symp-tomatic analogies between films and society at large – defining Westerns in terms of whether they corresponded to the ideologies of John Kennedy, Barry Goldwater or Richard Nixon. In a less grand and forceful way he also argued there is an analogy to be made between poker and the Western.[21] Judge Roy Bean gestures to a similar set of concerns; in a voiceover a character says, 'I reckon poker has as much to do with winning of the West as Colt's 45 or the prairie schooner . . . more a religion than a game.' But this is just a general statement suggestive that gambling was a premise of westward expansion. In Altman's film it works differently.

The card game, French argues, can act as a microcosm of the narrative, commencing with the initial set-up, continuing with the deal and progressing through the play, in which 'courses of action are undisclosed, towards a final confrontation between two men'.[22] *McCabe and Mrs Miller* undoubtedly fits such a paradigm, even as it rearranges how the analogy might be understood. Between the set-up and the reveal, the film configures the game as a tale of aspirational endeavour – the gambler remade as an entrepreneur.

This was an entirely novel proposition. When the titular character, played by Warren Beatty, first arrives in Presbyterian Church he withholds his name but quickly acquires one when it is assumed, with no evidence whatsoever, that he is John 'Pudgy' McCabe, a gunman with a 'big rep'. Though he doesn't deny he's McCabe, he does counter the idea of his being a gunman by declaring himself to be a businessman – just and only that. On the frontier, who is there to dispute one's given or proffered identity?

The black derby hat he wears might suggest McCabe's mercantilist bona fides, but his gold tooth indicates otherwise (the dental cap matching Faye Dunaway's in *Doc*). His business is to turn games of chance to his advantage. To do this is less about his skill with the cards than his ability to distract the attention of his fellow players. His unearned reputation as a killer, a gunman, has value because his business is precarious, his holdings no more than his horse, pack mule and bankroll. His most saleable asset is the front he presents to the world. Businessman or not, beyond the game of poker that he organizes, he is an entertainer; a ribald wit and raconteur. It is all a show. He is an actor, his character questionable. The table, with its red cloth covering, is his stage. The transactions he parlays are based on the promise of delivering pleasure – men's comforts – which is why he expands his activities into drink and prostitution.

On McCabe's arrival, the town is no more than a few clapboard buildings, dishevelled tents, a muddy thoroughfare and an unfinished church, which sits a little above and away from the centre of things. The reason for the nascent community is a nearby mining operation that the film studiously avoids documenting – at no point is the labour involved in getting zinc to the surface, its processing and transportation, depicted. Instead it is the building of the town that is of interest. By the film's end there is a plethora of businesses: an undertaker and a dentist, a dry goods store, a haberdasher and seamstress, a bakery, a cobbler and barber. The town becomes big enough to offer such specialized places of commerce, even an opium den maintained by its much enlarged Chinese community. Among all this industry, McCabe, the very model of the enterprising businessman, is the most active. He has built a bar, gambling house, brothel and bathhouse.

McCabe was alive to the possibilities the growing mining town offered, but it is Mrs Constance Miller (Julie Christie) who shows him how to invest his money, how to organize and run his operation along efficient and rational lines that will maximize profits. Her experience in the white slave trade proves as invaluable to his fortunes as the order she brings to his bookkeeping. By working with Sheehan (René Auberjonois), who runs the saloon, McCabe ensures competitors are kept at bay. The two control the town's market in consumables and services, but as business grows its profitability becomes visible to others.

The M. H. Harris & Shaughnessy Mining Company send representatives to Presbyterian Church to buy out Sheehan's and McCabe's holdings and interests. Sheehan sells up quickly and without fuss, spending his money on Mrs Miller's prostitutes, but McCabe, with the instincts of a gambler, tries to outwit the two men he calls 'gimpers'. His bluff is called, and the men walk away. The deal comes to nothing, his negotiating skills useless in the face of big capital. McCabe's appeal to a lawyer for help elicits only a homily: 'I'm talking about busting up these trusts and monopolies . . . Somebody's got to protect the small businessmen from these companies.' In the end it comes down to McCabe against the company thugs, an uneven match.

Despite carrying the reputation of a gunfighter, McCabe poses no apparent threat to the three assassins. They are specialists in their trade, he is *just* a businessman, whose muttered mantra, 'Pain and money', is about to become all about the pain and nothing about the money. The youngest of the thugs is a towheaded punk kid who calls out Keith Carradine's nameless cowboy. In his high-crowned hat with its rolled brim, boots, chaps and shearling jacket, the cowboy, embodying the conventional heroic image, is dressed like Robert Mitchum in *Blood on the Moon* (1948). Except unlike Mitchum's, Carradine's character is guileless and gormless – a deformed caricature of the mythic figure, which is compounded by his brutal and senseless killing. Altman made his cowboy a comic figure and then guns down the myth, the assassin a runty, psychopathic street rat. (The following year, Michael J. Pollard portrayed a similar punk killer in *Dirty Little Billy*.)

The film reviewer for *Playboy* was clear on what the film-makers were attempting: 'Shooting down all the old myths about how the West was won – by fearless lawmen who marched up Main Street and gunned down the bad guys – Robert Altman . . . shows pioneer life the way it really was.'[23] But was Altman's film just an attempt to show the real West or did he have even bolder ambitions? 'What's the film about?' a reporter for the *Los Angeles Times* asked Altman, who bridled at the question: 'I can't tell you what this film is about. I don't want to tell you what my point is, and I don't even want to know myself what my point is.'[24] But Altman relents, or rather plays games with the reporter: 'This picture is the most ordinary, common western that's ever been told. It's every event, every character, every western you've ever seen. I picked the story because it's the conventional thing.'[25] He then provides a synopsis of the film, which, he says, is a 'cliché': 'All I'm trying to say is, yeah, these things happened but they didn't happen that way.' Altman eventually resorts to metaphor: the film is about 'a guy who is riding his bicycle with no hands down the street past his girlfriend's house and he gets hit by a Mack truck and killed, and she doesn't see him. She's on the telephone talking to another guy, and that's what it is about.'[26] Which, if you think about it, is what the film is about.

'An appalling plague has been loosed on our films,' wrote John Simon in September 1971 for a *New York Times* article.[27] With Hollywood facing 'hard times' and the 'big' movies no longer affordable, the studios, 'impecunious and desperate', have come up with an answer: 'You make your movie small, with any old script and any new talent (or lack of talent), and you douse it liberally with pretentiousness.'[28] There would not be a problem if the film was *L'avventura* or *Persona*, but instead they turned out to be, he wrote, *Two-Lane Blacktop* or *The Hired Hand*. Alongside such 'pretentious horrors' that also included *Carnal Knowledge, Johnny Got His Gun, The Go-Between, Deep End* and *The Devils* is Robert Altman's *McCabe and Mrs Miller*: 'Here half the dialogue is delivered sotto voce out of the corners of people's mouths in a remote corner of the screen, or entirely off it.'[29] Efforts at concentrating were not rewarded,

for there is not much to see in the film and even less to hear – often no more than a pretentious ballad by Leonard Cohen, the Rod McKuen of the coach trade . . . The film, moreover, is full of plot elements that are left dangling like a forgotten Pauline; but one imagines the filmmaker pontificating, 'Such is life!' – as if art were supposed to be brute, undigested existence. Not that Altman's film is that either, crawling with audio-visual mannerisms as it is.[30]

From being crowned the 'King of Hollywood Hills' after the box office success of *M*A*S*H* (1970), the tide had turned against Altman, reported the reviewer for the *Independent Film Journal*: 'with this languorous, curious western the critics, almost to a man, have shot the director down.'[31] This critic, however, was not of a mind to put in the boot with all the others. The movie, he wrote,

eventually transcends its tediousness to become a film of definite clout, and features Altman's most controlled direction to date. It is an extraordinarily beautiful-looking film, and with its emphasis on setting and the recreation of a time and place (the Pacific Northwest, Circa 1900) Altman could be considered an American Visconti.[32]

That comparison would not have caused Simon to reconsider his opinion as he thought *Death in Venice*, despite 'all its homosexual trimmings', very old-fashioned posturing and Visconti to be a 'vulgar, campy poseur from way back'.[33]

If the male critics, 'to a man', had dismissed *McCabe*, then the film's production company, Warner Bros., could at least turn to two female New York critics to help boost the movie's promotion. In *New York Magazine* Judith Crist applauded the film, which she wrote was a 'frontier ballad about a gambling man and a Madame who could have made it big but didn't'.[34] The stars' glamour is hidden within the characters they play, who are so firmly located in the world they inhabit they might have been photographed by Matthew Brady:

> Never have the crowded, scruffy, sweat-saturated hotel-bar lobbies of the 1900 mining town been so smokily recreated, the canvas constructions and their fresh-wood replacements set so truly on the hard terrain, the loneliness of the encampments and the sordidness of its pleasuredomes made so relevant to the affairs of the ant-like humans taking over the territory and despoiling it and each other.[35]

Pauline Kael thought the film not just a fine approximation of what 'frontier life might have been', but a 'beautiful pipe dream – a fleeting diaphanous vision' of that world. What Simon saw as ambiguity, things left hanging, Kael viewed as indirection, a method used to throw the viewer 'off base'. It is not like other Westerns, but then it is also not much like other movies, instead it is a 'figment of the romantic imagination'.[36] Above all, the film is a 'step toward a new kind of naturalism', a technique that may seem mannered to those who are put off by the violation of custom . . . The fact is that Altman is dumping square conventions that don't work anymore: the spelled-out explanations of motive and character, the rhymed plots, and so on – all those threadbare remnants of the 'well-made' play which American movies have clung to.[37]

Siding with Kael and Crist, John Weisman, writing for *Rolling Stone*, thought the film 'the most outstanding American film of the year'.[38] His reasoning was twofold: first, by 'breaking up the traditional form of the western movie, Altman gives that genre a kind of life and spontaneity it has never before had'.[39] Second, he uses a style that is 'elliptical, and often just plain hard to get used to . . . Instead of the normal sequencing of events and steady building of characters, Altman supplies fleeting glimpses of people caught in off-guard moments and snatches of conversations not meant to be heard.'[40]

Playboy published a three-page pictorial using publicity stills from the film photographed by Steve Schapiro. An image of Beatty wearing his derby and bearskin coat, on horseback with the church behind him, is the lead image along with one of Christie sitting on a bed in a state of dishabille, looking bored. Unlike the Westerns of old, *McCabe* 'shows pioneer life the way it really was'.[41] But the magazine is little interested in the muddy streets, the new cut timber buildings, the incessant rain followed by snow, and turns to a sequence of shots of the prostitutes in the bathhouse in which the desaturated yellow-orange lighting used by Zsigmond has the reds heightened to exaggerate the impression that these are period photographs, not publicity stills.

The concern with recreating a past, suggesting a historical verisimilitude that is credible, occupied the film-makers during

Warren Beatty and Julie Christie in *McCabe and Mrs Miller* (1971).

the planning and preparation stages – setting, costuming and
hairstyles all played against type and convention. Carradine's
cowboy caricature is there in good part because his outfit reminds
viewers just how far removed in their dress the other characters
are from what he represents. Locating the story in the dank, for-
ested and mountainous Pacific Northwest, rather than in a dry
desert region, further removed the film from the formulaic, and
the prostitutes look like real women rather than mannequins
in bustier corsets and bustle dresses. The British accents in the
film – Mrs Miller's cockney contrasted with the rounded vowels
of Butler, the assassin played by Hugh Millais, and the Scottish
brogue of one of the prostitutes – all play their part in its babble of
voices, as they also underpin the idea of the frontier community

formed from an Anglo-Celtic diaspora. These were all elements that reviewers picked up on and highlighted alongside the actual look of the film – the desaturated hues that give the exteriors, mud paths, autumnal deciduous trees and fresh-cut lumber an ochre patina that complements the interiors, which are lit as if by the dim glow of oil lamps. McCabe's bearskin coat, which he hides within, and Mrs Miller's unruly tangle of hair further enhance the film's elemental and primal aesthetic, as does Butler's wolfskin coat.

Rolling Stone's critic discussed the film's visual 'tone' as being 'one of a daguerreotype or faded tintype. Exteriors are hazy, evocative of Seurat's painting. The interiors, pumped full of yellow, have the sweaty, salty feel of a closed room. Yet *McCabe* doesn't have the warm nostalgia of, say, *Butch Cassidy*.'[42] The town is a 'muddy, horseshit-in-the-street settlement. The people smell bad and look worse . . . In every way, Presbyterian Church is the realest town ever built for a movie.'[43] 'Sud away mine grime for 25 cents', reads a sign on the side of McCabe's bathhouse.

The overlapping dialogue, which made some conversations all but indecipherable, made worse by the steady throb of the wind, had a correlative in the intentional degrading of the image through 'flashing', a process of pre-exposing the film stock to give a slightly fogged appearance that also brought out detail in the dark areas and highlighted colour in the shadows. This antiquing of the image, especially so in the early scenes, gives an effect of viewing the world through gauze or the veil of rain and snow. The elements of the *mise en scène* combine with the generic transgressions to produce one of the era's most compelling attempts at an authentic recreation of America at the turn of the century. It is a significant achievement, but then, as if on a whim, Altman brings his edifice of historical reality tumbling down by laying on the soundtrack a thick serving of Leonard Cohen.

The anachronistic use of the Cohen recordings did not faze the *Rolling Stone* critic: 'The totality of Altman's vision is astounding. Instead of a formal score, there are sparse, heady songs by Leonard Cohen that don't evoke emotional response so much as they serve as literal comment about the world of McCabe. They are immediate, of the moment.'[44] Which is to say, Altman pulled in three tracks from Cohen's debut album, reaching only as far back as 1967 for music that was contemporary with The Beatles' *Sgt. Pepper* and Bob Dylan's *John Wesley Harding*. The effect was to produce a profound tension between the film's representation of the past and its present.

The trio of tunes – 'The Stranger Song', 'Sisters of Mercy' and 'Winter Lady' – are all the non-diegetic music in the film. There is a good deal of other music to be heard, especially fiddle playing, notably that which accompanies the dancing of an inebriated miner slip-sliding away on the frozen river, as well as in the bar – the player sitting back behind the action, picking out notes as if his violin were a mandolin. A late addition to the pleasures of the town's brothel is a music box with an autochanger for its multiple discs – a modern object to rival the steam traction engine and the hand-pumped vacuum cleaner. Elsewhere, unaccompanied singing is heard; a flute is played and the chimes outside Mrs Miller's rooms temporarily relieve the coarseness of the howling wind. Against the anachronism of Cohen's music, 'Beautiful Dreamer' gets at least two airings; Stephen Foster's parlour tune, published in the 1860s, is heard in more Westerns than just about any other melody.

For a set of pre-existing songs, the alignment of Cohen's music with the film's themes is remarkable, but then he had always dug deep into exploring emotional attachments that last just a small moment in time, and that's what the film covers too.[45] 'The Stranger Song' is given to McCabe, 'Sisters of Mercy' accompanies images of the prostitutes, and 'Winter Lady' follows around Mrs Miller. Altman originally considered using at least ten of Cohen's songs before deciding on just these three.[46] He clearly worked to put song and image together in an arrangement that was mutually beneficial. In this he succeeded; it is impossible to imagine the film without Cohen's atonal, sonorous odes to fleeting love.

A review of *Songs from a Room* (1969), Cohen's second album, made the somewhat harsh but not unwarranted point that 'it doesn't take a great deal of listening to realize that Cohen can't sing, period . . . It's monotonous in a literal sense of the word. He seems to be sort of dragging one tone slightly up and down the chromatic scale. His voice almost never has an edge to it.'[47] He can be 'matter of fact to the point of being dull', or he is 'obscure' and 'just irritating'.[48] The critic continued, 'Cohen sings with such lack of energy that it's pretty easy to conclude that if he's not going to get worked up about it, why should we.'[49] That lethargy effectively adds to the film's sense of time drifting, a correlative to Mrs Miller's opium dreams – the narcoticized dissembling of the senses that plays soft and hard against the rapid unfolding of events after McCabe's gambler's bluff fails and the corporation send in their hired thugs.

Poet, novelist, singer, which one was Leonard Cohen? asked the critic Arthur Schmidt, who reviewed his debut album for *Rolling Stone*. He thought there were three songs that transcend the three categories, one of which is 'The Stranger Song', the theme for McCabe the character: 'The simplicity of the imagery does not interfere with the feelings of the characters nor the situation, nor do the images crowd the loneliness.'[50] There is in some of his work 'a kind of faith in the regenerative power of degeneration, of sadness, perhaps even of evil'.[51] This view of Cohen matched Altman's with *McCabe*, especially the use of religious symbols. McCabe is that everyman Joseph looking for a manger, just as Mrs Miller and her girls are Mary Magdalene figures in 'Sisters of Mercy'. The songs tend to make manifest the film's iconography – the church that no one prays in, the sometimes Christ-like appearance of McCabe, especially with the pietà of Mrs Miller cradling him before the final showdown – which threatens to topple the film over into a symbolic mess.

This was what Simon objected to in his column in the *New Leader* when he doubled down on the idea of Altman's film as affected and conceited, reserving particular scorn for the film's poor continuity, which he thought was only further disrupted by the 'recurring balladeering of Leonard Cohen, the Rod McKuen of the pseudoliterate'.[52] McKuen was an immensely popular poet and singer – who also made a cameo appearance in Vincent Canby's *New York Times* review of the film. He is used as a representative of the mid-cult confection of the tepid, ingratiating and the pretentious that Dwight Macdonald had documented. Canby wrote: 'The intentions of *McCabe and Mrs Miller* are not only serious, they are also meddlesomely imposed on the film by tired symbolism, by a folk-song commentary on the soundtrack that recalls not the old Pacific Northwest but San Francisco's Hungry i [a nightclub renowned for giving a stage to comedians such as Mort Sahl and Lenny Bruce and music acts such as The Kingston Trio and Laura Nyro].'[53] Charles Champlin for the *Los Angeles Times* thought the film as 'uneven as the stare of a cheap mirror', but he wouldn't have missed it.[54] That ambivalence continued into his take on the use of Cohen's songs. He did not consider them, like Canby, to be any worthier than a performance by McKuen for a ladies' afternoon meeting in the Russian Tea Room, and he did think they were a 'welcome change from the symphony' usually used on Western soundtracks.[55] He qualified this, however, by stating that for his own taste Cohen was 'a mite too austere and artful'.[56] That would also be a fair summation of Altman's film.

A year earlier, Sam Peckinpah had played with superficially similar materials in *The Ballad of Cable Hogue*. The film begins with the titular character, played by Jason Robards, being relieved of his mule and water by his two travelling companions. He is left to wander in the arid wasteland. On the fourth day, he collapses. In a state of delirium he finds he has mud on his boots: he digs into the wet ground, a puddle forms in the hole and he relieves his thirst with the earthy brew. He has found water 'where it wasn't'. Perhaps the subsequent story is all a death dream. Such a hallucination would explain his unlikely romance with Stella Stevens's

Cover of Leonard Cohen's *McCabe and Mrs Miller* EP (1971).

good-hearted prostitute, Hildy; his long-planned vengeance; and his eventual forgiveness of the two who abandoned him to his fate. Illiterate, filthy, in worn and tattered clothing and without collateral, Hogue manages to secure a loan from a philanthropic banker (if that is not a contradiction in terms) and commodifies and then monopolizes the supply of water to wayfaring strangers and the stagecoach company. His making something from nothing is an American fable of the entrepreneur.

Cable Hogue is hopelessly sentimental, as only Peckinpah could be, and has a score to match, which was overseen by Jerry Goldsmith, who worked with Richard Gillis on four songs: 'Tomorrow (Is the Song I Sing)', 'Wait for Me, Sunrise', 'Butterfly Mornings' and 'Wildflower Afternoons'. Sometimes Gillis is heard, at other times the characters tunelessly sing the songs to themselves. They are as saccharine as Andy Williams's 'Marmalade, Molasses and Honey', a ghastly number that performs the same function in *The Life and Times of Judge Roy Bean* as 'Raindrops Keep Falling on My Head' did in *Butch Cassidy and the Sundance Kid*. In such company, Cohen's appearance on the *McCabe* soundtrack comes across as the very model of decorum and reserve, adult in its sentiment, mature in its intent and not at all the mid-cult of Rod McKuen.

'Now across America, the star of stars is Julie Christie,' was how *Vogue* introduced her in 1966.[57] She was the winner of the New York Critics' best actress award for *Darling*, in which the magazine thought she had the

> look of a heroine written by a man ... [I]n *Doctor Zhivago*,
> she plays what she looks: romantic, withy in spirit, sensu-
> ally aristocratic, sexually superb, infinitely wise, and
> hung about with the intimations of tragedy that threatens

such scramblings of the human and divine . . . she knows
everything, gives everything, forbids everything final, and
tomorrow will leave town.[58]

Vogue defined Christie as a romantic free spirit, sensual, erotic,
intelligent, beautiful, experienced and finally refusing commitment
– a male fantasy certainly, but one that suggests Christie might
play the female lead in a Hawks movie, a contemporary equivalent
of Lauren Bacall in *To Have and Have Not* (1944), Jean Arthur in
Only Angels Have Wings (1939) or Angie Dickinson in *Rio Bravo*
(1959). Writing in 1970 about 'The Hawksian Woman', Naomi Wise
defined his heroines against the limited roles given to women more
generally: 'In most of Hawks's adventure films, women play con-
sequential roles; in fact, the heroines are, if anything, superior to
the heroes. The good girl and bad girl are fused into a single, heroic
heroine, who is both sexual and valuable.'[59] Working through this
idea, Wise wrote:

> Hawks's films frequently show a merging of sexual roles
> for the benefit of both sexes – the women learn certain
> 'masculine' values while the men become 'feminized'.
> Frequently, the men have more to learn (and to gain) than
> the women, who are already mature at each film's begin-
> ning . . . The men tend to suffer from emotional blocks
> that keep them from full self-realization, while the women
> need merely to adjust to a particular situation.[60]

Beatty's and Christie's characters conform to this paradigm:
he needs her more than she needs him. As McCabe pursues his
romantic inclinations, Mrs Miller keeps their relationship to strictly

commercial transactions; even their lovemaking involves the exchange of money. She is the businessperson he claims to be, she the realist, he the romantic. McCabe's refusal to see the reality of the situation they find themselves in when he turns down the company's offer is not lost on Mrs Miller. She reads their predicament clearly and dispassionately. In the end she opts for the pipe dreams of the opium den rather than the mortal obliteration of the gunfight. Tomorrow she will leave town, McCabe is going nowhere.

The final tableaux of a frozen McCabe being covered in snow and the tracking shot into Mrs Miller's narcotized eye, the pair separate but linked through the parallel editing, confirm the film's anti-classical position, which rejects a neat resolution. The formation of the couple is now an impossibility. But, even in the moment of its negation of Old Hollywood, the film is still in thrall to the actors' star power. The ending confirms the image of Christie described by *Vogue*, which had regularly featured her in fashion spreads since she made her name with *Darling* (1965) – which, if set sixty or so years earlier, would have provided Mrs Miller's missing backstory, just as her role as Lara in *Doctor Zhivago* (1965) would have, too. Christie was a fetish for her times.

Christie's frizzed-out shock of hair in *McCabe and Mrs Miller* adds another layer to the fetishizing of her presentation, which functions much in the manner of the blonde ponytail she wore in David Lean's film, the mane and pelt a Freudian externalization symbolically covering the void beneath – the site of male arousal and fear. Photographed in 1970 by Richard Avedon for *Vogue*, Christie's new haircut caused the magazine's editor to become quite worked up. The style was a layered cut given to her by Barry of The Crimpers in London and then curled by Paul in New York, creating 'a downy blond innocence of curls, shaking out ringlets everywhere until it looked like the way children's hair does when it's tousled by a nice summer sleep. Delicious.'[61] All this was done, *Vogue* noted, just before shooting started on her new movie, 'The Presbyterian Church Wager'.

Three months later, and the film's title still not changed to *McCabe and Mrs Miller*, *Vogue* stayed with the hair totem when it did a similar profile of Christie's co-star, also photographed by Avedon:

> Growing a beard is a wilful, sometimes playful gesture for a man. It's a declaration of independence better suited to emperors and generals than servitors. It's the perfect insouciant move for Warren Beatty; his beard, which grows as thick, shiny, and chestnut-dark as his hair, is the perfect frame for the famous, boyish Beatty smile, the wicked gleam of the Beatty eyes.[62]

The film's main star was no more able to hide behind his beard, to lose himself in his character, than Christie managed with her cockney accent and her Elsa Lanchester *Bride of Frankenstein* hairdo.

One critic, spinning his review around a comparison of Bogart as Fred C. Dobbs and Beatty as McCabe, discussed the need for a director to balance comedy with despair:

> The hole in Fred C. Dobbs's hat may mock his pretensions to fierce, manly pride, but it dignifies them at the same time, for we cannot help but respect a man who wears so fiercely a hat so absurd. When the things are permitted merely to mock the characters, you get confusion or, at best, a 'spoof'. When the actuality works both ways, you get real pathos.[63]

The trouble with *McCabe*, wrote Jackson Burgess, is that Beatty is no Bogart:

> The air of commonplace madness which Bogart put into a line like, 'I'll show him he can't mess around with Fred C. Dobbs, nossir!' is not in Beatty's range. One problem is that he is ineluctably handsome. They say that a really beautiful woman cannot be funny; I think the proposition is even more true of a really handsome man. It is not Beatty's comedic talents which fail, however, but his ability to be at once mildly comic and deeply serious. He is a theatrical, even stagy, actor, and for this kind of gritty actuality film demands not an actor who does, but an actor who is: Bogart, Brando before he started reaching too hard, sometimes Sterling Hayden and Robert Mitchum. Beatty is in the line of Gable, not of Bogart.[64]

Being pretty or handsome is rarely conceived as a trait of the authentic, regardless of the dirt or hair used to hide the actor's beauty, but even as Altman failed with Beatty he succeeded with Christie. *McCabe and Mrs Miller* resonates between artifice and art, with Altman gambling that neither held a winning hand, so enabling the authentic to play alongside the anachronistic. All the while, he gestured to cultures low, middle and high as he toyed with sentiment and romance, but not so much as to obscure his withering story of modern capital and industry. With the moves he made, sleights of hand included, Altman showed he was a better card player, a better reader of his audience, than John 'Pudgy' McCabe.

7

Pat Garrett and Billy the Kid: Angels Descend and Graves Open

It will be terrible to see.

The Seventh Seal (dir. Ingmar Bergman, 1957)

'**I** don't know whether *Pat Garrett and Billy the Kid* will be a great rock 'n' roll western or merely a machismo wet dream,' *Creem*'s Dave Marsh wrote in his on-location report for America's hip rock journal.[1] The casting of Kris Kristofferson as Billy and Bob Dylan as Alias was a ready-made, much-repeated link between the counterculture and Old West gunfighters. But while there is no doubting that Dylan and Kristofferson were part of the rock establishment, and in the former's case its figurehead, whether or not they were rock 'n' roll outlaws is open to conjecture.

Neither star carried the attitude and style of a young Elvis or posed with the punkish threat of Gene Vincent; in Kristofferson's case he never had, and Dylan had not cut such a stance since 1966, when his motorcycle accident called an end to his aggressive, amphetamine-fuelled phase. What both *were* symptomatic of was the malaise rock found itself in as the 1960s turned into the 1970s. The second generation of rockers, personified by Dylan, Lennon and Jagger, who had followed the lines laid down by Presley, Chuck

Berry and Buddy Holly, were tipping into their thirties in a game that was defined by youth.

In his 1968 study *Bomb Culture*, Jeff Nuttall had written that Dylan was the 'first sign that popular music was transcending its commercial situation', an idea he located in the broad-based acceptance of the 'profound sourness' in the singer's delivery of his songs, an antidote to over-sweetened pop.[2] When the film was shot, Dylan was 32 years old, ten years had passed since that initial impact Nuttall had marked, and Kristofferson was four years older still. Talking to Robert Hilburn, screenwriter Rudy Wurlitzer told him, 'I always thought of Dylan as Billy the Kid. He even looks like Billy the Kid, very young-looking with that combination of coldness and detachment, then sudden warmth. He can have incredible vitality one minute yet be removed the next.'[3] A good part of the legend of Billy the Kid rests on his youth: 21 notches on his gun by the time he reached 21 years of age, when, in turn, Pat Garrett, 31, gunned him down. In his thirties, sullen, baby-faced, Michael J. Pollard just about pulled off the illusion of being a teenager in *Dirty Little Billy*, but, at 36, that was never an option for Kristofferson. Reporting from the film's set, Hilburn noted that Dylan was accompanied by his wife Sara and their five children.[4] It was a remark that aged him beyond his years. Kristofferson and James Coburn, 44 years old, were announced as co-stars as early as November 1972 in the *Los Angeles Times*; Dylan was confirmed at the start of December.[5] If the film's producers wanted a rock 'n' roller to play the Kid as a callow youth then they'd have cast Iggy Pop, but who would hang a big-budget movie on a noble savage with little or no name recognition outside the readership of *Creem*?

Dylan and Kristofferson could sell the movie. While not exactly universal, Dylan's appeal was broad enough and hip enough to attract the 16–30 age range of habitual filmgoers who increasingly filled the run-down inner-city theatres that family audiences had long abandoned in their flight to the suburbs. Kristofferson, it was no doubt assumed, similarly connected to the drive-in and Southern market that later 1970s fare like *Smokey and the Bandit* (1977) and the following year's *Convoy*, in which he starred and Peckinpah directed, would successfully exploit.

In the issue of *Creem* that carried Marsh's report, Nick Tosches had reviewed *Payday*.[6] Rip Torn's character has more than a few similarities to Harry Dean Stanton's in *Cisco Pike*. Both flared brightly and paid the hedonist's price for their pleasures. The counter to the picture of fame's victims was that promoted by Kristofferson – a man openly and honestly struggling with his addictions and frailties, rather than succumbing to them. Johnny Cash and Merle Haggard also played that side of the road, as did Waylon Jennings; he too featured in the July 1973 edition of *Creem*. 'If I was everything people make me out to be,' he told Chet Flippo, 'I'da been dead long ago.'[7] But ladies love outlaws.

In the photographs illustrating the spread, Jennings is dressed like a spruced-up version of one of Peckinpah's extras: cowboy boots, dark-hued Stetson, black leather pants and waistcoat. Flippo describes him as a 'renegade country singer . . . a man who knows what he wants and will take no shit, a man's man. An anachronism, too.'[8] Isn't such masculinity always a thing of the past? Jennings is playing a gig in Gallop, New Mexico, in a high school gym. It isn't Carnegie Hall, but he has chosen to play there. The most ardent members of his audience are young Navajos. He identifies with them and they with him: 'They respect him. He sings *to* them, not down to them.'[9] 'Perhaps', Flippo continued, 'it was a historical warp that united them as opposite poles of an ethos: a century ago they might have been braves and he an outlaw but they would have shared a common freedom and a certain frontier ethic.'[10] Jennings, Flippo wrote, had rejected and renounced the Nashville establishment as relics who disrespected Hank Williams: 'Well those relics *couldn't make it now*,' said Jennings, and then echoed Pat Garrett's mantra: 'They still can't see that times have changed.'[11]

Peckinpah was not interested in using the Western as an allegory of the 1960s counterculture and the generation gap; his film was not going to be *Easy Rider* or *Five Easy Pieces* on horseback, but it would be about that anachronistic masculinity Flippo saw in Jennings. The ageing of his legendary protagonists was intentional, times had changed. That was his theme. Paul Seydor, author of a history of the film, argues that the maturation of the legend's key protagonists was based on Peckinpah's decision to make his story centre on Garrett rather than Billy.[12] Following a tendency in critical discussions of Peckinpah, Seydor provides a biographical reading of the film, writing that the casting of Coburn was done to better align Garrett's and Peckinpah's ages.[13] But more important than any vanity project that Peckinpah might have been indulging, which I doubt anyway, is that the main characters have lived long enough to credibly carry the film's theme and its concomitant that the story was about the end of days.

The attenuation of youth is the tale told; it is not a story of youth's promise. As to historical truth, in response to an early draft of the screenplay Peckinpah wrote: 'Because we are dealing with a legend everyone seems to feel that it must be authentic. I am not interested in authenticity. I am interested in drama.'[14] Kevin Thomas caught the essence of *Pat Garrett and Billy the Kid* in his review for the *Los Angeles Times*: 'Never has Peckinpah made his recurrent preoccupation, the death of the Old West, suggest so strongly that it also signifies the beginning of the end of freedom in America . . . [The film] is not against law and order but quietly asks who it serves.'[15]

Coburn told the writer Garner Simmons that 'the interesting thing about Kris was the boyish quality he brought to the part of Billy . . . Sam saw the kind of brash naiveté in Kris that really made Billy come alive on screen.'[16] That 'boyishness', however, is conveyed by a mature man. Quoting that exchange between Coburn and Simmons, Seydor also considered Peckinpah's casting decision to be motivated by a need to suggest a sense of dissipation in Billy's character, something that the director had heard in songs like 'Sunday Mornin' Comin' Down' and 'Help Me Make It through the Night'.[17] 'All my bottoms are ups – in the end,' Kristofferson told a *Chicago Tribune* reporter. *Cisco* had been a 'fiasco' but he was learning the ropes, starting from scratch with acting and the movies.[18]

The idea of Kristofferson playing a character whose youth is in his past is accentuated in the description of him given by the *Tribune* reporter: 'His 5-foot-11, 170-pound frame seems cherubic and slightly abandoned to flab. The smile isn't quite there and hints at more serious, but inarticulate thoughts.'[19] Kristofferson brought with him to the figure of Billy a vulnerable-toughness that one reporter who witnessed his debut at the Troubadour thought similar to what 'F. Scott Fitzgerald did in another age', writing that 'Kristofferson is a romantic (rather than political) spokesman for the time. His music is filled with loneliness, struggle and irony. But there are also moments of triumph.'[20] Such responses to his work added to the sense of correctness in casting him and, according to the *Tribune* reporter, it was also because 'the time is ripe for plain-faced heroes with working-class backgrounds. America is getting back to its roots again after washing the pretty boys out of its hair, and nobody could be more basic than Kris.'[21]

Whatever authenticity he had been accredited with, and however plain-faced he may have been, Kristofferson's working-class credentials were always a complete fiction. He was, as Craig McGregor wrote in the *New York Times*, 'A middle-class drop out', like Ramblin' Jack Elliott and Bob Dylan and other 'contemporary "folk" artists . . . And like them, he seems to have undergone a long process of identity transfer: having rejected their own background, they have been forced to discover a new persona for themselves.'[22] The down-home side of his persona was part of his act, but it was not so well carried off that he could fool all the people all the time. In the sleeve notes to a collection of Kristofferson's song demos, Merle Haggard, who *was* the very thing Kristofferson posed as, wrote, 'you can tell he doesn't expect anything and here he is getting everything. He's always been that way.' Like Nicholson's character in *Five Easy Pieces*, Kristofferson was a privileged dropout, a fully paid-up member of the bourgeoisie who liked to go slumming with the wild boys and was practised at passing as a John Doe figure (if that was what you wanted from him).

The appeal of Kristofferson's suggestion of authenticity was not denied by reporters for the British and American music press, but it counted for little against the presence of Dylan in the cast of *Pat Garrett*. *Melody Maker*'s Michael Watts joined the film set in Durango, Mexico, and all but short passages of his long account of his time south of the border was taken up with Dylan. He accepted that Dylan was cast because of his potential box office appeal and that the choice enabled the possibility of dramatizing the 'old America meeting the new, the traditional values of the West encountering the pop surrealism of the East. It was a symbolic meeting of two vastly different generations, of two attitudes to life.'[23] He thought the crucial aspect was that 'he is the aging and long-appointed prophet, who has grown old and increasingly distant in a role which for years has held for him no relevance, yet which seems effectively to have constrained his talents.'[24] Since his self-imposed quasi-retirement from public life, with no tours and only intermittent recording, Dylan 'has been away too long now to return to the heart of the action with the same pertinence as before, even if he wished to'.[25] The movies, Watts thinks, might be Dylan's way out and path back to a valid creative profile.

Media access to any of the principal actors was limited, and in Dylan's case just plain out of the question, so screenwriter Rudy Wurlitzer acted as an intermediary for the visiting rock critics. He told Watts:

Pat and Billy were two gunmen who essentially felt a kinship but had chosen two diametrically opposed roles in life, the former as a sheriff, the latter as an outlaw. Thus they were symbols of a changing America in the last century: the one a roving free spirit, symbolising the pioneer nature of the Old West; the other selling out to the Establishment for a steady job and security, representing, therefore, the solidifying respectability of the new America.[26]

But for Dylan his role was more personal, as Watts explained:

He was a whole era of youth coiled into one man and now slowly winding down into the years past 30, and the consciousness of this had escaped no one, least of all him, with his eyes set straight and stonily to the front lest he

be forced to pick up those curious sidelong glances, as a
magnet does iron filings.[27]

However much Dylan tried to avoid eye contact, his very presence on the set left him impuissant, powerless to alter the fact of
his myth: 'Durango . . . it's a strange dark place to make a film,'
Wurlitzer told Watts. '"Everyone gets so exposed." He whispered
the last sentence.'[28] The temptation was to search constantly for
parallels in the story the film told, and in the legendary figure
of Billy, with the lives and careers of its three key protagonists,
Peckinpah, Dylan and Kristofferson. They were there, but if you
cared to look more coolly at all the action then the message was
more sanguinary than celebratory.

'Rock Stars on Film? It's Mind-Blowing!' was the headline
given to Lillian Roxon's review of *Pat Garrett* in New York's *Sunday
News*. Her review began with a disclaimer: 'I'm not a film critic, and
I really can't tell you if Sam Peckinpah's *Pat Garrett and Billy the Kid*
is a good film. Probably not. It moves a little slowly.'[29] New York
correspondent for the *Sydney Morning Herald*, Roxon also wrote
the weekly 'The Top of Pop' column for the *News*. If she could not
speak with authority on film, she could tell you all you needed to
know about the pop and rock scenes. Should a Dylan fan see this
film? she asked. 'All I can say is yes, absolutely. Don't think twice
about it. My mind is still shattered from the experience of seeing
"him" on the screen.'

> Remember in the old days when they never used to want
> to show Jesus on the screen, and you had to be content
> with a view of His back or a disembodied hand? Then
> one day, it was OK, and you got this really weird feeling

looking at Jeffrey Hunter as Jesus in *King of Kings*. There was something about his eyes.

I want to warn you right now that there's nothing God-like about Bob's appearance in the film. Quite the opposite, but somehow *that* was what was mind-shattering – to see him, after all these years of mystery and veneration, the prophet of our generation, as a punk kid, a very punk kid, a kid that would have difficulty getting into Max's Kansas City, let alone the lobby of the Sherry Netherland, a place he could probably buy if he felt like it.

What you see on the film, and this is why I love it and think it's historically important for those of you too young to have that perspective, is not the Guru Dylan, or the father and family man, the millionaire songwriter, the culture hero, but the kid who came to New York from Minnesota back in the early '60s.[30]

For Roxon, Dylan on-screen loses ten years. Times had clearly changed – 'the nostalgia of it knocks you for a loop.'[31]

She did not much care for the film's attempts at historical accuracy – she thought it would be a better film, funnier certainly, if Kristofferson's character had been coupled with Brigitte Bardot or Sophia Loren. The film would also have benefited if 'all those endless bearded outlaws' had been 'played by The Band':

In the best movie tradition, there could have been cameo appearances by other rock notables. David Crosby as the crazed religious fanatic jailer who got his in the end. Manager Albert Grossman as the wily bartender. Carole King as Ruthie Lee . . . The Allman Brothers could have walked onto the set of this film without raising an eyebrow. The spry old retainer who brings Kris his horse after he escapes the gallows reminded me for all the world of Papa John Creach. Even James Coburn reminds me of an older version of former *Creem* magazine editor Dave Marsh. Same even features and watchful expression. In this context, Kris Kristofferson is very satisfying as Billy the Kid, galloping around, acting out his fantasies and having a good time. Only Loudon Wainwright III has a more homicidal grin.[32]

Roxon flowed on, finding parts for Janis Joplin and Jim Morrison, if they hadn't died. Her point was that the film provided an answer to the question, long asked by the rock community, 'we want to make a film, but how can we make one that's different from other rock and roll films?'[33] Roxon's recasting of Peckinpah's film certainly took a step towards answering Marsh's question about whether it was a 'great rock 'n' roll Western or merely a machismo wet dream'.[34] It was neither, exclusively, but if it had been as Roxon imagined it wouldn't have been quite so much of the latter.

Pat Garrett and Billy the Kid is about the monetization of the West, the fencing in of the range, and the limits commercial opportunity puts on choice. It is about moral turpitude and violence, as practised by individuals and by corporations; and it is about friendship pure and tainted. And, because it is Peckinpah, it is about masculinity. These are the themes most often identified in critical interventions, but they are arguably all subservient to a core concern with death. The world Billy and Garrett inhabit is not in transition, it has already ended. 'These are the cats who ran out of

Covers of the Eagles' *Desperado* LP (1973) and Donnie Fritts's
Prone to Lean LP (1974).

territory and know it,' *Rolling Stone* reported Peckinpah as saying, 'but they don't bend, refuse to be diminished by it. They play their string out to the end.'[35]

Towards the film's conclusion, Peckinpah appears before his own camera. He is making a child's coffin. Garrett pauses and acknowledges him; the director looks off-screen and tells him to get it done. Long delayed, Garrett's final assignation with Billy is about to play out and his rendezvous with myth is about to begin. Unlike the knight in Bergman's *Seventh Seal*, who, facing death, continues to pursue his quest for knowledge only to discover that the end itself holds no secrets, is in fact the absolute converse of knowing, Garrett refuses to search for answers. He does not ask questions of death, he just acts, and then only to postpone the final, fatal decision to kill Billy and thus himself. Whatever ability he had for self-reflection he has expunged, like his mirror image that he shoots after the assassination. Garrett's philosophy is solipsistic; he is but a pawn in life's chess game, his scheming never going further than the next move he is required to make.

The film begins, at least as Peckinpah envisioned it, at the end, with the assassination of an older Pat Garrett by the forces he had aligned himself with and for whose gold and grace he had betrayed his friendship with Billy. Processed in monochrome, the images of Garrett's death are intercut with a scene from years before, set in 1881 in Fort Sumner, where Billy and his boys are killing the day by drinking and shooting the heads off chickens buried in the dirt up to their necks. The death scene will be replayed at film's end, creating a framing effect, a formal affirmation of the film's theme of life as a series of returns.

In a Fort Sumner cantina, the estranged friends share a glass of whisky. Pat gives Billy his ultimatum: quit the territory, go to

Mexico or in five days he will come for him. The electorate, the Sante Fe Ring, want Billy gone. Times *have* changed, and Garrett tells Billy he aims to change with them, but if he ever had the choice to make such a change it has long since gone. Both men are anachronisms, out of place and out of time, it's just that Garrett's string will take a little longer to play out.

After a shoot-out at a small, isolated ranch building, Billy is captured and jailed in Lincoln. In the street outside a scaffold has been erected, children swing in its noose and the Stars and Stripes flutters on a flagpole nearby. The juxtaposition of the elements is as heavily overloaded in its symbolism as an isolated shot of Billy on horseback, hindered in his drift by a barbed wire fence. Such images are signposts, but ones with little value because the characters are already at the end of the world. They have nowhere to go but into the void.

As he again sets off in pursuit of Billy, Garrett deputizes Alamosa Bill and coaxes Sheriff Cullen Baker to aid him in his quest. The two are played respectively by Jack Elam and Slim Pickens. Both are killed, both deaths taking on an elegiac dimension, extended and sentimentalized. When Garrett encounters him, Cullen is working on a boat, which, when finished, he hopes to use to float out of the territory, but the vessel he is fashioning is in truth the coffin that will ferry him across the Styx. Alamosa's casket will be made from a cottonwood door, entry and exit.

The casting of elderly Western stalwarts Elam and Pickens was echoed with bit parts for Chill Wills, Gene Evans, Dub Taylor and Elisha Cook Jr. The latter two are placed as if holding a seat in God's shabby, flea-infested waiting room. These old men carry with them the stink of carrion, the promise of their youth, if they ever had that, lost to madness. When the two are beaten by the Sante Fe's stooge, Poe, to elicit the whereabouts of the Kid, Peckinpah creates a genuine sense of the brutality of the new order. But elsewhere, where a memento mori aesthetic, like the child's coffin he is shaping, was called for to better exemplify the pathos he was trying to capture and create through the use of these character actors, Peckinpah instead too readily traded in a lachrymose, Victorian sentimentality. This is especially true of his favoured trope of portraying Mexican peasants as salt-of-the-earth paragons of untrammelled virtue, a romanticization that colours purple the death of Paco (Emilio Fernández), whose dying words to Billy are about his dream of a house with a vine-covered veranda. Such sentimentality exists to soften the male narcissism of Peckinpah's collection of sociopaths, but it also blights the film's grave's-edge philosophy.

At one point Billy says, 'There's gonna be some hard times coming down,' but his hombres can barely raise a response. Range-worn and beaten, only Pat and Billy can muster the energy for a shave. Every other character looks as if they have not seen a razor in a month of Sundays; even Dylan sports a little peach fuzz on his cheeks. Garrett grows and crops moustaches between scenes, showing little care for continuity. The Kid alone is clean-shaven.

While the supporting cast look like they have been baked in the dirt of New Mexico, barely discernible from the adobe walls they lean against, Billy and Pat are at times costumed in raven black, giving them definition and a distinctiveness. But where Garrett wears his three-piece, matching hat and boots with an air of a boulevardier stepping out onto the boardwalk after his toilette, the Kid doesn't seem to be able to keep his pants clean or his white shirt tail tucked in. Through such devices – costume, male grooming, the grey in Pat's hair against the dark of Billy's – Peckinpah establishes a generational divide between the two protagonists. Yet Billy is no callow youth.

Two years on from his role in *Cisco Pike*, Kristofferson has put on a little weight. He has got jowly, puffy cheeks push his already deep-set eyes back further into his head. He looks like he has the onset of an alcoholic's bloat, has been to one too many parties. He plays his part as if he were suffering a loss of appetite for life, even if against Harry Dean Stanton, with whom he is reunited here, he maintains a certain youthfully dissolute appearance. Living, for Billy, has become a dull business full of longueurs and passages of ennui.

Breaking bread with Governor Wallace (Jason Robards) and the Sante Fe Ring, Garrett turns down their offer of paying a bounty on the Kid. His principles are performative, after the fact. He has already sold out Billy and all he once believed in. Was this where Dylan now found himself? It was a question somewhat posed by the rock critics who visited the set.

Dave Marsh in his report on the film shoot in Durango and his review that followed a month later considered Peckinpah the 'greatest contemporary American director' and that 'his Westerns are virtually unmatched in the history of the movies', but *Pat Garrett and Billy the Kid* was a mess: clumsy, confused, amateurish and sloppy. 'This may not be entirely Peckinpah's fault – being saddled with four rock stars may be enough to defeat the very best – but it is Peckinpah who is going to have to live with the failure, not Kris Kristofferson, Bob Dylan, Rita Coolidge or Donnie Fritts.'[36] Rounding up a small run of recent Western releases, Jon Landau in *Rolling Stone* reviewed the film alongside *High Plains Drifter* (Clint Eastwood) and *Kid Blue* (James Frawley). He argued that Peckinpah's themes, were reductive, 'unambiguous' with 'simplistic values; straight choices: conform or die':

Peckinpah is interested only in the reverberations of the past: he disdains the details of storytelling, characterization and acting style . . . He photographs every frame in a luscious way that cries out for consideration as visual mythology, but his inattention to anything that might make it such leaves his movie looking more like a lavish, coffee-table edition of a Classics Illustrated comic book.[37]

And Dylan? He is 'history's most nervous cowboy', and even if his part is 'minuscule and his role barely defined', his 'mere presence is compelling'. But Dylan does not save the film, which Landau thought a 'very bad movie'.[38]

In the following month's edition of the magazine, Landau reviewed the soundtrack album, which he wrote was an 'extension of its myth-destroying predecessor *Self-Portrait*, a record which further eliminated the possibility of anyone placing Bob Dylan on a pedestal'.[39] Though Landau did not make this point, Dylan was, like Billy, going in ever-decreasing cycles, perpetuating an act of self-annihilation. The album did have its supporters. Paul Nelson thought it 'reinvestigated the old myths, albeit mostly without words. "Knockin' on Heaven's Door" and especially the instrumental, "Final Theme," are songs well suited for either weddings or funerals' – a given value, however, that suggested he wasn't that convinced of its merits.[40]

In his *New Musical Express* review of the soundtrack album, Roy Carr was not prone to play with ambiguity: 'What I have before me constitutes yet another chapter in the decline of perhaps the most important individual performer of the last 25 years.'[41] Carr continued, 'It is as though he was purposely attempting to commit professional and artistic suicide . . . Seemingly, only one cut

Sam Peckinpah and Rudy Wurlitzer on the set of *Pat Garrett and Billy the Kid* (1973).

emerges from those highly publicized midnight-to-dawn tequila-soaked Mexico City sessions – the rest of the pap being hastily slung together in beautiful downtown Burbank.'[42] Those Mexican recording sessions had been heavily trailed in the music press, suggesting this was the real business, the true creative reason for the coming together of such talent below the border.

Chet Flippo's on-location report for *Rolling Stone* began with him witnessing the scene where chickens are used for target practice. Wurlitzer told the reporter that he had only one hen in his script, but Peckinpah upped the quota. The hip author is put up against the visionary director, and both are contrasted with John Wayne, whose Batjac productions were shot nearby to where much of *Pat Garrett and Billy the Kid* was being staged. Peckinpah appeared to be spinning out of control, the film was behind schedule and over budget. Wurlitzer told Flippo that the director's job was to turn the prosaic into something flashy, so that the audience was not aware of the genre's banality. 'That's Westerns, though,' he said.[43]

Peckinpah is only nominally in charge, and Dylan and his entourage duck out of a preview screening of *The Getaway* the director has organized. The band of musicians and actors head off to Mexico City for a 'recording session because that's heavier'.[44] Dylan told the writer,

> Rudy needed a song for the script. I wasn't doing anything. Rudy sent the script, and I read it and liked it and we got together and he needed a title song. And then I saw *The Wild Bunch* and *Straw Dogs* and *Cable Hogue* and liked them. The best one is *Ride the High Country*. Sam's really, like he's the last of a dying breed. They don't hire people like that to make movies anymore. So I wrote that song real quick and played it for Sam and he really liked it and asked me to be in the movie. I want now, to *make movies*. I've never been this close to movies before. I'll make a hell of a movie after this.[45]

Like Peckinpah's Billy, Dylan was playing to type even as he pushed back against convention and expectation. In his report of the recording session, Flippo noted that Dylan's singing initially recalled his *Another Side* era, but then he began to play with the song. Wurlitzer got all lit up by Dylan's shifting style: 'Hey man, do you dig what he's *doing*? He's *changed* the song. He's being perverse, man. See, he got fucked and now he's gonna do it *his* way.'[46] But where did that way lead? Dylan is so burdened with his own legend that it diminished him as it aggrandized his past achievements. All that could be seen is all that he was. The best of him was behind him, just as it was for Billy. It was indeed terrible to see.

Conclusion:
Bring Me the Head

Stax Records began a new promotional campaign in 1973, one that drew on an existing understanding that its artists were the genuine, authentic item: 'GUTS is the music you feel. Not just hear. Music from the guts of America. From Memphis. From Stax. R&B, Pop, Rock, Gospel, when it's Stax, it's guts. Honest, basic, straight. Like Stax itself.' And like dirt, guts signified an essential truth – it was the real that countered the phoney. Against the pop blandishments made by other companies, Stax recordings were visceral – somatic music that hit you in the belly. *Bring Me the Head of Alfredo Garcia* (1974) was similarly marketed as having 'GUTS': 'You've either got them, or you don't. Sam Peckinpah had the guts to bring a new kind of violent reality to the screen in *The Wild Bunch* and *Straw Dogs*.' Praised and attacked, his latest film will also 'provoke controversy' but, like its maker, it is 'uncompromising, unyielding, uncensored. In short, it's got guts.' It was film and music promoted as elemental, instinctual and physical – the real.

The campaign for *Alfredo Garcia* also sold the film as a 'new classic in the mold of *Treasure of Sierra Madre*' – the ghost of Fred C. Dobbs still haunted American movies. *Variety* thought the film a 'turgid melodrama' that, despite the 'vast carnage' unleashed, had a 'nothing impact':

> One could possibly get carried away with the apparent philosophical ideas churned over in the script – irrational human goals achieved through extraordinary human labor, all for nothing. There is a passing script reference to the lead character in *Treasure of the Sierra Madre*, which nobody in grammar school film class will miss, but any attempt to hang this inferior film on its spiritual source will require the most specious intellectualizing.[1]

Intellectually specious or not, *Alfredo Garcia* proceeds on the idea held by Bennie (Warren Oates) that 'no man loses all the time'. His belief that the odds are not always stacked against him, that he isn't a loser, drives Bennie to pursue the reward of $10,000 for the head of Alfredo Garcia. His ambition will cost the lives of many, himself included as well as that of Elita (Isela Vega), the woman he has promised to marry and who was once Garcia's lover.

The walls of Bennie's rundown Mexican apartment are decorated with nude pin-ups, tourist postcards and multiple lottery tickets. One day tomorrow he'll pick a winner. John Huston's 1948 adaptation of B. Traven's *The Treasure of the Sierra Madre* (1927) opens on a close-up of a list of the winning numbers in the Mexican national lottery. Reading down the list and not finding his number, Fred C. Dobbs (Humphrey Bogart) shreds his losing tickets. His luck will later change, and he uses his winning capital to fund a gold prospecting trip that grants him riches beyond his wildest dreams. His good fortune, however, is an illusion, a self-deception, and before he can spend a penny of it, he will lose

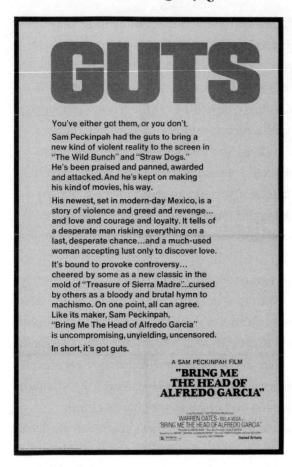

Poster for
*Bring Me the
Head of Alfredo
Garcia* (dir. Sam
Peckinpah, 1974).

everything and his life; if it wasn't for bad luck he wouldn't have any luck at all.

Looking for information on Garcia, hoodlums Johnny Quill (Gig Young) and Sappensly (Robert Webber) drop into the bar where Bennie entertains American tourists. Bennie sees a way of turning his luck by staking a claim on the reward. Asked for his name, Quill tells Bennie it is 'Dobbs, Fred C. Dobbs'. But it is Bennie who is the deluded character that better fits Dobbs's profile, not Quill. Like Dobbs, Bennie thinks he can hit pay dirt and find his fortune in a hole in the ground – in his case a grave occupied by the recently killed Garcia. He needs only to collect on the dead man's head.

After *Pat Garrett and Billy the Kid*, Kris Kristofferson and his bandmate Donnie Fritts made a return appearance in Peckinpah's picture as two beer-bellied dirt bikers who interrupt Bennie and Elita's picnic on their journey to Garcia's resting place. Held off the road beside Bennie's beat-up red convertible Chevrolet Impala, the couple's second picnic of the day is spoiled when the two bikers appear like uninvited guests at a wedding. The would-be rapists are the antithesis of the outlaw figures Kristofferson and Fritts had played in *Pat Garrett*; they are the scum of the earth who would violate Elita as Bennie would the body of Garcia. Bennie

Humphrey Bogart as Fred C. Dobbs in *The Treasure of the Sierra Madre* (dir. John Huston, 1948).

kills them both, but the disturbance caused to the couple's repast is not settled. Justifying his actions, Bennie explains to Elita that

> There's nothing sacred about a hole in the ground or the man who's in it. Or you, or me. Listen. The church cuts off the feet, fingers, any other goddamn thing from the saints don't they? Well Alfredo's our saint. He's the saint of our money. And I'm gonna borrow a piece of him. I got a chance – a ticket . . . There ain't no more chances.

If he had heeded the perilous warning the bikers carried, he might have turned back to try his luck another day, but Bennie figures this is his last good chance.

Bennie and Garcia look enough alike – same dark hair and moustache – that they could, in a tavern's interior shadows, be mistaken for one another. The first time Bennie sees his mirror image, Garcia is dead. As he tries to disinter his double's cadaver, Bennie is hit on the head by a shovel. He awakes in the grave beside Garcia's decapitated body and the corpse of Elita, the woman they had both loved. The entwined bodies make their first and last physical threesome in the cemetery, a triad of lost souls unmatched in the iconography of contemporary horror films or in comic books like Warren's *Eerie* and *Creepy*, which trade in such tropes of the wretched.

Reaching for the light, Bennie's hand breaks through the grave's tumulus, out of the dirt that loosely covers him and his two lovers. Gasping for air, he spits out the soil that fills his mouth; the undead is resurrected. Following the revenger's trail, Bennie reclaims Garcia's head from those who had taken it from the shared grave, and the body count begins to mount. Bennie's once white suit is now blackened and filthy beyond recognition, its ruin matching the decaying, fly-blown head of Alfredo, which bounces around on the car seat beside him, his constant and true companion.

After a night at his apartment, still maintaining the one-way conversation with Garcia, Bennie takes the head in a picnic basket to the mobsters' hotel. The wicker carrier recalls the time, on a blanket under a tree beside the highway, that he proposed to Elita as they ate and drank and spoke of their dreams. Garcia's head, he believed, was the means to realize those visions; instead it despoiled and destroyed everything he cared for. Now, closing in on the finale, Bennie is again dressed in the clothes he had worn when first he had visited the hotel to find out the price on Garcia's head. These are the same clothes he had been wearing when united with Garcia and Elita in their shared grave, but this set is new. His jacket and trousers are pressed, the white buckled shoes are clean, and his shirt ironed. This angel of vengeance clothed in white slubby linen kills all the room's occupants and then flies off to end his waning reverie at the ranch of the patrician who ordered the beheading of Alfredo Garcia. Like Gashade in *The Shooting*, Bennie has circled back on himself to face his own death. Like Fred C. Dobbs, Bennie was born to lose, his chances all played out.

The film's final image is the view down the barrel of a machine gun – a peephole into the abyss. Bennie belongs in the same gallery of beautiful losers alongside Kansas in *The Last Movie*, Bobby Dupea in *Five Easy Pieces*, G.T.O., The Driver and The Mechanic in *Two-Lane Blacktop*, the titular characters in *The Hired Hand, Cisco Pike, McCabe and Mrs Miller, Pat Garrett and Billy the Kid* and *Dirty Little Billy* – American dreamers, American failures.

That figuration of loss and defeat was replayed in the films made after these films, and not just in a continuation of similar stories

Warren Oates as Bennie in *Bring Me the Head of Alfredo Garcia* (1974).

and poor box office returns like Monte Hellman's *The Cockfighter* (1974), starring the redoubtable Warren Oates and supported by other Hellman alumni Harry Dean Stanton, Laurie Bird and Millie Perkins, but also there in the less artistically ambitious movies actors like Fonda went on to appear in. Exploitation pictures that Fonda must have thought he had left choking on the exhaust fumes of *Easy Rider*, movies like *Dirty Mary, Crazy Larry* (1974), *Race with the Devil* (1975, co-starring Oates), *Killer Force* (1976) and *Outlaw Blues* (1977). Fun some of these films may be, while other roles in *Two People* (1973) and *92 in the Shade* (1975, again with Oates) may have been more credible, but the trip he went on from *The Hired Hand* to *The Cannonball Run* (1981) was a fall from grace. Dennis Hopper may not have found equivalent employment, and there is a deal of merit in his performances in *Kid Blue*, *Tracks* and

The American Friend, but he was still a good way from rising again to the ambition of *The Last Movie*. It would be a long climb back before his role in *Blue Velvet* (1986) and his direction on the underrated *The Hot Spot* (1990) turned things around. Jack Nicholson would become a parody actor, a caricature of his former self in *One Flew Over the Cuckoo's Nest* (1975) and *The Shining* (1980), to name but only two of his endless stream of scene-stealing romps. Robert Altman went from one genre pastiche to another, a *reductio ad absurdum* of *McCabe and Mrs Miller*, with *The Long Goodbye* (1973) and *Buffalo Bill and the Indians, or Sitting Bull's History Lesson* (1976). *Nashville* (1975) only proved how good *Payday* was. Kris Kristofferson ended up in the cab of a truck with Ali McGraw on Peckinpah's risible *Convoy* (1978). They joined Peter Fonda in cross-country road races in which they were lapped continuously by Burt Reynolds in his *Smokey and the Bandit* franchise.

Easy Rider's duck shooters had become the topic and audience for the new-New Hollywood and an end point as ignoble as any rock 'n' roll had reached before punk took it back to its beautiful-dirty roots. Finishing the eastward journey away from Hollywood that Hellman's, Fonda's and Hopper's protagonists and, most especially, the midnight cowboy Joe Buck had begun, Martin Scorsese, with *Mean Streets* (1974) and *Taxi Driver* (1976), made New York once more a viable alternative to the LA conglomerates as he worked the same streets The New York Dolls occupied and that were later traversed by Patti Smith, Television and The Ramones.

Chasing the coat-tails of the 1960s doyen of New York independent filmmakers, Shirley Clarke, in the 1980s, Spike Lee, Jim Jarmusch, Susan Seidelman, Lizzie Borden, Bette Gordon, Kathryn Bigelow and Maggie Greenwald also paced Manhattan's sidewalks, producing a cycle of American art films that, in his more lucid days,

Poster for *Variety* (dir. Bette Gordon, 1983).

Hopper might have prophesied: *She's Gotta Have It* (1986), *Do the Right Thing* (1989); *Stranger than Paradise* (1984), *Down by Law* (1986); *Smithereens* (1982), *Desperately Seeking Susan* (1985); *Born in Flames* (1983), *Working Girls* (1986); *Variety* (1983); *The Loveless* (1981), *Near Dark* (1987); *The Kill-Off* (1990) and *The Ballad of Little Jo* (1993). But things were not the same as when Hopper set out on his auteurist adventures, and even he could not have missed that the larger number of these films were made by women (and two by an African American man). The art cinema of New Hollywood was based on the irresolvable contradiction that its revolutionaries were the problem, not the answer. In the end, the American art film did not belong to the blonde-haired, blue-eyed boys of California, Hollywood's privileged progeny clothed in the pitch that defileth; it belonged to those who had been assiduously ignored in films like *Two-Lane Blacktop*, *The Last Picture Show* and *Five Easy Pieces*. Ruby Mae Brown had that figured right.

Select Filmography

À bout de souffle (dir. Jean-Luc Godard, 1960)

The American Dreamer (dir. L. M. Kit Carson and Lawrence Schiller, 1971)

L'avventura (dir. Michelangelo Antonioni, 1960)

The Ballad of Cable Hogue (dir. Sam Peckinpah, 1970)

Bande à part (dir. Jean-Luc Godard, 1964)

Bonnie and Clyde (dir. Arthur Penn, 1967)

Breakaway (dir. Bruce Conner, 1966)

Bring Me the Head of Alfredo Garcia (dir. Sam Peckinpah, 1974)

Butch Cassidy and the Sundance Kid (dir. George Roy Hill, 1969)

Cisco Pike (dir. Bill L. Norton, 1971)

Deadlock (dir. Roland Klick, 1970)

Dirty Little Billy (dir. Stan Dragoti, 1972)

Easy Rider (dir. Dennis Hopper, 1969)

El Topo (dir. Alejandro Jodorowsky, 1970)

Five Easy Pieces (dir. Bob Rafelson, 1970)

Flaming Creatures (dir. Jack Smith, 1963)

From Hell to Texas (dir. Henry Hathaway, 1958)

Head (dir. Bob Rafelson, 1968)

The Hired Hand (dir. Peter Fonda, 1971)

Jules et Jim (dir. François Truffaut, 1962)

Kustom Kar Kommandos (dir. Kenneth Anger, 1965)

The Last Movie (dir. Dennis Hopper, 1971)

The Last Picture Show (dir. Peter Bogdanovich, 1971)

The Life and Times of Judge Roy Bean (dir. John Huston, 1972)

McCabe and Mrs Miller (dir. Robert Altman, 1971)

The Maltese Falcon (dir. John Huston, 1941)

Midnight Cowboy (dir. John Schlesinger, 1969)

Model Shop (dir. Jacques Demy, 1969)

Pat Garrett and Billy the Kid (dir. Sam Peckinpah, 1973)

Payday (dir. Daryll Duke, 1973)

Performance (dir. Donald Cammell and Nicolas Roeg, 1970)

Ride in the Whirlwind (dir. Monte Hellman, 1966)

Ride the High Country (dir. Sam Peckinpah, 1962)

Scorpio Rising (dir. Kenneth Anger, 1963)

Seven Men from Now (dir. Budd Boetticher, 1956)

The Shooting (dir. Monte Hellman, 1966)

The Treasure of the Sierra Madre (dir. John Huston, 1948)

The Trip (dir. Roger Corman, 1967)

Two-Lane Blacktop (dir. Monte Hellman, 1971)

Where Did Our Love Go? (dir. Warren Sonbert, 1966)

The Wild Angels (dir. Roger Corman, 1966)

The Wild Bunch (dir. Sam Peckinpah, 1969)

Zabriskie Point (dir. Michelangelo Antonioni, 1970)

References

Introduction: Dirt for Dirt's Own Sake

1 Anthony Scaduto, *Bob Dylan* (London, 1973), p. 19.
2 Ibid., p. 13
3 Ibid., p. 19.
4 Bob Dylan, *Chronicles, Volume One* (London, 2004), p. 60.
5 Kenneth Tynan, 'The Man and The Myth', *Playboy* (June 1966), pp. 111, 168–70, 172. 'The Man and The Myth' is collected in Kenneth Tynan's posthumously published *Profiles* (London, 2007), pp. 196–203.
6 Ibid.
7 Ibid.
8 Ibid.
9 Ibid.
10 Ibid.
11 Ibid.
12 Ibid.
13 Bosley Crowther, 'The Career and the Cult', *Playboy* (June 1966), pp. 111–12, 158, 160–62, 164–5.
14 Ibid.
15 Ibid.
16 Ibid.
17 Ibid.
18 In a *Variety* review of *Two-Lane Blacktop*, Oates's G.T.O. was described thus: 'In many ways the character and performance is not unlike that of Humphrey Bogart's Dobbs in *Treasure of the Sierra Madre*. In fact, until the ending, there's more than this one similarity.' Murf, 'Pictures: *Two-Lane Blacktop*', *Variety* (23 June 1971), p. 46.
19 Crowther, 'The Career and the Cult'.
20 For further reading on the youth scene on the Strip, see 'Six Faces of Youth', *Newsweek* (21 March 1966), p. 64. Ken Reich, 'Crackdown Quiets Teens on Strip', *Los Angeles Times* (5 June 1966), p. ws1.

21 Mary Reinholz, 'Model Living, West Hollywood Style', *Los Angeles Times* (16 July 1967), pp. A36–8.

22 Patrick McNulty, 'Is This Any Way to Start an Airline?', *Los Angeles Times* (26 November 1967), p. B27; Arne D. Anderson, 'There's Enough Gold . . .', *Los Angeles Times* (25 August 1968), p. A32; Patrick McNulty, 'Which Way to El Arco?', *Los Angeles Times* (12 April 1970), p. M20; Lawrence Dietz, 'He Blue Denim', *Los Angeles Times* (30 August 1970), p. K7.

23 Domenic Priore, *Riot on Sunset Strip: Rock 'n' Roll's Last Stand in Hollywood* (London, 2015).

24 Ibid., pp. 18, 94.

25 In the film, the band's music was replaced by Corman with the more psychedelic mutterings of The Electric Flag.

26 Peter Stanfield, *Hoodlum Movies: Seriality and the Outlaw Biker Film Cycle, 1966–1972* (New Brunswick, NJ, 2018).

27 Ibid., p. 29.

28 George Melly, *Revolt into Style: Pop Arts in the 50s and 60s* (Oxford, 1989), p. 91.

29 Nik Cohn, *Pop from the Beginning* (London, 1969), p. 141.

30 Ibid., p. 144.

31 Nick Tosches, 'The Sea's Endless, Awful Rhythm and Me Without Even a Dirty Picture', in *Stranded: Rock and Roll for a Desert Island*, ed. Greil Marcus (New York, 1979), pp. 5–6.

32 Robert Christgau, 'Can't Get No Satisfaction', *Creem* (January 1973), pp. 30–35, 84.

33 Greil Marcus, 'Epilogue: Treasure Island', in *Stranded*, ed. Marcus, pp. 288–9.

34 Cohn, *Pop from the Beginning*, p. 145.

35 Ibid.

36 Ibid., p. 149.

37 Stanley Booth, *Dance with the Devil: The Rolling Stones and Their Times* (New York, 1984), p. 154.

38 Ibid., p. 215.

39 Tynan, 'The Man and The Myth'.

40 Ibid., p. 154.

41 Ibid., p. 180.

42 Ibid., p. 242.

43 James R. Shepley, 'A Letter from the Publisher', *Time* (8 December 1967), p. 15.

44 Ibid.

45 Stefan Kanfer, 'Hollywood: The Shock of Freedom in Films', *Time* (8 December 1967), p. 66.

46 Ibid.

47 Ibid.

48 Ibid.

49 See Robert Benton and David Newman, 'The New Sentimentality', *Esquire* (July 1964), pp. 25–31, a proclamation for the new that makes abundant references to Truffaut and Godard as well as citing Bogart as a key transitional figure: 'Bogart says a man can both care and not give a damn.'

50 Kanfer, 'Hollywood'.

51 Ibid.

52 Ibid.

53 Ibid.

54 Dennis Hopper, 'Into the Issue of the Good Old Time Movie Versus the Good Old Time', in Peter Fonda, Dennis Hopper and Terry Southern, *Easy Rider: Screenplay* (New York, 1969), p. 9.

55 Ibid.

56 Ibid., pp. 9–10.

57 Andy Warhol and Pat Hackett, *Popism: The Warhol Sixties* (London, 1981), p. 41.

58 Ibid., p. 42.

59 Ibid., p. 297.

60 Sonbert quoted in 'Warren Sonbert: *Where Did Our Love Go?*', www.tate.org.uk, accessed 24 June 2022.

61 Robert Christgau, '*Easy Rider*'s Soundtrack', reprinted in Fonda, Hopper and Southern, *Easy Rider*, pp. 22–5.

62 Ibid.

63 Ibid.

64 Lillian Roxon, *Lillian Roxon's Rock Encyclopedia* (New York, 1971), pp. 446–7.

65 Christgau, '*Easy Rider*'s Soundtrack'.

66 Quote reproduced in an advertisement for *Easy Rider* run in *Los Angeles Free Press* (15 August 1969), p. 32.

67 Paul Schrader, 'Review: *Easy Rider*', *Los Angeles Free Press* (25 July 1969), pp. 26, 32.

68 Ibid.

69 Johnny Rogan, *The Byrds: Requiem for the Timeless* (Ipswich, 2012), pp. 285–7, 366.

70 Ibid., p. 375.

71 Richard Maltby, '"A Brief Romantic Interlude": Dick and Jane Go 3½ Seconds of the Classical Hollywood Cinema', in *Post-Theory: Reconstructing Film Studies*, ed. David Bordwell and Noel Carroll (Madison, WI, 1996), pp. 434–59.

72 Shelley Benoit, 'Prototype For Hollywood's New Freedom', *Show* (March 1971), pp. 24–6.

73 Ibid.

74 Horace McCoy, *I Should Have Stayed Home* (London, 1996), p. 8.

75 Ibid, p. 184.

1 *The Hired Hand*: Circling Back to the End Again

1 'Review: The Hired Hand', *Playboy* (October 1971), p. 46.
2 Alan Sharp, *The Hired Hand* (London, 1971), p. 11.
3 Ibid., pp. 6–7.
4 Ibid., p. 8.
5 Ibid., p. 95.
6 George Melly, 'Boring Away in the West', *The Observer* (7 November 1971), p. 30.
7 Sharp, *The Hired Hand*, p. 131.
8 Lawrence Linderman, '*Playboy* Interview – Candid Conversation', *Playboy*, XVII/9 (September 1970), pp. 85–106, 278–9.
9 Ibid.
10 Howard Junker, 'Maui Boogie: Starring Peter Fonda and the Seven Sacred Pools', *Rolling Stone*, 82 (13 May 1971), pp. 28–32. A similar interview partly set on Fonda's boat was conducted by Tom Burke, 'Peter Fonda Will Survive: Yes, He Will', *Cosmopolitan* (September 1971), pp. 144–8.
11 John Weisman, 'Fonda and Hellman: Whatever Happened to The Garden of Eden?', *Rolling Stone*, 92 (30 September 1971), p. 50.
12 Ibid.
13 Ibid.
14 Ibid.
15 Ibid.
16 Ibid.
17 Ibid.
18 Michael Kasindorf, 'He Blew It', *Newsweek* (2 August 1971), pp. 75–6.
19 David Pirie, 'The Hired Hand', *Monthly Film Bulletin* (January 1971), pp. 240–41.
20 Roger Greenspun, 'Peter Fonda Directs and Is Cast as Hero', *New York Times* (12 August 1971), p. 29.
21 Charles Champlin, 'Hired Echoes Rider Theme', *Los Angeles Times* (18 August 1971), p. G1.
22 Edwin Miller, '6 Bit by the Theater Bug!' *Seventeen* (July 1962), p. 68.
23 Ibid.
24 Ibid.
25 Hedda Hopper, 'Hopper Picks Best of New Faces', *Los Angeles Times* (30 December 1962), p. A4.
26 Edwin Miller, 'Peter Fonda on His Own', *Seventeen* (August 1963), pp. 208–9, 294, 296.
27 Ibid.

28 Ibid.
29 George Waldo, 'Star's Actor-Sons Reveal Hopes', *Los Angeles Times* (10 February 1963), p. B4.
30 Personality Posters advertisement, *Seventeen* (May 1967), p. 242.
31 'Actor's Son Surrenders on Marijuana Charge', *Los Angeles Times* (21 June 1966), p. SF8.
32 'Beauty Bulletin', *Vogue* (1 August 1966), p. 127.
33 'Men in Vogue', *Vogue* (1 August 1968), p. 71.
34 Kevin Thomas, 'Fonda Son Has Fresh Teen View', *Los Angeles Times* (26 November 1966), p. 19.
35 Ibid.
36 Ibid.
37 Ibid.
38 'Order Restored to Sunset Strip after Officers Seize 67', *Los Angeles Times* (28 November 1966), p. 3.
39 'Trial of Fonda's Son Ends as Jury Splits in Verdict', *New York Times* (20 December 1966), p. 46; 'Peter Fonda Freed in Marijuana Case', *New York Times* (28 December 1966), p. 34.
40 'Peter Fonda Freed in Dope Case, Gets Scolding by Judge', *Los Angeles Times* (28 December 1966), p. 3.
41 'Henry Fonda Testifies for Son on Marijuana Charge', *Los Angeles Times* (13 December 1966), p. 3.
42 Cecelia Ager, 'Peter Fonda: Was This Trip Necessary?', *New York Times* (20 August 1967), pp. D11, 15.
43 Ibid.
44 Ibid.
45 Ibid.
46 'Mitchell Lifton Plans Ambitious Film Sked', *Variety* (11 February 1970), p. 29.
47 'Henry Passes Role to Pete Fonda', *Variety* (15 April 1970), p. 22.
48 Writer Harry Joe Brown Jr, who had an associate producer credit on the film, took court action in the summer of 1973 claiming the film's producers had underpaid him for the script, which he sold to Pando Co. for $150,000. 'Writer Sues, Thinks Trio and U Under-Paid Him on *The Hired Hand*', *Variety* (13 June 1973), p. 4.
49 'Peter Fonda to Star, Direct Pando Co.'s *Hired Hand*', *Boxoffice* (11 May 1970), p. 12; 'Fonda Feature Under Way', *Boxoffice* (8 June 1970), p. W7.
50 'New York Soundtrack', *Variety* (3 June 1970), p. 6.
51 Diana Lurie, 'Actresses Who Are Real People', *Life* (29 May 1970), pp. 40–47.
52 'The Actresses', *Newsweek* (7 December 1970), pp. 73–4.
53 Syd Cassyd, 'Hollywood Report', *Boxoffice* (15 June 1970), p. 10.

54 'Look to Universal for Your Future', *Independent Film Journal* (30 September 1970), p. 7; 'Calendar of Feature Releases', *Independent Film Journal* (14 October 1970), p. 1376.
55 'Hollywood Sound Track', *Variety* (23 June 1971), p. 47.
56 'Feature Review', *Boxoffice* (12 July 1971), p. 11.
57 'Film Reviews', *Variety* (7 July 1971), p. 14.
58 Ibid.
59 Ibid.
60 'The Exhibitor Has His Say', *Boxoffice* (14 August 1972), p. A3.
61 'Peter Fonda's Conditions', *Variety* (14 July 1971), p. 1.
62 Robert B. Frederick, 'Peter Fonda Spews Scatology & Raps in Gabfest That's Put-On & Put-Down', *Variety* (11 August 1971), p. 5.
63 Ibid.
64 Jack Kindred, 'On Peter Fonda's Tour', *Variety* (13 October 1971), pp. 1, 53.
65 Ibid.
66 Romany Bain, 'Peter Fonda', *She* (January 1972), pp. 24–5.
67 Vincent Canby, 'If James Taylor and Peter Fonda Flop', *New York Times* (19 September 1971), p. D1.

2 *The Last Movie*: Dennis Hopper's Three-Ring Circus

1 Tony Crawley, '*Game* Interview: Dennis Hopper', *Game*, III/10 (October 1976), pp. 20–24, 28–31.
2 Ibid.
3 Ibid.
4 Ibid.
5 Terry Southern, 'The Loved House of the Dennis Hoppers', *Vogue* (1 August 1965), pp. 138–43, 153, 162, 164.
6 Mark Rozzo, *Everybody Thought We Were Crazy: Dennis Hopper, Brooke Hayward, and 1960s Los Angeles* (New York, 2022), p. 225.
7 Ibid.; Southern, 'The Loved House', p. 142.
8 Ibid.
9 Ibid.
10 Ibid.
11 Ibid.
12 Ibid.
13 'Vogue's Own Boutique', *Vogue* (15 March 1968), p. 136.
14 John Coplans, 'Art Bloom', *Vogue* (1 November 1967), pp. 184–7, 232–3.
15 Joan Didion, 'People Talking About', *Vogue* (15 February 1967), pp. 94–5.
16 Southern, 'The Loved House', p. 153.
17 Didion, 'People Talking About', p. 95.
18 John C. Mahoney, 'Hopper's *Last Movie* a Film within a Film', *Los Angeles Times* (15 March 1970), pp. 1, 23–5.

19 Dennis Hopper, 'Into the Issue of the Good Old Time Movie Versus the
   Good Old Time', in Peter Fonda, Dennis Hopper and Terry Southern,
   Easy Rider: Screenplay (New York, 1969), pp. 7–11.
20 Peter Bart, 'A Groovy Kind of Genius?', *New York Times* (10 July 1966),
   p. 81.
21 Ibid.
22 'At 27, Peter Fonda Parades His Bit: Nonconformity', *Variety* (22 June
   1966), pp. 7, 18.
23 'International Soundtrack: Mexico', *Variety* (22 October 1969), p. 38.
24 Pauline Kael quoted in Peter L. Winkler, *Dennis Hopper: The Wild Ride
   of a Hollywood Rebel* (London, 2011), p. 177.
25 'Universal Bathes in Fountain of Youth', *Variety* (10 December 1969),
   p. 3.
26 Rick Setlowe, 'MCA Backs Pair of Newcomers; Cheap Features Gotta See
   Books', *Variety* (31 December 1969), p. 3.
27 Ibid.
28 Ibid.
29 Ibid.
30 Ibid.
31 Michael Goodwin, 'In Peru with Dennis Hopper Making *The Last Movie*',
   Rolling Stone (UK edn) (16 April 1970), pp. 22–8. Tony Crawley liked this
   quote so much he plagiarized two-thirds of it for his '*Game* Interview'.
32 Goodwin, 'In Peru', p. 23; Alix Jeffry Chinchero, 'A Gigantic Ego Trip for
   Dennis Hopper?', *New York Times* (10 May 1970), pp. 11, 99; Tom Burke,
   'Dennis Hopper Saves the Movies', *Esquire* (1 September 1970), np.
33 Brad Darrach, 'The Easy Rider Runs Wild in the Andes', *Life* (UK edn)
   (20 July 1970), pp. 58–64.
34 Ibid., p. 61.
35 Ibid.
36 Ibid., p. 64.
37 Goodwin, 'In Peru', p. 25.
38 Ibid.
39 Edwin Miller, 'Dennis Hopper Makes *The Last Movie* in Peru', *Seventeen*
   (July 1970), pp. 92–3, 136–7.
40 Ibid.
41 Mahoney, 'Hopper's *Last Movie*', pp. 1, 23–5.
42 Ibid.
43 Ibid.
44 Ibid.
45 Dick Adler, 'Five Directors in Search of a Renaissance', *Los Angeles Times*
   (15 November 1970), p. W16.
46 See Guy Flatley, 'D-e-n-n-i-s H-o-p-p-e-r', *New York Times* (18 October
   1970), p. D13.

47 Wayne Warga, 'Dennis Hopper Wound Up in Cutting Room', *Los Angeles Times* (7 March 1971), pp. 01, 22–3.
48 Charles Champlin, 'Documentary on Hopper', *Los Angeles Times* (18 June 1971), p. E24.
49 Murf, 'Review: *The American Dreamer*', *Variety* (14 April 1971), p. 16.
50 Ibid.
51 Ibid.
52 For more on non-theatrical film screenings on campus and the history of *The American Dreamer*, see the booklet notes that accompany the Etiquette Pictures 2015 release of the film on disc, Chris Poggiali, '*The American Dreamer* and the Heyday of Campus Film Programming'.
53 The advertisement ran in the *Los Angeles Times* (24 October 1971), p. P15.
54 Thomas Quinn Curtiss, 'Hopper's *Last Movie* at Venice Avoids Son-of-*Easy Rider* Tag', *New York Times* (30 August 1971), p. 35; Ian Cameron, 'Glum Viewing at Film Fest', *Los Angeles Times* (8 September 1971), p. H11.
55 Mosk, 'Venice Film Fest: *The Last Movie*', *Variety* (8 September 1971), p. 16.
56 'Dennis Hopper Unwinds at Venice Fest: Personal Pix vs Hard Dollars', *Variety* (22 September 1971), p. 20.
57 'International Soundtrack: Paris', *Variety* (6 October 1971), p. 28.
58 Charles Champlin, 'Hopper Loose in the Allegorical Jungles', *Los Angeles Times* (27 October 1971), p. E1.
59 Ibid.
60 Ibid.
61 Vincent Canby, 'Hopper Cast as a Mythic Film Cowboy', *New York Times* (30 September 1971), p. 58.
62 Ibid.
63 Ibid. Some readers *had* found value in Hopper's allegory and did think the real and the surreal could hang together. In a letter to the *Los Angeles Times*, Blair H. Allen wrote: 'I'm having second thoughts about movies like *A Clockwork Orange*. The youth slugaway slaying in Los Angeles and the rape of a woman in Cucamonga were right out of the film's script. Violent sadistic thrill crimes seem to be exploding across the nation in the wake of ultraviolent films, which makes Dennis Hopper's film *The Last Movie* even more prophetic about the influence of movies on our lives – the unreal becoming the real . . . between the two becoming thinner every day.' 'Letters', *Los Angeles Times* (20 February 1972), p. AA10.
64 Nat Freedland, 'Mamas and Papas: Four Rugged Individualists Getting Back Together', *Los Angeles Times* (5 December 1971), p. Z26.
65 *Los Angeles Times* (24 October 1971), p. P15.
66 Champlin, 'Hopper Loose in the Allegorical Jungles', p. E1.
67 'Review: The Last Movie', *Independent Film Journal* (30 September 1971), p. 48.

68 Ibid.
69 Ronald Gold, 'How "New" Is the New Art Film?', *Variety* (27 October 1971), p. 40.
70 Ibid.
71 Ibid.
72 Alex Cox, 'Scene Missing', booklet that accompanied the limited-edition Blu-Ray release of *The Last Movie* (Indicator, 2019).
73 See Tom Folsom, *Hopper* (New York, 2013), pp. 174–85; and Winkler, *Dennis Hopper*, pp. 174–9.
74 Shelley Benoit, 'Prototype for Hollywood's New Freedom', *Show* (March 1971), p. 26.
75 'Picture Grosses: Broadway', *Variety* (6 October 1971), p. 18.
76 'Picture Grosses: Broadway', *Variety* (13 October 1971), pp. 8, 12.
77 'Picture Grosses: Broadway', *Variety* (27 October 1971), p. 8.
78 Marcia Seligson, 'American Notebook', *New York Times* (25 October 1970), p. BR16.
79 Adverts for the film's Los Angeles run initially promoted a soundtrack as being 'available on Uni records and tapes' but reference to the LP was quickly excised, see *Los Angeles Times Calendar* (24 October 1971), p. 15.
80 Gene Handsaker, 'Critics, Public Are Wrong', *San Francisco Examiner* (29 October 1971), p. 31. Also in Long Beach's *Independent* (5 November 1971), p. 39.
81 Handsaker, 'Critics, Public Are Wrong'.
82 Todd Mason, 'Dennis Hopper Steps beyond *Easy Rider*', *San Francisco Examiner* (5 December 1971), p. 218.
83 'Youth Shuns Youth-Lure Films', *Variety* (3 November 1971), pp. 1, 48.
84 'Youth Film Market a B.O. Mirage', *Variety* (29 November 1971), pp. 1 and 68.
85 Beverly Walker, 'Go West, Young Man', *Sight and Sound* (Winter 1971), pp. 22–5.
86 Ibid.
87 Ibid.
88 Ibid.
89 Ibid.
90 Display advertisement in *Los Angeles Times* (2 May 1972), p. G18.
91 Foster Hirsch, 'You're Wrong If You Write Off Dennis Hopper', *New York Times* (24 October 1971), p. D11.
92 Geoff Brown, 'Reprieve for the Wayward Offender', *The Times* (23 October 1982), p. 27.
93 'Hopper Will Attend Fete', *Los Angeles Times* (16 March 1972), p. 113.
94 Ibid.

3 *The Last Picture Show, Five Easy Pieces* and *Payday*: Cowboy Rhythm on KTRN

1 'Review: The Last Picture Show', *Independent Film Journal* (30 September 1971), p. 54.

2 Ibid.

3 Ibid.

4 Rita Mae Brown, '*The Last Picture Show*: Male Trip in Black and White', *Off Our Backs* (30 June 1972), p. 8.

5 Ibid.

6 Ibid.

7 Ibid.

8 Jan Dawson, '*The Last Picture Show*', *Sight and Sound* (Spring 1972), pp. 107–8.

9 John Weisman, 'Thrilling Days of Yesteryear: Texas in the Fifties', *Rolling Stone* (25 November 1971), pp. 64, 66.

10 Ibid., p. 66.

11 Dawson, '*The Last Picture Show*', pp. 107–8.

12 'The historical perspective which Bogdanovich has allows him to put us in touch with our feelings about old movies and forces us to revaluate them . . . [His] use of a classical narrative and style forces us to see these methods are still viable, that they still have the power to move and affect us, even when applied to instances of sexual candor and human misery which were missing from the movies of our past. Thus, he not only rekindles our love for old movies, he enriches it.' John Kane, 'America: Two Ways of Looking at It', *Creem* (January 1972), pp. 42–4.

13 Robe, 'New York Film Festival: *The Last Picture Show*', *Variety* (6 October 1971), p. 16.

14 Charles Champlin, 'Movies Were Better Than Ever in Picture', *Los Angeles Times* (14 November 1971), pp. W1, 18, 70.

15 Vincent Canby, 'A Lovely *Last Picture Show*', *New York Times* (17 October 1971), pp. D1, 20.

16 Robe, '*The Last Picture Show*', p. 16.

17 Ibid.

18 Ross Macdonald, *The Underground Man* (London, 2012), p. 203.

19 Jack Ammon, '*Five Easy Pieces* Rolls in Canada', *Variety* (14 January 1970), p. 30.

20 Ibid.

21 Gold, 'Review: *Five Easy Pieces*', *Variety* (16 September 1970), p. 15.

22 Ibid.

23 Ibid.

24 Ammon, '*Five Easy Pieces*', p. 30.

25 Nick Tosches, 'Country Crap Exposed!' *Creem* (July 1973), pp. 52–3.

References

26 Jon Landau, 'Payday: Documentary Realism in Country and Western Drama', Rolling Stone (12 April 1973), p. 66.
27 'Review: Payday', Variety (17 January 1973), p. 20.
28 Roger Greenspun, 'Payday Traces Country Singer on the Road', New York Times (23 February 1973), p. 22.
29 Kim Newman, Wild West Movies: How the West Was Found, Won, Lost, Lied about, Filmed and Forgotten (London, 1990), p. 45.
30 Charles Champlin, 'Twang of Truth in Payday', Los Angeles Times (16 March 1973), p. F1.
31 Peter Schjeldahl, 'Payday Doesn't Shortchange You', New York Times (11 March 1973), p. 131.

4 The Shooting, Ride in the Whirlwind and Two-Lane Blacktop: Who's Monte Hellman, You Ask?

1 A. H. Weiler, 'Murder, Family Style', New York Times (10 May 1970), p. 99.
2 Kevin Thomas, 'Monte Hellman and Hollywood's Best-Kept Secret', Los Angeles Times (4 October 1970), p. Q1.
3 Ibid.
4 Ibid.
5 Ibid.
6 Ibid.
7 Ibid.
8 Ibid.
9 Ibid.
10 Ibid.
11 'World Film Showcase', Variety (11 May 1966), p. 1.
12 'Elite Film Mags Stage Paris Retrospectives', Variety (7 February 1968), p. 26.
13 'Avignon's New Stress on Films', Variety (17 July 1968), p. 18.
14 'Paris Highbrow Mag's Year's "Bests" Show Big-Budget U.S. Pix Admired', Variety (26 April 1969), p. 26.
15 'International Soundtrack', Variety (2 April 1969), p. 37.
16 'Shooting Makes North American Debut at Montreal Film Festival', Boxoffice (15 August 1966), p. K1.
17 Ibid.
18 Ibid.
19 'Ride in the Whirlwind', Variety (2 November 1966), p. 6.
20 Ibid.
21 Ibid.
22 Beverly Walker, 'Two-Lane Blacktop', Sight and Sound (Winter 1970), pp. 34–6.

23 Ibid.
24 Ibid.
25 Ibid.
26 Ibid.
27 'Sets Crowded', *Variety* (29 March 1967), p. 17; 'If Music of Cash Forthcoming, Think U Will Hark to "Offbeat"', *Variety* (12 July 1967), p. 7; Syd Cassyd, 'Hollywood Report', *Boxoffice* (15 January 1968), p. 18; 'Hollywood Happenings', *Boxoffice* (17 June 1968), p. W4.
28 See Peter Stanfield, 'Notes toward a History of the Edinburgh International Film Festival, '69–'77', *Film International*, vi/4 (Summer 2008), pp. 62–71.
29 Edinburgh International Film Festival programme (1970), p. 61.
30 Ibid.
31 'The Man Who Brought the Film Festival back To Life', *The Scotsman*, reproduced in the EIFF Press Dossier, 1970, np. Copies of the press dossiers for each year of the festival are held by the British Film Institute library, London.
32 Interview conducted with Lynda Myles, London (25 September 2007).
33 Edinburgh International Film Festival programme (1975), p. 78.
34 'Show-A-Rama Will Honor Columbia', *Boxoffice* (23 February 1970), p. 9; 'Nicholson Completes 2 Films', *Boxoffice* (27 April 1970), p. w5; 'Films on Campus', *Billboard* (27 March 1971), p. 84.
35 'Monte Hellman Pair Get Belated Release; At First Too Offbeat', *Variety* (19 January 1972), p. 32.
36 Thomas, 'Monte Hellman and Hollywood's Best-Kept Secret'.
37 *Variety* reported on Hellman's acquisition of the rights to Beckett's play: 'Set Godot for Coast', *Variety* (10 July 1957), p. 124.
38 Kent Jones, '"The Cylinders Were Whispering My Name": The Films of Monte Hellman', in *The Last American Picture Show: New Hollywood in the 1970s*, ed. Thomas Elsaesser, Alexander Horwath and Noel King (Amsterdam, 2004), pp. 165–94.
39 Ibid., p. 166.
40 Ibid., p. 169.
41 Michael Atkinson, booklet essay, *Ride in the Whirlwind/The Shooting* (Criterion Blu-Ray, 2014).
42 Ibid.
43 Michael Atkinson, '*The Shooting* and *Ride in the Whirlwind*: We Can Bring a Good Bit of Rope', www.criterion.com, 10 November 2014.
44 Chuck Stephens, 'Moebius Dragstrip: Monte Hellman Circles Back', *Film Comment* (March–April 2000), pp. 52–65.
45 Ibid.
46 Ibid.
47 Ibid.

48 Ibid.
49 J. Hoberman, *Vulgar Modernism: Writing on Movies and Other Media* (Philadelphia, PA, 1991).
50 Ibid., p. 23.
51 Ibid.
52 Ibid.
53 Ibid., p. 32.
54 Hellman told Beverly Walker for her *Sight and Sound* piece that the original screenplay by Adrien Joyce was based on a Jack London short story, but I have not been able to trace it. That idea of the film having a decidedly legitimate literary provenance comes across as yet another smokescreen to hide its lowly status as a crossover Western suspense.
55 Critic Jonathan Rosenbaum has staked something of a claim to the term 'acid western', linking it to the three Hellman pictures as well as *El Topo*, *The Last Movie* and *Greaser's Palace* (1972) and Jim Jarmusch's *Dead Man* (1995), among other movies and novels. He writes: 'What I partly mean by "acid Westerns" are revisionist Westerns in which American history is reinterpreted to make room for peyote visions and related hallucinogenic experiences, LSD trips in particular.' Jonathan Rosenbaum, *Dead Man*, BFI Modern Classics (London, 2000), p. 51. The term is used in a similar manner by Nick Pinkerton in his discussion of Hellman, 'Way Out West', *Sight and Sound* (January 2015), pp. 94–5.
56 The note about the research Nicholson undertook is in Beverly Walker, 'Two-Lane Blacktop', p. 36.
57 The quotation is from Aljean Harmetz, 'Monte's Turn for the Big Time', *New York Times* (16 May 1971), pp. D11, 16.
58 '*The Shooting* and *Ride in the Whirlwind*, a pair that might be called existential westerns'. Shelley Benoit, 'On the Road with the New Hollywood', *Show*, II/1 (March 1971), p. 16.
59 Sylvia Townsend, *Bumpy Road: The Making, Flop, and Revival of Two-Lane Blacktop* (Jackson, MS, 2019), p. 57.
60 'The most remarkable thing about this film, a "road" picture, is its R rating. There is a total lack of nudity, sex and violence.' 'Opinions of Current Productions', *Boxoffice* (28 June 1971), p. A11. In 1971, *Playboy* ran a pictorial survey of recent sex and nude scenes in the movies, which suggests just how nonconformist *Two-Lane Blacktop* was in its avoidance of such things. Arthur Knight and Hollis Alpert, 'Sex in Cinema 1971', *Playboy* (November 1971), pp. 160–75, 186, 264, 266, 268, 270, 272, 274, 276–7.
61 Ian Penman, 'Lost Highway', *Sight and Sound* (February 2012), pp. 26–9.
62 Ibid.
63 Ibid.
64 Ibid.

65 'James Taylor: One Man's Family of Rock', *Time* (1 March 1971), pp. 45–53.
66 Ibid.
67 Benoit, 'On the Road', p. 17.
68 Penman, 'Lost Highway', p. 28.
69 Murf, 'Pictures: *Two-Lane Blacktop*', *Variety* (23 June 1971), p. 46. See also Susan Braudy, 'James Taylor, a New Troubadour', *New York Times* (21 February 1971), pp. SM28–34.
70 Benoit, 'On the Road', p. 22.
71 Rudolph Wurlitzer and Will Cory, *Two-Lane Blacktop* (New York, 1971), pp. 50–51.
72 Ibid., p. 16.
73 Michael Watts, 'The Man Called Alias', *Melody Maker* (3 February 1973), pp. 28–30.
74 John Weisman, 'Fonda and Hellman: Whatever Happened to the Garden of Eden?' *Rolling Stone*, 92 (30 September 1971), p. 50. In April 1971, *Esquire* had pitched *Two-Lane Blacktop* as its film of the year; by July, it had backtracked on that opinion: 'the film is vapid: the photography arch and tricky and naturally, therefore, poorly lit and unfocused; the acting (only one part is played by a professional) amateurish, disingenuous and wooden; the direction inverted to the degree that fundamental relationships become incidental to the film's purpose. The script has become the victim of the auteur principle.' 'Editor's Notes', *Esquire* (July 1971), np. Like *Esquire*, Kevin Thomas, who had first hailed Hellman in the *Los Angeles Times*, now turned against him: 'The trouble with *Two-Lane Blacktop* is, while being about people who cover a lot of territory without really getting anywhere, it goes nowhere itself.' Kevin Thomas, 'Big Street Racers', *Los Angeles Times* (15 July 1971), p. F1. Not all critics found the film problematic. Clive Hodson in the British underground paper *oz* thought it fulfilled the promise of *The Shooting*, which bore comparison with Franz Kafka and Jean-Paul Sartre, and it revealed the phoniness of *Easy Rider*. *Two-Lane Blacktop*, he wrote, 'provides a healthy slice of post-Dylan culture'. It is the 'Great Amerikan Movie'. Clive Hodson, *oz*, 42 (May 1972), np. New York's *Independent Film Journal* also strongly recommended the film: 'Monte Hellman's beautiful movie about car freaks. The best of the road films and the most compassionate' (22 July 1971), p. 14. Less celebratory but still positive was Vincent Canby, 'Cross-Country Ride', *New York Times* (8 July 1971), p. 30. Other New York-based critics were less hospitable: 'N.Y. Critics Opinions', *Variety* (14 July 1971), p. 5. *Playboy*'s reviewer thought the film offered 'less depth and clarity' than the published screenplay, but still considered it a worthy film: 'Hellman isn't telling a story, he's using actors as props to create a kind of primitive social poetry – uniquely American and uncannily

persuasive – in which the automobile becomes a potent substitute for power, sex, home and even mother.' 'Review: *Two-Lane Blacktop*', *Playboy* (September 1971), pp. 48, 50. See also Townsend, *Bumpy Road*, pp. 115–16.

75 Benoit, 'On the Road', p. 23. Her article is reproduced in the booklet accompanying the Masters of Cinema Blu-Ray release of *Two-Lane Blacktop* (2012).

5 *Cisco Pike*: Kris Kristofferson Has Got a Great Future Behind Him

1 Craig McGregor, 'I'm Nobody's Best Friend', *New York Times* (26 July 1970), p. 68.

2 'Watching Dennis Hopper's *The Last Movie* is a dismally disappointing and depressing experience. As a piece of film-making it is inchoate, amateurish, self-indulgent, tedious, superficial, unfocused and a precious waste not only of money but, more importantly, of a significant and conspicuous opportunity,' wrote Charles Champlin. Hopper and the film would never recover from such a critical mauling; however, Champlin did find elements to admire within the chaos, especially the scene where two women perform a lesbian sex act for visiting Yankee businessmen (and their wives), which he thinks 'powerful, and lost', and Kovács's cinematography. But if the whole was to work, it 'required an icy intellectual rage and control which does not seem to be where Hopper is at'. Rumours, he reports, are that Universal will withdraw the film after its test run at the Regent in Westwood and recut the film. Charles Champlin, 'Hopper Loose in the Allegorical Jungles', *Los Angeles Times* (27 October 1871), pp. E1, 15.

3 McGregor, 'I'm Nobody's Best Friend'.

4 'Nashville Cats', *Sunday Times* (20 February 1972), p. 76.

5 'Los Angeles', *Boxoffice* (22 June 1970), p. w5; 'Toronto', *Billboard* (25 July 1970), p. 56.

6 He also recorded three songs for the *Ned Kelly* (1970) soundtrack, supervised and composed by Shel Silverstein, but none made the cut of the film. Silverstein's 'Blame It On the Kellys' was a little later refashioned by Kristofferson as the lead track on his debut, 'Blame It On the Stones', which suggested an easy-going interchangeability between historical outlaws and modern-day rock 'n' rollers that would eventually be exploited more fully in his casting as Billy the Kid.

7 At the Troubadour he was second on the bill to headliner Linda Ronstadt, who was introduced to readers as 'a singer with a shape as sensual as her voice' by Robert Hilburn, a critic who felt more at home appraising a woman's body than her voice. 'Country-Rock Vocalists

Nightclub Headliners', *Los Angeles Times* (25 June 1970), p. E16. The
pair were held over for a second week at the venue, *Los Angeles Times*
(30 June 1970), p. F11. Commentary on the audience Kristofferson was
attracting is found in Robert Hilburn, 'Atmosphere, Talent Key to Club's
Success', *Los Angeles Times* (2 August 1970), pp. M1, 12.

8 John S. Wilson, 'Natural Storyteller Ramble in Song', *New York Times*
(21 August 1970), p. 22.

9 Kristofferson and Dylan's pal Bob Neuwirth make cameo appearances
in a profile of Joplin. Julie Smith, 'Janis Joplin and the Saturday Night
Swindle', *Los Angeles Times* (12 July 1970), p. D2.

10 Paul Hemphill, 'Kris Kristofferson Is the New Nashville Sound', *New
York Times* (6 December 1970), pp. 54, 137–8.

11 Ibid.

12 Ibid.

13 John S. Wilson, 'Kristofferson Sings Sad Songs at Recital Here', *New York
Times* (1 January 1971), p. 18.

14 'Poets Host Weakened Sagehens Tomorrow', *Los Angeles Times*
(4 November 1955), p. C2. At fourteen years old he is listed as being
among a group of scouts who had visited Mt Diablo. 'Troop 1', *San Mateo
Times* (1 May 1951), p. 6. He appeared in the paper's school notices in
1953, pictured preparing for a balloon-shaving competition (9 April
1953), p. 11.

15 'Glove Eliminations Continue', *Los Angeles Times* (6 January 1958), p. C8.
Kristofferson is pictured knocking out his opponent in the *Pomona
Progress Bulletin* (22 January 1958), p. 32.

16 Cal Whorton, 'Kristofferson "Smartest" Glover', *Los Angeles Times*
(27 January 1958), p. C4.

17 'Leo King Scores Pair of Kayoes', *Los Angeles Times* (29 January 1958),
p. C3.

18 'Pomona Pair Hope to Score with Two Songs', *Los Angeles Times*
(13 July 1958), p. SG14.

19 British rock 'n' roll historian Rob Finnis kindly provided me with further
details of Kristofferson's brief dalliance as a London pop sensation: 'In
early 1959, Paul Lincoln, co-owner of the 2i's Coffee Bar in Soho, placed
an ad in the *Daily Mirror*. "If you have TALENT, ring this number." Among
those who responded was Kris Kristofferson, a 22-year-old American
would-be folk singer studying at Oxford. Lincoln signed him up and
placed him with the fledgling Top Rank label (an offshoot of the cinema
chain), where he was teamed with Tony Hatch, who would later produce
(and very often write) many hits, including 'Downtown' by Petula Clark.
Three or four tunes were recorded. Amazingly, *Time* magazine wrote
Kristofferson up in an article . . . in which he was pictured sporting an
immaculate crew cut. Unfortunately, prior to his English sojourn, Kris

had recorded an extremely obscure folk single for a one-man operation in Los Angeles. Alerted by the *Time* article, the owner kicked up a fuss, probably hoping for a pay-off. In fact, Top Rank simply walked away, leaving Kris and Paul Lincoln high and dry. The session was lost and nothing more was heard of Kristofferson until 1966–7. Paul Lincoln was always fondly remembered by Kristofferson, who would periodically enquire as to his whereabouts and well-being. I've no doubt that he probably put in an appearance or two at the 2i's during the above period.' Rob Finnis, email to the author, 7 March 2021. An example of Kristofferson's blues-tinged lyrics is included in the piece, see 'The Old Oxonian Blues', *Time*, LXXIII/14 (6 May 1959), p. 69.

20 'News in Brief', *Disc* (16 May 1959), p. 16.

21 Wilkin had co-authored songs with Kristofferson, notably 'Delta Day (No Time To Cry)', which as Bucky Wilkin he released as a B-side in March 1968. His debut solo album, *In Search of Food Clothing Shelter and Sex*, released in 1970 has two songs featured in *The Last Movie*, 'Me and Bobby McGee' and 'My God and I'. He also contributed three recordings to the soundtrack to Kit Carson's documentary on Hopper, *The American Dreamer*, including 'The Screaming Metaphysical Blues', the song that gets quoted in *Rolling Stone*'s long piece on *The Last Movie*.

22 Robert Hilburn, 'Ray Stevens – He's Full of Surprises', *Los Angeles Times* (20 October 1969), p. C23; Robert Hilburn, '1969 Was Year of Cash and Country', *Los Angeles Times* (25 January 1970), pp. 44, 57.

23 Roy Reed, 'Country Music Becomes Concerned', *New York Times* (19 April 1970), p. 49.

24 Robert Hilburn, 'A Rhodes Scholar Finds Song Niche', *Los Angeles Times* (15 June 1970), p. F19.

25 '*Cisco Pike*', *Independent Film Journal*, LXVIII/12 (11 November 1971), p. 8.

26 Ibid.; Gerald Ayres, 'Cisco Pike and Its Parts', in Bill L. Norton, *Cisco Pike: Screenplay* (New York, 1971), p. 4.

27 Ibid.; Jacoba Atlas, 'The Cycle Becomes a Maze', in Norton, *Cisco Pike*, p. 9.

28 It was reported by *Billboard* that the film was to be named after his album *Silver Tongued Devil and I*: 'a last-minute change was made to take advantage of Kristofferson's current hit album . . . which also provides most of the soundtrack.' Nat Freedland, 'Rock and Roll Film Past Woodstock', *Billboard* (28 August 1971), p. 28.

29 Stephen Farber, '*Cisco* Isn't Just Another Dope Movie', *New York Times* (6 February 1972), p. D15.

30 Kevin Thomas, 'Kristofferson as Passe Rock Star', *Los Angeles Times* (11 February 1972), p. H12.

31 Murf, 'Cisco Pike', *Variety* (3 November 1971), pp. 16, 24.

32 Ayres, '*Cisco Pike* and Its Parts', pp. 1–2.

33 Ibid., p. 7.

34 Atlas, 'The Cycle Becomes A Maze', p. 9.

35 Ibid.

36 Norma Whittaker, 'Interview with Bill Norton', in Norton, *Cisco Pike*, p. 33.

37 Andrew Loog Oldham, *2Stoned* (London, 2003), p. 163.

38 Ibid.

39 '*Cisco Pike*', *Independent Film Journal*, p. 8.

6 *Dirty Little Billy*: Scuffling on Madison Ave

1 The May pre-release review in *Variety* suggests there was originally a scene that flashbacked to Berle's childhood, but if there was it had been excised by the time of the film's release in November. The length listed for its Paris preview is 100 minutes; the general-release print was seven minutes shorter. Mosk, 'Film Reviews', *Variety* (17 May 1972), p. 28; George Lazarus, 'Mary Wells Goes Hollywood', *Chicago Tribune* (5 October 1972), p. C10. Though first shown in Paris after the film was taken to Cannes, it was not screened at the festival. Michel Ciment wrote that this 'remarkable Western' was pulled so as not to compete with other American films: Michel Ciment, 'Cannes 1972', *Positif* (July 1972), pp. 31–3.

2 Susan Nelson, 'Whatever Happened to the Grand Old Studio? Warner Bros.', *Chicago Tribune* (13 October 1974), pp. J73–4, 76. One of the earliest announcements of the movie was by A. H. Weiler, 'Can They Clean Up with *Dirty Little Billy*?', *New York Times* (21 June 1970), p. 93.

3 Betty Liddick, 'Advertising Woman Bringing Personal Sell to Film-making', *Los Angeles Times* (10 February 1972), pp. 12, 10.

4 Ibid.

5 'Profile: Charles Moss', *Broadcasting* (20 November 1972), p. 99.

6 Liddick, 'Advertising Woman'.

7 Thomas Frank, *The Conquest of Cool: Business Culture, Counterculture, and the Rise of Hip Consumerism* (Chicago, IL, 1997), p. 124.

8 Ibid.

9 Ibid., p. 126.

10 Ibid., p. 129.

11 'San Francisco Gets Little Billy Bally', *Boxoffice* (23 October 1972), p. A1.

12 Vincent Canby 'How the West Was, and How Elvis Is?', *New York Times* (17 June 1973), np.

13 Ibid.

14 For a fuller account of its etymology and the history of its use in American films, see Peter Stanfield, 'Punks! JD Gangsters', in *The Cool and the Crazy: Pop Fifties Cinema* (New Brunswick, NJ, 2015), pp. 135–61.

15 Stanley Burch, 'C. W. Moss Blossoms Out as Billy the Kid', *Daily Mail* (1 June 1971), pp. 14–15.

16 'Booking Guide', *Boxoffice* (13 November 1972), p. B7.

17 Mosk, 'Film Reviews', *Variety* (17 May 1972), p. 28.

18 Ibid.

19 Ibid.

20 Gene Siskel, '*Dirty Little Billy*: A Life Of Grime', *Chicago Tribune* (12 December 1973), p. C8.

21 Joyce Haber, 'Dirty Bill a New Bonnie, Clyde?', *Los Angeles Times* (18 January 1971), p. G10.

22 Olli Lagerspetz, *A Philosophy of Dirt* (London, 2018), p. 49.

23 Mike Gormley, 'Iggy: "At First, I Was in the Mood to Self-Destruct"', *Detroit Free Press* (21 September 1969), pp. 29–30.

24 A. H. Weiler, 'Legend of Gunslinging Kid Explored in Film', *New York Times* (19 May 1973), p. 28.

25 Canby, 'How the West Was'.

26 Jay Cocks, 'Sick Shooter', *Time* (13 November 1972), p. 107.

27 Ibid.

28 Beth Ann Krier, 'Costume Design Revolution', *Los Angeles Times* (18 March 1971), p. G1.

29 Ibid.

30 Ibid.

31 Ibid.

32 'Showmandiser', *Boxoffice* (5 November 1972), p. A1. Reporting that Dragoti had signed Burland for the film's score, *Billboard* noted he will 'utilize instruments popular in the West in the 19th Century, such as harpsichord, dulcimer and tack piano'. 'New York', *Billboard* (26 February 1972), p. 15. As for Pollard's musical ambitions, it was reported elsewhere that he was recording an album of 'music by his pals', who included Bob Dylan, Kris Kristofferson, Stevie Winwood and Paul McCartney. He was scheduled to sing on *The Johnny Cash Show*. Haber, 'Dirty Bill', p. G10.

33 Review section, *Independent Film Journal*, LXX/12 (13 November 1972), p. 29.

34 Ibid.

35 Ibid.

36 Kevin Thomas, 'Dirty Billy Smudges Legend', *Los Angeles Times* (25 January 1973), p. G17.

37 Donald Lyons, 'Hitler and Billy the Kid', *Rock Scene* (November 1973), p. 38.

38 Ibid.

39 Ibid.

40 'Columbia Pictures Presents . . .', *Variety* (13 December 1972), pp. 12–13.

41 Lazarus, 'Mary Wells Goes Hollywood', p. C10.

42 Marylin Bender, 'America's Corporate Sweethearts', *New York Times* (20 January 1974), pp. 1, 4. With half its investment being amortized, the box-office failure of the film hit the company's shares, which otherwise would have been $0.27 higher at $2.31. Philip H. Dougherty, 'Advertising: Anti-Memo Drive', *New York Times* (23 January 1974), p. 53.

43 A. H. Weiler, '*Wounded Knee* to Aid Indians', *New York Times* (24 June 1973), p. 117.

44 Don Carpenter, *The Murder of Frogs and Other Stories* (Mineola, NY, 2020), pp. 203–4.

45 Joel W. Finler, *The Hollywood Story* (London, 1988), p. 43.

46 John Simon, *Movies into Film: Film Criticism, 1967–1970* (New York, 1971), p. 177.

47 Ibid., p. 178.

7 *McCabe and Mrs Miller*: Pipe Dreams – Lows and Highs

1 André Bazin, 'The Evolution of the Western', in *What Is Cinema?*, vol. II, trans. Hugh Grey (Berkeley, CA, 1971), pp. 150–51.

2 Ibid., p. 155.

3 André Bazin, 'The Western; or The American Film Par Excellence', in *What Is Cinema?*, vol. II, pp. 140–48.

4 André Bazin, 'The Beauty of a Western', in *Cahiers du cinéma*, vol. I: *The 1950s: Neo-Realism, Hollywood, New Wave*, ed. Jim Hillier (Cambridge, MA, 1985), pp. 65–7.

5 Ibid., p. 66.

6 André Bazin, 'An Exemplary Western', in *Cahiers du cinéma*, vol. I, pp. 170–72.

7 Bazin, 'The Beauty of a Western', p. 167.

8 Bazin, 'An Exemplary Western', p. 171.

9 Ibid., p. 172.

10 See, for example, Jim Kitses, *Horizons West* (London, 1969); Edward Buscombe, 'The Idea of Genre in American Cinema', *Screen*, XI/2 (March–April 1970), pp. 33–45; Philip French, *The Western: Aspects of a Movie Genre* (London, 1973); David Lusted, *The Western* (London, 2003); Steve Neale, *Genre and Hollywood* (London, 1999).

11 Andrew Patrick Nelson, *Still in the Saddle: The Hollywood Western, 1969–1980* (Norman, OK, 2015).

12 French, *The Western*, p. 129.

13 Ibid.

14 'Review: *Doc*', *Playboy* (November 1971), p. 50.

15 Gary Engle, '*McCabe and Mrs Miller*: Robert Altman's Anti-Western', *Journal of Popular Film* (Fall 1972), pp. 268–88.

16 Charles Champlin, 'Review: *McCabe and Mrs Miller*', *Los Angeles Times* (1 August 1971), pp. Q1 and 20.
17 Ibid.
18 Ibid.
19 'Review: *McCabe and Mrs Miller*', *Playboy* (October 1971), p. 52.
20 Ibid.
21 French, *The Western*, p. 130.
22 Ibid.
23 'Bets and Bawds', *Playboy* (September 1971), pp. 103–5.
24 Ray Loynd, '*Wager*, Robert Altman's Deep-Freeze Western', *Los Angeles Times* (7 March 1971), pp. O1, 16–17.
25 Ibid.
26 Ibid.
27 John Simon, 'An Appalling Plague Has Been Loosed on Our Films', *New York Times* (19 September 1971), p. D13.
28 Ibid.
29 Ibid.
30 Ibid.
31 'Review: *McCabe and Mrs Miller*', *Independent Film Journal* (22 July 1971), p. 16.
32 Ibid.
33 Simon, 'An Appalling Plague', p. D13.
34 Reprinted in its entirety along with Pauline Kael's review as an advert promoting the film in *Variety* (30 June 1971), pp. 18–19.
35 Ibid.
36 Ibid.
37 Ibid
38 John Weisman, 'They're a Strange, Pitiful, Slick Pair, *McCabe and Mrs Miller*', *Rolling Stone*, 91 (16 September 1971), p. 50.
39 Ibid.
40 Ibid.
41 'Bets and Bawds', p. 103.
42 Ibid.
43 Ibid.
44 Ibid.
45 'Disconcertingly . . . it is Leonard Cohen's gentle ballad "The Stranger" that introduces and accompanies Robert Altman's latest film . . . Disconcertingly but appropriately, to the point where one suspects Altman of extrapolating his scenario from the song rather than from Edmund Naughton's novel . . . its mood is closer to that of Cohen's writing, with its transitions from obscenity to finely wrought metaphor in the evocation of fear, tentatively raised hopes and final impenetrable

loneliness.' Jan Dawson, '*McCabe and Mrs Miller*', *Sight and Sound*, XL/4 (Autumn 1971), p. 221.

46 Robert Christgau, 'Stranger Songs: The Music of Leonard Cohen in *McCabe and Mrs Miller*', www.criterion.com, 5 October 2016.

47 Alec Dubro, 'Review: *Songs from a Room*', *Rolling Stone*, 33 (17 May 1969), p. 16.

48 Ibid.

49 Ibid.

50 Arthur Schmidt, 'Review: *The Songs of Leonard Cohen*', *Rolling Stone*, 7 (9 March 1968), p. 21.

51 Ibid.

52 John Simon, 'Danger from Below', *New Leader* (12 July 1971), p. 24.

53 Vincent Canby, 'Review: *McCabe and Mrs Miller*', *New York Times* (25 June 1971), p. 17.

54 Champlin, 'Review: *McCabe and Mrs Miller*', p. Q1.

55 Ibid., p. Q20.

56 Ibid.

57 'People Are Talking About', *Vogue* (1 February 1966), pp. 138–9.

58 Ibid.

59 Naomi Wise, 'The Hawksian Woman', *Take One*, III/3 (January–February 1971), reprinted in *Howard Hawks: American Artist*, ed. Jim Hillier and Peter Wollen (London, 1996), pp. 111–12.

60 Ibid., pp. 113–14.

61 'Julie Christie Has the Layered Haircut', *Vogue* (15 August 1970), pp. 106–7.

62 'Beauty Bulletin', *Vogue* (15 November 1970), pp. 146–7.

63 Jackson Burgess, 'Review: *McCabe and Mrs. Miller*', *Film Quarterly* (Winter 1971/2), pp. 49–53.

64 Ibid., p. 52.

8 *Pat Garrett and Billy the Kid*: Angels Descend and Graves Open

1 Dave Marsh, 'Duel to the Death: *Pat Garrett and Billy the Kid*', *Creem* (July 1973), pp. 22–5, 74.

2 Jeff Nuttall, *Bomb Culture* (London, 2018), p. 59.

3 Robert Hilburn, 'Peckinpah Lures Dylan from behind Wall of Privacy', *Los Angeles Times* (19 February 1973), pp. VI, 52.

4 Ibid.

5 Mary Murphy, 'Movie Call Sheet', *Los Angeles Times* (13 November 1972), p. D19, and 'Dylan Debut', *Los Angeles Times* (5 December 1972), p. C19.

6 Nick Tosches, 'Country Crap Exposed!', *Creem* (July 1973), pp. 52–3.

7 Chet Flippo, 'Waylon Jennings', *Creem* (July 1973), pp. 34–7, 75–6.
8 Ibid.
9 Ibid.
10 Ibid.
11 Ibid.
12 Paul Seydor, *The Authentic Death and Contentious Afterlife of 'Pat Garrett and Billy the Kid': The Untold Story of Peckinpah's Last Western* (Evanston, IL, 2015), p. 145.
13 Ibid.
14 Ibid., p. 144.
15 Kevin Thomas, 'A New Aspect of Old West', *Los Angeles Times* (24 May 1973), p. G17.
16 Garner Simmons, *Peckinpah: A Portrait in Montage* (Austin, TX, 1982), p. 182.
17 Seydor, *The Authentic Death*, p. 176.
18 Rex Reed, 'Meanwhile, Back at the Corral with Kris and Clan', *Chicago Tribune* (15 April 1973), p. E15.
19 Ibid.
20 Robert Hillburn, 'Kris Kristofferson at the Troubadour', *Los Angeles Times* (10 June 1971), p. 17.
21 Reed, 'Meanwhile', p. E15.
22 Craig McGregor , 'I'm Nobody's Best Friend', *New York Times* (26 July 1970).
23 Michael Watts, 'The Man Called Alias', *Melody Maker* (3 February 1973), pp. 28–30.
24 Ibid.
25 Ibid.
26 Ibid.
27 Ibid.
28 Ibid.
29 Lillian Roxon, 'Rock Stars on Film? It's Mind-Blowing!', *Sunday News* (27 May 1973), Leisure section, p. 9.
30 Ibid.
31 Ibid.
32 Ibid.
33 Ibid.
34 Marsh, 'Duel to the Death', p. 22.
35 'Bob and Kris Team in Billy the Kid Film', *Rolling Stone*, 125 (4 January 1973), p. 10.
36 Dave Marsh, film review, *Creem*, V/3 (August 1973), pp. 58–9.
37 'Roundin' Up the Hot New Westerns', *Rolling Stone*, 138 (5 July 1973), pp. 74, 75.
38 Ibid.

39 Jon Landau, 'Dylan Redefines Himself: Merely Awful', *Rolling Stone*, 142 (30 August 1973), p. 80.
40 Kevin Avery, *The Life and Writings of Paul Nelson* (Seattle, WA, 2011), p. 99.
41 Roy Carr, review of original soundtrack, *New Musical Express* (25 August 1973), p. 36.
42 Ibid.
43 Chet Flippo, 'Dylan Meets the Durango Kid: Kristofferson and Dylan in Mexico', *Rolling Stone*, 130 (15 March 1973), pp. 46 and 48.
44 Ibid.
45 Ibid.
46 Ibid.

Conclusion: Bring Me the Head

1 Murf, 'Review: *Bring Me the Head of Alfredo Garcia*', *Variety* (7 August 1974), p. 18.

Select
Bibliography

Bazin, André, *What Is Cinema?*, vol. ii, trans. Hugh Grey (Berkeley, CA, 1971)
Booth, Stanley, *Dance with the Devil: The Rolling Stones and Their Times*
    (New York, 1984)
Bordwell, David, and Noel Carroll, eds, *Post-Theory: Reconstructing Film*
    Studies (Madison, WI, 1996)
Cohn, Nik, *Pop from the Beginning* (London, 1969)
Dylan, Bob, *Chronicles, Volume One* (London, 2004)
Elsaesser, Thomas, Alexander Horwath and Noel King, eds, *The Last*
    American Picture Show: New Hollywood in the 1970s (Amsterdam, 2004)
Finler, Joel W., *The Hollywood Story* (London, 1988)
Folsom, Tom, *Hopper* (New York, 2013)
French, Philip, *Westerns: Aspects of a Movie Genre* (London, 1973)
Godfrey, Nicholas, *The Limits of Auteurism: Case Studies in the Critically*
    Constructed New Hollywood (New Brunswick, NJ, 2018)
Hillier, Jim, ed., *Cahiers du cinéma*, vol. i: *The 1950s: Neo-Realism, Hollywood,*
    New Wave (Cambridge, MA, 1985)
Hoberman, J., *Vulgar Modernism: Writing on Movies and Other Media*
    (Philadelphia, PA, 1991)
Kitses, Jim, *Horizons West* (London, 1969)
Lusted, David, *The Western* (London, 2003)
Marcus, Greil, ed., *Stranded: Rock and Roll for a Desert Island* (New York,
    1979)
Melly, George, *Revolt into Style: The Pop Arts in the 50s and 60s* (Oxford, 1989)
Neale, Steve, *Genre and Hollywood* (London, 1999)
Nelson, Andrew Patrick, *Still in the Saddle: The Hollywood Western, 1969–1980*
    (Norman, OK, 2015)
Newman, Kim, *Wild West Movies: How the West Was Found, Won, Lost, Lied*
    About, Filmed and Forgotten (London, 1990)
Norton, Bill L., *Cisco Pike: Original Screenplay* (New York, 1971)

Nystrom, Derek, *Hard Hats, Rednecks, and Macho Men: Class in 1970s American Cinema* (Oxford, 2009)

Oldham, Andrew Loog, *2Stoned* (London, 2003)

Priore, Domenic, *Riot on Sunset Strip: Rock 'n' Roll's Last Stand in Hollywood* (London, 2015)

Rogan, Johnny, *Byrds: Requiem for the Timeless* (Ipswich, 2012)

Roxon, Lillian, *Lillian Roxon's Rock Encyclopedia* (New York, 1971)

Rozzo, Mark, *Everybody Thought We Were Crazy: Dennis Hopper, Brooke Hayward, and 1960s Los Angeles* (New York, 2022)

Scaduto, Anthony, *Bob Dylan* (London, 1973)

Seydor, Paul, *The Authentic Death and Contentious Afterlife of 'Pat Garrett and Billy the Kid': The Untold Story of Peckinpah's Last Western* (Evanston, IL, 2015)

Simmons, Garner, *Peckinpah: A Portrait in Montage* (Austin, TX, 1982)

Simon, John, *Movies into Film: Film Criticism, 1967–1970* (New York, 1971)

Stanfield, Peter, *The Cool and the Crazy: Pop Fifties Cinema* (New Brunswick, NJ, 2015)

——, *Hoodlum Movies: Seriality and the Outlaw Biker Film Cycle, 1966–1972* (New Brunswick, NJ, 2018)

Townsend, Sylvia, *Bumpy Road: The Making, Flop, and Revival of Two-Lane Blacktop* (Jackson, MS, 2019)

Tynan, Kenneth, *Profiles* (London, 2007)

Warhol, Andy, and Pat Hackett, *Popism: The Warhol Sixties* (London, 1981)

Winkler, Peter L., *Dennis Hopper: The Wild Ride of a Hollywood Rebel* (London, 2011)

Photo
Acknowledgements

The author and publishers wish to express their thanks to the sources listed below for illustrative material and/or permission to reproduce it.

Allstar Picture Library Limited/Alamy Stock Photo: p. 77; Archivio GBB/ Alamy Stock Photo: p. 188 (*top right*); Bibliothèque nationale de France, Paris: p. 188 (*bottom*); Fairchild Archive/Penske Media via Getty Images: p. 87; Granger – Historical Picture Archive/Alamy Stock Photo: p. 56; Heritage Auctions, HA.com: pp. 18, 43, 98, 108, 146, 167, 183, 203, 246; private collection: p. 188 (*top left*).

Index

Page numbers in *italics* refer to illustrations